LEARNING AND TEACHING THE WAYS OF KNOWING

LEARNING AND TEACHING THE WAYS OF KNOWING

Eighty-fourth Yearbook of the National Society for the Study of Education

PART II

By

THE YEARBOOK COMMITTEE
AND
ASSOCIATED CONTRIBUTORS

Edited by

ELLIOT EISNER

Editor for the Society

KENNETH J. REHAGE

Distributed by THE UNIVERSITY OF CHICAGO PRESS • CHICAGO, ILLINOIS

The National Society for the Study of Education

Founded in 1901 as successor to the National Herbart Society, the National Society for the Study of Education has provided a means by which the results of serious study of educational issues could become a basis for informed discussion of those issues. The Society's two-volume yearbooks, now in their eighty-fourth year of publication, reflect the thoughtful attention given to a wide range of educational problems during those years. A recently inaugurated series on Contemporary Educational Issues includes substantial publications in paperback that supplement the yearbooks. Each year, the Society's publications contain contributions to the literature of education from more than a hundred scholars and practitioners who are doing significant work in their respective fields.

An elected Board of Directors selects the subjects with which volumes in the yearbook series are to deal, appropriates funds to meet necessary expenses in the preparation of a given volume, and appoints a committee to oversee the preparation of manuscripts for that volume. A special committee created by the Board performs similar functions for the Society's paperback series.

The Society's publications are distributed each year without charge to more than 3,000 members in the United States, Canada, and elsewhere throughout the world. The Society welcomes as members all individuals who desire to receive its publications. For information about membership and current dues, see pages 295-96 of this volume or write to the Secretary-Treasurer, 5835 Kimbark Avenue, Chicago, Illinois 60637.

The Eighty-fourth Yearbook includes the following two volumes:

Part I: *Education in School and Nonschool Settings*
Part II: *Learning and Teaching the Ways of Knowing*

A complete listing of the Society's previous publications, together with information as to how earlier publications still in print may be obtained, is found in the back pages of this volume.

Library of Congress Catalog Number: 84-062254
ISSN: 0077-5762

Published 1985 by
THE NATIONAL SOCIETY FOR THE STUDY OF EDUCATION

5835 Kimbark Avenue, Chicago, Illinois 60637

First Printing, 6,500 Copies

Printed in the United States of America

Officers of the Society
1984-85

(Term of office expires March 1 of the year indicated.)

HARRY S. BROUDY

(1985)
University of Illinois, Champaign, Illinois

MARGARET EARLY

(1986)
Syracuse University, Syracuse, New York

ELLIOT W. EISNER

(1986)
Stanford University, Stanford, California

JOHN I. GOODLAD

(1987)
University of California, Los Angeles, California

A. HARRY PASSOW

(1985)
Teachers College, Columbia University, New York, New York

RALPH W. TYLER

(1987)
Director Emeritus, Center for Advanced Study in the Behavioral Sciences
Stanford, California

KENNETH J. REHAGE

(Ex-officio)
University of Chicago, Chicago, Illinois

Secretary-Treasurer

KENNETH J. REHAGE

5835 Kimbark Avenue, Chicago, Illinois 60637

The Society's Committee on Learning and Teaching the Ways of Knowing

ELLIOT EISNER

(Chairman)
Professor of Education and Art
Stanford University
Stanford, California

BENNETT REIMER

Professor of Music
Northwestern University
Evanston, Illinois

ROBERT J. STERNBERG

Professor of Psychology
Yale University
New Haven, Connecticut

ELIZABETH VALLANCE

Assistant Professor of Education
Director of Academic Outreach
Kansas State University
Manhattan, Kansas

Associated Contributors

RUDOLPH ARNHEIM

Professor Emeritus of the Psychology of Art
Harvard University
Cambridge, Massachusetts

ELLEN BERSCHEID

Professor of Psychology
University of Minnesota
Minneapolis, Minnesota

JEROME BRUNER

George Herbert Mead Professor of Psychology
New School for Social Research
New York, New York

DAVID R. CARUSO

Post Doctoral Fellow, Department of Psychology
Yale University
New Haven, Connecticut

B. JEAN CLANDININ

Assistant Professor, Faculty of Education
University of Calgary
Calgary, Alberta, Canada

MICHAEL COLE

Professor of Developmental Psychology
Laboratory of Comparative Human Cognition
University of California, San Diego
La Jolla, California

F. MICHAEL CONNELLY

Professor, Ontario Institute for Studies in Education
Toronto, Ontario, Canada

DWAYNE E. HUEBNER

Visiting Professor of Christian Education
Divinity School, Yale University
New Haven, Connecticut

BRUCE KEEPES

South Australian College of Advanced Education
Adelaide, South Australia

HERBERT M. KLIEBARD

Professor of Education
University of Wisconsin, Madison
Madison, Wisconsin

JILLIAN MALING

Principal, South Australian College of Advanced Education
Adelaide, South Australia

NEL NODDINGS

Associate Professor of Education
Stanford University
Stanford, California

D. C. PHILLIPS

Professor of Education and Philosophy
Stanford University
Stanford, California

VINCENT ROGERS

Professor of Education
University of Connecticut
Storrs, Connecticut

Acknowledgments

The National Society for the Study of Education deeply appreciates the contributions of all who have had a part in the preparation of this volume. Elliot Eisner, a member of the Society's Board of Directors, graciously accepted the responsibility of preparing the proposal for this Yearbook. Following acceptance of the proposal by the Board, he organized a committee to assist with further planning, solicited contributions from the several authors, and edited the manuscripts as they came to him. The work of Professor Eisner and his committee, as well as that of all the contributors, was done under severe constraints of time and is therefore all the more deserving of our gratitude.

Eunice Helmkamp McGuire has assisted with the preparation of the manuscripts for publication and, in addition, has prepared the indexes for the volume. We are especially grateful to her.

The Society is pleased to present this book as Part II of its Eighty-fourth Yearbook.

KENNETH J. REHAGE
Editor for the Society

Editor's Preface

Planning for this volume, *Learning and Teaching the Ways of Knowing*, was predicated on several assumptions. First, the mind is not given at birth, but rather is shaped by the experiences a growing human has during the course of his or her life. Second, the potential of mind is not yet fully understood. What humans have the capacity to think about is related to the context in which they live. Since contexts change, the capacities of mind themselves alter. Third, the roads to knowledge are many. Knowledge is not defined by any single system of thought, but is diverse. What people know is expressed in the cultural resources present in all cultures. Fourth, the school has a special responsibility to develop the mental potential of the young. The major vehicles it employs to achieve this end—intentionally or not—are the curriculum of the school and the quality of teaching that the school provides.

This Yearbook was formulated during a period in which two important movements were occurring simultaneously in American society. One of these movements is conservative in character and looks to the past as a major source of priorities for schooling. The other movement is emanating from the work of those who are currently studying human thinking and intelligence and who are developing new ideas about the potential of the mind. The specific manifestations of the former are to be found in the back-to-basics movement in American schools. Many citizens in the United States believe that our schools have not been achieving the results that children deserve and that our society needs. As a result of these public views there has been a call to return to what is truly basic in education. For many, what is basic are the three R's: Reading, 'Riting, and 'Rithmetic. Rather than viewing educational needs as expansive, these people take just the opposite tack: the solution to educational problems is reductive. We have been asked as educators to focus on less, not more. We are urged to teach by direct instruction, by didacticism, and in some cases by drill and practice. We are to look to yesteryear to regain the educational quality that people apparently believe has recently been lost.

Yet, while these "solutions" are being proposed to cure the ills of American schooling, new views of mind have rapidly been developing. I speak here of developments in cognitive science, in the study of human creativity, in the specialized functions of the brain, and in new conceptions of intelligence and knowledge. The gap between the view backward and the view forward could not be greater. An anxious public urges a limited educational focus in order to regain what it believes it has lost. New developments in psychology, philosophy, and education point to a broadened scope for the development of mind.

The committee for this Yearbook believes that, while children must of course learn to read, write, and compute skillfully, the full development of *only* those skills in no way does children justice. They are capable of more, and schools must try to optimize what students can learn.

To express such a view is to display a commitment; it is not to articulate what it means for education. What does it mean to say that there is a practical, or a spiritual, or a formal way of knowing? And what do these ways of knowing mean for curriculum, or teaching, or teacher education, or educational evaluation? It is the intention of this volume to share with the reader some answers to these questions. The answers provided, as in all educational scholarship, are tentative. The authors provide their reflective views of the state of affairs as they see them, fully expecting that these views will change as further work is undertaken in the domains about which they write.

The Yearbook is organized in three parts. Part One highlights the efforts at school reform in the first half of the twentieth century and thus provides a context for the chapters that follow. Part Two consists of eight essays, each focusing upon a particular mode of knowing. Each is written by a scholar whose previous work has been concerned with the topic. The chapters are designed to explore the nature of a particular mode of knowing within the context of education. The essays in Part Three are intended to explore the relevance of these various modes of knowing for several of the major concerns of schools: teaching, curriculum, and evaluation.

In this Yearbook we are attempting to push the boundaries of the ways in which we think about the educational possibilities of schools. The educational ends we embrace are shaped by our values and our values are shaped, in part, by what we believe we can accomplish and by what we are able to imagine. We hope this volume will contribute to both aims—that it will widen our view of what we can achieve in schools and that it will expand our vision of the possibilities of education.

ELLIOT EISNER
January, 1985

Table of Contents

Part Three

Implications for Educational Practice

Part One
A PERSPECTIVE ON TWENTIETH-CENTURY CURRICULUM REFORMS

CHAPTER I

What Happened to American Schooling in the First Part of the Twentieth Century?

HERBERT M. KLIEBARD

The Current Debate

Over a period of several years two main traditions have dominated the way in which American education has been seen and interpreted. The older tradition has been to focus on the story of how American education expanded from elitist traditions, borrowed largely from Europe, to encompass the great mass of children and youth in the United States. American education, from this perspective, is the story of a gradual transformation from a selective and class-biased system to one much more in harmony with popular American democracy. In general, the data for this story are drawn from the ever-increasing numbers of students who were entering the schoolhouse doors. It is, in one sense, a very dramatic story, the story of an experiment in mass public education extending at least to secondary schools—an experiment that many people would insist is still under way and where the results are still inconclusive.

Associated with that tradition, or perhaps a part of it, is the identification of American schooling with American political democracy. Popular education is seen as the principal vehicle for individual opportunity in this country and for social mobility generally. It is the way the poor, immigrants, and racial minorities could make their way in the world, and it is primarily for their sake that the expansion of schooling and curriculum reforms were undertaken. While deficiencies and poor educational policies can be detected here and there, they were by and large identified and overcome. In the end, a democratic school system wins out over elitist and class-dominated interests.

Within the past fifteen or twenty years, a new and very different story has been told, largely by a group of historians often identified as radical revisionists. Sometimes using neo-Marxist class analysis, these historians have interpreted the course of American education as one in which dominant class interests have been consistently served through the schools. Not only have the schools been used by these classes to create a large and available labor force, but the schools have consciously or unconsciously served as a breeding ground for the inculcation of obedience to authority, acceptance of specialization in work, and competitiveness leading even to intragroup hostility. The real nature of modern industrial society has been carefully hidden from successive new generations of Americans, and the schools, therefore, have been the site for the perpetuation of the political and social status quo.

In their interpretation, the revisionists have struck (although they have not always stated it in this form) a very real weakness or two in the traditional tale of American education. In the first place, in their effort to demonstrate the extension of educational opportunity through the expansion of schooling, traditionalists have tended to ignore what was taught once the children entered the classroom doors in such large numbers. This is admittedly a very difficult task. Even in the contemporary context, very little is known about what lies behind the printed syllabi and courses of study that are regularly issued by state departments of education and local school districts. This lack of understanding is reflected in the current efforts at school reform which are stated in terms of increasing the number of credits required for graduation or adding a unit of English here and one of science there, all done in the absence of any knowledge of what is taught under those labels. It is in this sense that a study such as John Goodlad's performs a very valuable service by, if nothing else, telling us something as to what teachers and students are actually doing.[1] How much more difficult it must be, however, to present a credible picture of what happened in schools even a few years ago. It is much easier to tell the story in terms of attendance rolls and numbers of school buildings.

Second, it must be admitted that at least some traditionalists have told a rather naive and sometimes self-serving story. Educational leaders at the state and national levels, although not lacking in certain humanitarian impulses, could not have been as uniformly high-principled as they are frequently portrayed. Like politicians, industrialists, labor leaders, and scientists, they numbered among them those who served dominant class interests or simply self-interest. It can be taken for granted that educational rhetoric will carry allusions to humanitarian causes and "meeting the needs of children" as well as to democratic principles and a better world. But one has to be able to see beyond that rhetoric and attempt to assess the real thrust of any proposed reform. And, in general, schools as social institutions can be expected to mirror to a large extent the established social values and almost inevitably serve the function of social stability.

For the most part, the competing interpretations of the traditionalists and the revisionists have revolved around the question of whether progressive education, allegedly the dominant educational movement in the twentieth century, has been predominantly a movement to transform a staid and functionally inert curriculum into one that could serve the new population of students marching through the school gates or whether, under that guise, it has essentially made the curriculum an even more potent instrument for dominant class interests and for repression of the poor, women, and minority groups. Almost invariably lost in the debate over that question is whether there was any such thing as a progressive education movement in the first place. This is not simply to raise the issue of whether the term "progressive" is an appropriate one to designate the movement, but whether there was anything cohesive enough to be defined as a movement by any name. It is in this sense that the traditionalists and the revisionists may be debating a question that does not (or need not) exist. What may be needed is not a decision one way or the other as to how to characterize the progressive education movement but an analysis of what movements did actually exist and how they functioned. What could emerge from such an analysis is not a picture of educational reformers, who, although they may have had somewhat diverse interests, nevertheless banded together in what amounted in the long run to a reasonably unified reform effort, but a picture of opposing, even warring, interest groups struggling with one another over control of the American curriculum. Seen in this light, the question is not one of whether the progressive education movement was fundamentally progressive in character and effect or fundamentally repressive; it raises questions of what interest groups banded together with what common purposes, whose interests did they serve, what battles were fought among them over what issues, and, perhaps most important, what compromises were reached. American education in the twentieth century, in other words, does not have to be seen as a triumph of the forces of good over the forces of evil or vice versa, but as an undeclared detente among fundamentally opposing reform groups. Such a conclusion may not be as dramatic or even as appealing as a paeon of praise or a sweeping denunciation, but it may bring us closer to an understanding of how American schooling got that way.

Portents of Change

That the beginning of the twentieth century coincided with a massive effort at educational reform can hardly be doubted. Americans had long been uncomfortable with the classical humanist curriculum that had been inherited from Europe. As early as the eighteenth century, Benjamin Franklin's academy reflected an impatience with "chapeaux bras," subjects merely ornamental. Modern foreign languages were more useful than the classical ones, and subjects like surveying and navigation needed a place alongside masterpieces of literature and formal grammar. Modest successes were achieved here and there in changing the curriculum along utilitarian lines. In the nineteenth century, the academy, a popular (although not really public) form of secondary education that included practical subjects, became the dominant form of secondary education in the country. The Morrill Act of 1862 set up land-grant colleges that were required to include along with the regular academic curriculum such useful subjects as agriculture and mechanic arts.

But what happened as the twentieth century came into view was of quite a different order. Changes in the American social fabric, which had actually been under way for several decades, suddenly were thrust into the American consciousness, and the impending arrival of a new century only served to underscore the notion that a new world was in the making. There was, of course, the fact of industrialization and the accompanying urbanization. There was not only the sharp increase in the volume of immigrants at the end of the nineteenth century but the shift in immigration from northern to eastern and southern Europe, a matter of some consternation to American leaders and social planners.

The social changes themselves have been well documented, but they do not in themselves explain why their impact should have been felt so keenly at the turn of the century nor why so many Americans should have seen in school reform the response to those changes. Most of these changes had been going on since the mid-nineteenth century and even before. Part of the answer may lie in the fact that the changes, although not new, were becoming visible to larger numbers of Americans. There was, for example, a tremendous growth in popular journalism in the late nineteenth century, including both magazines and newspapers, and also the powerful influence created by the rapid advance of railroads as a means of relatively cheap and reliable transportation. Both these developments, in addition to the continued growth of cities, were significant factors in the transformation of American society from one characterized by relatively isolated self-contained communities into an urban, industrial nation. The decade of the 1870s, for example, was a period in which the sheer number of newspapers in America doubled, and, by 1880, *The New York Graphic* published the first photographic reproduction in a newspaper, portending a dramatic rise in readership. Between 1882 and 1886 alone, the price of daily newspapers dropped from four cents per copy to one cent, due largely to the success enjoyed by Joseph Pulitzer's *New York World*, and the introduction in 1890 of the first successful linotype machine promised even further growth. In 1872, only two American daily newspapers could claim a circulation of over 100,000, but, by 1892, four more newspapers exceeded that figure.[2] A world beyond the immediate community was rapidly becoming visible to millions of Americans.

But it was not newspapers alone that were bringing this new consciousness to Americans in the late nineteenth century. Magazines as we know them today began publication around 1882, and, in fact, the circulation of weekly magazines in America exceeded that of newspapers in the period that followed. By 1892, for example, the circulation of *Ladies Home Journal* had reached an astounding 700,000.[3] Neither should book readership be ignored. Edward Bellamy's utopian and socialist-leaning novel, *Looking Backward*, sold over a million copies in 1888, giving rise to the growth of organizations dedicated to the realization of Bellamy's ideas. The printed word, unquestionably, was intruding on the insulation that had characterized American society in an earlier period. Industrialization and urbanization may have been going on for some time, but its impact was probably being felt by a relatively small segment of the population before newspapers and magazines began to bring word of vice and corruption in the cities and a generally decaying America to millions of citizens.

Of at least equal importance to mass circulation journalism was the effect on American consciousness of the growth of railroads in the late nineteenth century. By 1880, the east and the midwest had adopted four feet, eight inches as the standard track gauge, but the overwhelming majority of southern track lines were five feet, and the western states had laid very narrow track lines in the early 1800s. By 1883, however, leaders of the railroad industry had created the system of standardized time zones that we use today, and by the end of that decade, most railroad track in the United States had become standardized. In 1889, the United States already had 125,000 miles of railroad in operation, whereas Great Britain had only about 20,000 miles and Russia 19,000. As Robert Wiebe has pointed out, "The primary significance of America's new railroad complex lay not in the dramatic connections between New York and San Francisco, but in the access a Kewanee, Illinois, or an Aberdeen, South Dakota, enjoyed to the rest of the nation and the nation to it."[4] Like mass journalism, railroads were penetrating the towns and villages across the United States not only creating new industries and new markets but changing social attitudes and remaking our sense of what kind of world we were living in.

Early Reform Efforts

With the society in such a rapid state of flux, it should not be surprising that the matter of what we teach our children in school should also come under scrutiny. It should also not be surprising, given the diversity of ideological and political positions of the time, that the agendas for reform of the American curriculum in the twentieth century should not simply differ from one another in matters of detail, but even present contradictory positions and fundamentally opposing directions.

The situation after the turn of the century, in other words, appears to be a more complicated one than was first supposed. Not one, but at least three identifiable reform movements seem to have arisen during the course of the twentieth century to challenge the old humanism in education, and this may account for the fact that such totally divergent interpretations have evolved regarding what is commonly called progressive education. Each appealed to a special constituency, and to complicate matters further, the readiness for change on the part of the largest constituency of all, the teachers and school administrators who populated the ever increasing number of schools, may have been so intense as to include antagonistic reforms pointing in clearly different directions for American schooling. Although leading figures in the various reform movements were engaged in open strife, school people were, in many cases, gleefully placing their stamp of approval on all of them. What seemed to be important on the part of school people was not a clear ideological position or a coherently constructed curriculum but simply keeping up with the times. While one may find isolated examples of a school curriculum that followed a consistent ideological line, for the most part, what emerged as the American curriculum in the twentieth century was a hodge-podge of contradictory reforms patched on to the conventional humanist curriculum.

The dominant reform group was the social efficiency educators. Their appeal was multifaceted. First, they held out the promise of replacing the largely useless subjects that had dominated the humanist curriculum with subjects that were tied to the actual activities that human beings performed. Teaching subjects to people who would not use them was simply a waste, and a proper system of schooling would see to it that the curriculum would be tied as closely as possible to the activities that the child would one day perform. Such a conception of schooling required "a large variety in output,"[5] since not all people would be doing the same thing in life, and, therefore, the school had to prepare not one kind of person, but many, in order to meet the varied demands of a complex industrial society. Efficiency was important, therefore, in two senses. First, schooling should not be wasteful by trying to teach children things that they would not in fact use; and second, the society itself could be made much more efficient if the schools self-consciously and diligently performed their task of filling the social slots with those individuals who were most suited to occupy them. The schools would become the instrument, in other words, by which people occupied their appropriate rungs on the social ladder.

Beyond the potent appeal to efficiency, the social efficiency educators claimed the full and powerful backing of science. In fact, the leading figures in the movement saw themselves as bringing the light of science to a system of schooling that had been dominated by antiquated and futile speculation. Typical of this position was that of John Franklin Bobbitt. In his first book, Bobbitt provided the most explicit and at the same time most concise explication of the theory:

> The central theory is simple. Human life, however varied, consists in the performance of specific activities. Education that prepares for life is one that prepares definitely and adequately for these specific activities. However numerous and diverse they may be for any social class, they can be discovered. This requires that one go out into the world of affairs and discover the particulars of which these affairs consist. These will show the abilities, attitudes, habits, appreciations, and forms of knowledge that men need. These will be the objectives of the curriculum. They will be numerous, definite, and particularized. The curriculum will then be that series of experiences which children and youth must have by way of attaining those objectives.[6]

Almost every sentence in Bobbitt's summary of the theory marks off a vital facet of what was the ascendant mode of thinking about American schooling in the twentieth century. There was first its simplicity. That simplicity was expressed largely in a conception of curriculum planning that could be reduced to a series of steps. There was also the appeal to specificity, an ideal drawn from the scientific management movement of Frederick Winslow Taylor as well as the psychological theory of connectionism of Edward Lee Thorndike. Imbedded in Bobbitt's description of the essentials of the theory was the mechanism by which the curriculum would actually be constructed, a mechanism that Bobbitt was convinced was "a scientific technique."[7] *Activity analysis* or, as it was sometimes called, job analysis, consisted of a procedure whereby one first created an inventory of the "particulars" that comprised human life. These were the things that people in fact did, and those things would be converted into curricular objectives. The next step was simply to create that "series of experiences" that would most efficiently achieve each objective. Inherent in this approach, therefore, was an immense broadening of the scope of schooling. Bobbitt proposed that his approach be applied to all the activities in which human beings engage, to "their civic activities; their health activities; their recreations; their language; their parental, religious, and general social activities." The scope of schooling would be nothing less than "the mosaic of full-formed human life."[8]

The social efficiency reformers, then, were characterized first by their appeal to sheer efficiency, an appeal that was derived most directly from the scientific management movement but which pervaded all aspects of American life in the early twentieth century.[9] Efficiency, as filtered through the lens of scientific management, was closely identified, almost indistinguishable, from science. In fact the appeal to science in general was such a potent one in the late nineteenth and early twentieth centuries that hardly any reform movement could succeed without some allusion to it. In the case of social efficiency, however, the identification with science was so complete that many of the leading figures in the movement such as Bobbitt, W. W. Charters, and David Snedden proudly wore the badge of "scientific-curriculum makers" on their sleeves.

The second of the major reform movements, actually co-existing with the first, was the child-centered educators. Their appeal was also to science, but it was a far different science from the scientific precision drawn from the model of industry that was the focus of the social efficiency educators. Their science was one that was developmentally attuned to the true nature of the child. The schooling that they envisioned was not one in which the school would mold children in a manner consistent with the demands of industrial society but one in which the natural order of development of the child would provide the keys to the riddle of what should be taught. It was a science infused with a high romanticism.

The first great leader of the developmentalists was the preeminent American psychologist, G. Stanley Hall. Earlier educational movements such as the Froebelians and, most particularly, the American Herbartians, had achieved notable success in trying to draw attention to the child as the key to a renewed American schooling. In the 1870s the cause of child-study had gained impetus through the criticism of American education advanced by Charles Francis Adams,[10] especially by his efforts to draw attention to the child's mental habits as a way of bringing the light of science to a benighted pedagogy. Adams's high praise for the work of Colonel Francis Parker in the Quincy,

Massachusetts, school system not only brought Parker national prominence, but seemed to indicate that drudgery and repression were not, after all, necessary concomitants of schooling. Parker had not simply introduced a much greater measure of freedom for the child than was typical of the regimented schools of the time. He had, essentially, discarded the old course of study in favor of one that was congenial to the child's penchant for play and activity.

But it was not until Hall returned from Germany in 1880 that the developmentalists found the champion who would make them a potent force in American education. Under his leadership, child-study flourished in the 1890s. In 1894, Hall was able to announce at the annual meeting of the National Education Association that "unto you is born this day a new Department of Child Study."[11]

There was general agreement, of course, among the developmentalists that schools thwarted the child's basic need for activity by treating children as passive receptacles and presenting them with a program of studies that ran contrary to their natural tendencies and predilections. To some reformers, this meant simply the introduction of more active pursuits such as manual training or industrial education and more considered attention to recreation and play activities. But Hall had a much grander scheme in mind, and although Hall covered himself in the armor of science, it is significant that his curriculum ideas were drawn, not so much from the scientific data so diligently collected by him and his fellow psychologists, as from his metaphysical, even mystical, assumptions about the alleged relationship between the stages in individual development and the history of the human race.

From his early period of study with the German disciples of Herbart, Hall returned to the United States convinced of the validity of the doctrine of culture-epochs applied to pedagogy. Culture-epochs theory posited the notion that the child, almost literally, recapitulates in his or her individual development the states that the whole human race had traversed throughout the course of history. In Hall's mind, that recapitulation had strong mythic overtones:

> The principle that the child and the early history of the human race are each a key to unlock the nature of the other applies to almost everything in feeling, will, and intellect. To understand either the child or the race we must constantly refer to the other. This same principle applies also to all spontaneous

activities. Thus in seeking the true principle of most education we must not only study the plays, games, and interests of the child today, but also compare these with the characteristic activities of early man. . . . The child relives the history of the race in his act, just as the scores of rudimentary organs in his body tell the story of its evolution from the lower forms of animal life. . . . The all-dominant, but of course main unconscious will of the child is to relive this past, as if his early ancestors were struggling in his soul and body to make their influences felt and their voice heard.[12]

Hall was a masterful and charismatic teacher, and his call to arms for a system of schooling based on the true nature of the child attracted many devoted disciples and an army of followers. His vision of what schooling was to become in the twentieth century differed enormously from the calculated elimination of waste and the strong concern for a stable social order that were the key ingredients in the social efficiency movement. High romanticism and a faith in the natural order of development, not order and efficiency, were his keynotes.

In time, however, Hall's leadership of the child-study movement, which had once been so stirring and seemingly full of promise for success, met with some sharp reversals as the new century began.[13] Hall's pseudo-scientific approach to the study of the child had been more or less exposed, and his mystical belief in race recapitulation as a basis for a curriculum built on natural law had fallen out of favor. William James's 1899 series of lectures on the relationship between psychology and school practice seemed at times almost a direct attack on the claims that Hall had once boldly set forth for the redirection of the curriculum through the psychological study of the child. In what almost appears to be a direct reference to Hall, James felt that there was "a certain fatality of mystification laid upon the teachers of our day,"[14] even going so far as to say that in his "humble opinion there *is* no 'new psychology' worthy of the name."[15] Emphasizing that teaching is an art and not a science, James was wary of Hall's optimism about turning psychological laws into pedagogical recipes:

> I say moreover that you make a great, a very great mistake, if you think that psychology, being the science of the mind's laws, is something from which you can deduce definite programmes and schemes and methods for immediate schoolroom use.[16]

With someone of the immense stature of James joining other major critics in the psychological world, such as Hugo Munsterberg,[17] Hall's prominence among psychologists and child-centered educators rapidly diminished. A once promising cause needed a new leader, and William Heard Kilpatrick, a philosopher rather than a psychologist, was quickly catapulted into that role.

Without a doubt, the single most dramatic event in the revival of the child-centered movement was the appearance in the September 1918 issue of *Teachers College Record* of an article with the unpretentious title, "The Project Method."[18] Written by a faculty member at Teachers College, Columbia University, the article caused such an immediate sensation that the Teachers College Bureau of Publications was obliged to distribute an astounding 60,000 reprints. Exactly why that particular article aroused such an explosion of interest was not exactly clear at the outset. The extension of the project idea beyond the field of vocational agriculture had been going on for some time. Part of the answer, to be sure, lay in Kilpatrick's unusually felicitous style, an inspiring way with words that ultimately helped him become the most popular professor in Teachers College history. But beyond the easy cadence of his writing, Kilpatrick was able to rekindle the diminishing hope that the developmentalists had once ignited—that somewhere in the child lay the key to a revitalized system of schooling.

If anything, Kilpatrick's call to arms was the antithesis of the hard efficiency that characterized the social efficiency movement. Although Kilpatrick was usually careful to indicate that the project method of organizing the curriculum was consistent with what he continued to call the "laws of learning," his primary emphasis was that "education be considered as life itself and not as a mere preparation for later living," a position fundamentally opposed to what scientific curriculum makers like Bobbitt and Charters were espousing. "We of America," Kilpatrick declared, "have for years increasingly desired that education be considered as life itself and not as a mere preparation of later living."[19] Instead of a curriculum broken down into its most minute units and then reassembled into the most efficient arrangement possible, Kilpatrick boldly proposed "the conception of wholehearted purposeful activity proceeding in a social environment," or, in short, "the hearty purposeful act" as the basis around which the curriculum would be built.[20]

Some Reforms Achieved

As the twentieth century progressed, these two conflicting reform movements existed alongside one another each scoring a victory now and then but with the original humanist curriculum showing surprising resilience. What started as the project method evolved into the activity curriculum or as it was sometimes called the experience curriculum. "Wholehearted purposeful activity" never replaced the subject as the basic unit in the school curriculum as Kilpatrick earnestly hoped. But *within* the various subject areas, one can detect the influences of these movements. In its early years, the *General Science Quarterly* devoted itself almost exclusively to reorganizing the teaching of science around projects rather than around abstract principles or an array of factual information about the natural world. The idea was to take advantage of the curiosity that children and youth experience about their world as a way of leading into the spirit of scientific inquiry. Such major figures in the teaching of English as John De Boer and Wilbur Hatfield carried on the same crusade in their field, eventually culminating in the influential *An Experience Curriculum in English*,[21] issued by the National Council of Teachers of English. To the extent that the child-study movement achieved any success, it tended to lie in the reorganization of studies within existing subject matter rather than as a substitute for it. The subject, not "the hearty purposeful act," remained the basic building block of the curriculum of American schools throughout the twentieth century.

The victories won by the social efficiency interest group were more numerous and, in some sense, more dramatic. Like the developmentalists, they also achieved some success in reorganizing existing subjects along their own lines. Scientific studies, such as that represented by Edward Lee Thorndike's *The Teacher's Word Book*,[22] strongly influenced the teaching of reading as did comparable studies in other subjects by people like S. A. Courtis in arithmetic. But by far, the most complete single victory in the battle for American schooling was vocationalism. When the prestigious Committee of Ten headed by Charles W. Eliot, the president of Harvard University, reported in 1893, there was no attention to the teaching of vocational subjects. To the members of that Committee, the best preparation for life lay in those academic subjects that were most conducive to training the mind, and it was in terms of the development of the intellect that they saw the function of American schooling. Just a quarter of a century later, when the Commission on the Reorganization of Secondary Education issued its famous Cardinal Principles of Secondary Education, preparation for earning a livelihood was not only prominently mentioned, but was listed as one of the seven aims by which the Commission is most remembered.

The immediate precursor to the emergence of vocational education as a central function of American schools was the manual training movement. Led by professors who were initially concerned with the training of engineers, such as John O. Runkle of the Massachusetts Institute of Technology and Calvin O. Woodward, Dean of the O'Fallon Polytechnical Institute at Washington University, the movement, in its early stages, presented itself as completing a liberal education, not replacing it. "It is scarcely necessary," Woodward declared in 1885, "to add that the 'New' education includes the 'Old.' We tear down no essential parts of the old temple."[23] In general, manual training was not seen in terms of direct trade training but in terms of "education through the hand."

Even in the face of reluctance of education leaders to accept a definition that equated manual training with direct trade training in the nineteenth century, the movement toward specific vocational education proceeded apace once the new century began. It was, in the long run, the immediate benefits of occupational skills rather than the remote values associated with the completing of a liberal education by educating through the hand that had the greater appeal. That appeal in fact was so great that the major impetus for vocational education began to shift from the relatively obscure journals of education and other professional forums to the larger social and political arena. One turning point was the founding in 1896 of the National Association of Manufacturers, which from the outset made school policy a centerpiece of its deliberations. Of particular concern to the National Association of Manufacturers was competition for world markets from Germany, and Germany's system of separate and specialized technical schools was held in such high esteem that, one year after its founding, the NAM annual convention adopted a resolution declaring that since technical education was so critical to the development of industry, its members should support "manual training or other technical schools."[24]

By 1906, the National Society for the Promotion of Industrial Education had been founded with express purpose of influencing American schooling in the direction of vocational education. At first, the exact direction that the movement would take was not clear, but under the guidance of such prominent members of the social efficiency group as David Snedden and Charles Prosser, it soon became a major lobbying force for trade training in the public schools. In 1907, President Theodore Roosevelt wrote to the president of the new society, Henry S. Pritchett, that the American school system had been "well-nigh wholly lacking on the side of industrial training, of the training which fits a man for the shop and farm. . . . We of the United States must develop a system under which each individual citizen shall be trained so as to be effective individually and as an economic unit, and fit to be organized with his fellows so that he and they can work in efficient fashion together."[25] The passage of the Smith-Hughes Act in 1917 not only assured a generous supply of federal money for vocational education in the United States, but marked a significant victory for social efficiency educators who saw vocational education as the linchpin in a program that would prepare youth, not only for jobs, but for all the duties of life. In the years to come, prominent social efficiency educators played significant roles in the administration of the programs that were initiated under the Smith-Hughes Act. The victory that vocational education represented was not limited simply to the addition of subjects designed to prepare youth for particular jobs. It affected other aspects of schooling as vocationalism became a central function of schooling. Subjects like business English and commercial arithmetic are indications that there was a vocationalizing of other aspects of the curriculum as well.

A Third Reform Thrust

With the advent of the Great Depression of the 1930s a new interest group emerged, the social meliorists. Actually, their ancestry can be traced to some of the educational writings of the great American sociologist, Lester Frank Ward, in the late nineteenth century, but their influence through the first two decades of the twentieth century was so minimal as almost to be nonexistent. They existed more as an undercurrent of protest than as a major force for changing the schools. Their central doctrine revolved around the idea that the schools could play a central role in social progress, even in the reconstruction of American society. The economic devastation created by the depression lent credence to their doctrines, and their leaders, such as George S. Counts and Harold Rugg, were thrust into the limelight.

It is likely, however, that even at the height of their popularity, the influence of the social meliorists has been exaggerated. Their leadership was limited largely to certain faculty at Teachers College, Columbia University, and their vision of a new society built on a reconstructed economic system was treated warily by school people. *Social Frontier*, their semiofficial journal, was full of lively, even fascinating, debates about the relationship between schooling and an emerging new society, but reached only a small audience of intellectuals.

The major exception to their apparent lack of success in changing the course of American schooling was the famous series of social studies textbooks written by Harold Rugg. Published by Ginn and Company, the series was nothing short of a phenomenon. After undergoing a series of experimental versions, the first volume, not published until August of 1929, sold over 20,000 in the remaining four months of that year. In 1930, 60,000 volumes were sold. Overall, in the decade between 1929 and 1939, books in the series sold 1,317,960 copies, and an additional 2,287,000 workbooks were sold in the same period.[26]

The success of Rugg's *Man and His Changing Society* was all the more remarkable in view of the breadth of its vision and the departure from conventional approaches to the subject. Most visible, from a curriculum perspective, was the ambitious attempt to reorganize all of the conventional social science disciplines into one organized field of study. History, geography, economics, political science were all made part of a grand plan to understand human civilization. In the context of the times, it was also remarkably bold in terms of the topics covered. Great attention was given, for example, to the contribution of immigrants and to America being a nation of immigrants. In that context, the plight of forced emigration from Africa by blacks was prominently featured. One volume reported in graphic detail the cruelties that blacks endured on their way to America. In one account, a story told by James Morley, a gunner on the ship *Midway*, is reported:

I have seen them under great difficulty of breathing. The women, particularly, often got upon the beams to get air, but they are generally driven down, because they were taking air from the rest. I have seen rice held in the mouths of sea-sick slaves until they were about strangled. I have seen medicine thrown over them in such a way that not half of it went into their mouths. The poor wretches were wallowing in their blood, hardly having life, and with blows from a whip, the cat-o'-nine-tails.[27]

Inequalities in wealth and general material condition also were featured. One page showed two contrasting scenes of residential neighborhoods. The heading under one said, "This is one of the fine residential neighborhoods in Washington, D.C. Notice the wide, well-kept cement boulevard, the trees, the neat hedges, the large, well-built houses, and the automobile." The caption on the photograph below it read: "This is another neighborhood in Washington, D.C. Notice the broken pavement in the alley, the lack of trees, the old tenements, and the carts."[28] In another set of photographs illustrating a chapter called "The Changing American Family," one illustration showed a woman in a white laboratory coat with the subscript: "Many women find that their housework does not keep them sufficiently occupied, so they enter industry, business, or the professions."[29] Another illustration, showing a man and a woman working together on washing dishes, indicates: "This was a rare sight in 1890. It is not unusual today."[30]

Rugg vigorously opposed activity analysis, the mainstay of the social efficiency educators. He saw his series as representing the work of "frontier thinkers" whose vision extended beyond the present to a purified democracy of the future. Like other social reconstructionists, he saw the schools in the forefront of changing the social order. Almost immediately, however, his work attracted concerted opposition, and by 1941, the drive to take the Rugg textbooks out of the public schools had achieved remarkable success. When the Binghamton, New York, board of education voted to drop the series, one newspaper reported under the heading, POISON TEACHING, "The action of the Binghamton, N.Y., board of education in ousting the misnamed 'social science' text-books of Professor Harold Rugg, of Columbia University, will call attention anew to the necessity of seeing that our American children are not being TROJAN HORSED INTO COMMUNISM or any allied collectivist theories."[31] The social reconstructionist ideal enjoyed one notable success in the Rugg textbooks over the course of one decade and then seemed to collapse almost overnight.

John Dewey as Critic

John Dewey is regarded with some justification as the transcendent figure in American education of the twentieth century, but his position in relation to the three major reform movements of the twentieth century is difficult to encapsulate. He has at various times been identified with all of them, but the significance of his opposition to major planks in their platforms has been seriously underestimated.

Dewey, for example, was fundamentally opposed to what may be the most central doctrine of the social efficiency educators—that education is a preparation for what lies ahead. As Bobbitt made this point, "Education is primarily for adult life, not for child life. Its fundamental responsibility is to prepare for the fifty years of adulthood, not for the twenty years of childhood and youth."[32] Dewey regarded his own position as one that "contrasted sharply" with any doctrine based on education as preparation. He objected to placing children on a "waiting list," a kind of probation for "another life." That kind of education, he insisted, has no motive power and puts "a premium on shilly-shallying and procrastination," instead of capitalizing on the natural powers of attention and energy that children bring with them to school. In the end, he claimed, "the principle of preparation makes necessary recourse on a large scale to the use of adventitious motives of pleasure and pain" just because a remote future has no power to direct children's energies. It has cut itself off, he claimed, from the "possibilities of the present."[33] Resort to a system of education based on preparation also, in Dewey's view, subverted the ethical force of education. "Who can reckon up the loss of moral power," Dewey once said, "that arises from the constant impression that nothing is worth doing in itself, but only as a preparation for something else, which in turn is only a getting ready for some genuinely serious end beyond."[34]

Dewey also emerged, strangely enough, as probably the principal opponent of what became the greatest triumph of the social efficiency educators, vocational education. In a debate that he inadvertently initiated with David Snedden in the pages of *New Republic* three years before the passage of the Smith-Hughes Act, Dewey deplored the admiration frequently directed to the dual system of vocational and academic education in Germany, declaring the German educational system to be "frankly nationalistic," something "extraordinarily irrelevant to American conditions."[35] Snedden in his reply seemed genuinely dismayed by Dewey's firm opposition. He denied that vocational education would mainly aid employers, arguing that the benefits of greater productive capacity would ultimately be shared by the workers. In the end, Dewey concluded that his differences with Snedden, the quintessential social efficiency educator, were "not so much narrowly vocational as . . . profoundly political and social." "The kind of vocational education in which I am interested," Dewey insisted, "is not one which will 'adapt' workers to the existing industrial regime; I am not sufficiently in love with the regime for that."[36]

Dewey's reaction to the child-study movement as represented by Hall was anything but enthusiastic. He felt that their claim to converting scientific data on the child into educational prescriptions was grossly exaggerated. He was critical of the idea that science could be converted into "usable recipes, ticketed and labeled for all pedagogical emergencies."[37] Much of the then current interest in the child, Dewey felt, was an outgrowth of German romanticism, which included a belief that childhood was somehow tied to the "childhood of humanity," that it was associated with "a lost Garden of Eden," and, in an apparent reference to Hall, that a return to childhood somehow was connected with idyllic, primitive conditions. Much of it, Dewey thought, was mere sentimental primitivism.[38]

Even when Kilpatrick took over the leadership of the child-centered movement and gave it his project method stamp, Dewey remained rather skeptical of its prospects. Dewey was never completely sanguine about the traditional subject orientation of the curriculum, but his main objection lay in the fact that subjects were conventionally presented to children as finished products and in a form that emphasized their isolation from one another rather than their interrelationships. Knowledge, he thought, ought to appear in the curriculum as vital and interconnected and interdependent. It was not their intellectual content that Dewey objected to but their lack of it. The "subjects grow superficial," he said, "and their multiplication brings weariness to the spirit and the flesh."[39]

Although the project alternative to the subject offered some promise, Dewey felt that projects frequently involved too short a time span and were often casually arrived at. "In short," he said, "they are too trivial to be educative." The knowledge that is gained in that context, he thought, is too often of "a merely technical sort, not a genuine carrying forward of theoretical knowledge."[40] In the end, what Dewey seemed to be rejecting was the project organization as a substitute for the subject as the basic unit in the school's curriculum. What he was advocating was a thorough reconstruction of the subject so that it should appear in the school's curriculum in a much more intellectually respectable form. Additionally, the problem of the isolation of the subjects from one another was something that could be addressed without abandoning subjects altogether.

Dewey's differences with social reconstructionists were much more subtle. For one thing, Dewey shared the political leanings of colleagues like Counts and Rugg, and he had always seen the schools as a force in shaping a better society. Basically, he felt, however, that schools were not a powerful enough instrument to change existing social conditions by themselves. "I do not think," he said, "that the schools can in any literal sense be the builders of a new social order. But the schools will surely, as a matter of fact, and not of ideal, *share* in the building of the social order of the future according as they ally themselves with this or that movement of existing social forces."[41] In other words, Dewey saw as a precondition the existence of forces of change that the schools could choose to support. In the context of the political agitation that characterized the 1930s, there was little doubt in his mind that such forces were coming into being. Dewey was suspicious, however, about education that aimed at a specific solution to the problems that plagued American democracy, and he was unalterably opposed to indoctrination in the schools, which some social reconstructionists appeared to support. He felt that indoctrination worked only in those countries where a political change had already taken place. "There is an important difference," he said, "between education *with respect to a new social order* and indoctrination into settled convictions about that order."[42] What he wished that schools would accomplish in this regard was a fine-grained analysis of present social conditions as a way of getting people to participate aggressively in changing society for the better.

The influence of Dewey as a symbol of school reform in general was undoubtedly greater than the impact of his specific ideas. But schooling did change in the first part of this century. The fact that there were three distinctly different reform thrusts, however, makes it difficult to establish any clear-cut direction. If anything, the social efficiency reformers achieved the most notable successes, but evidence of the impact of the other groups also exists here and there. What emerged after half a century of reform was the patchwork that is the American curriculum today.

Footnotes

1. John Goodlad, *A Place Called School* (New York: McGraw-Hill, 1984).

2. F. L. Mott, *American Journalism: A History of Newspapers in the United States through 250 Years, 1690-1940* (New York: Macmillan, 1941), p. 506.

3. Ibid., p. 507.

4. Robert H. Wiebe, *The Search for Order, 1877-1920* (New York: Hill and Wang, 1967), p. 47.

5. Ellwood P. Cubberly, *Public School Administration* (Boston: Houghton Mifflin, 1916), p. 338.

6. Franklin Bobbitt, *The Curriculum* (Boston: Houghton Mifflin, 1918), p. 42.

7. Ibid.

8. Ibid., p. 43.

9. Samuel Haber, *Efficiency and Uplift: Scientific Management in the Progressive Era 1890-1920* (Chicago: University of Chicago Press, 1964).

10. Charles Francis Adams, *The New Departure in the Common Schools of Quincy and Other Papers* (Boston: Estes and Lauriat, 1879).

11. G. Stanley Hall, "Child Study," in *National Educational Association Journal of Proceedings and Addresses, 1894*, p. 173.

12. G. Stanley Hall, "The Natural Activities of Children as Determining the Industries in Early Education," in *National Educational Association Journal of Proceedings and Addresses, 1904,* pp. 443-44.

13. Dorothy Ross, *G. Stanley Hall: The Psychologist as Prophet* (Chicago: University of Chicago Press, 1972), pp. 341-367.

14. William James, *Talks to Teachers* (New York: Holt, 1899), p. 6.

15. Ibid., p. 7.

16. Ibid.

17. Hugo Munsterberg, *Psychology and Life* (Boston: Houghton Mifflin, 1899).

18. William Heard Kilpatrick, "The Project Method," *Teachers College Record* (September 1918): 319-35.

19. Ibid., p. 323.

20. Ibid., p. 320.

21. W. Wilbur Hatfield, *An Experience Curriculum in English* (New York: D. Appleton-Century, 1935).

22. Edward Lee Thorndike, *The Teacher's Word Book* (New York: Teachers College, 1921).

23. Calvin O. Woodward, "Manual Training in General Education," *Education* 5 (1885): 614.

24. National Association of Manufacturers, *Proceedings* (1897): 92.

25. Roosevelt to Pritchett, in "A Symposium on Industrial Education," *National Society for the Promotion of Industrial Education Bulletin,* September 1907, p. 6.

26. Elmer O. Winters, "Harold Rugg and Education for Social Reconstruction," Doct. diss., University of Wisconsin, 1968, p. 91.

27. Harold Rugg, *Our Country and Our People: An Introduction to American Civilization* (Boston: Ginn and Company, 1938), p. 117.

28. Harold Rugg, *An Introduction to Problems of American Culture* (Boston: Ginn and Company, 1931), p. 53.

29. Ibid., p. 132.

30. Ibid., p. 133.

31. *Milwaukee Sentinel,* 13 June 1940.

32. Franklin Bobbitt, *How to Make A Curriculum* (Boston: Houghton Mifflin, 1924), p. 8.

33. John Dewey, *Democracy and Education* (New York: Macmillan, 1916), pp. 63-64.

34. John Dewey, *Moral Principles in Education* (Boston: Houghton Mifflin, 1909), pp. 25-26.

35. John Dewey, "Education *vs.* Trade Training," *New Republic* 3 (1915): 42-43.

36. John Dewey, "Dr. Dewey Replies," *New Republic* 3 (1915): 72.

37. John Dewey, "Criticisms Wise and Otherwise on Modern Child Study," in *National Educational Association Journal of Proceedings and Addresses,* 1897, pp. 867-68.

38. John Dewey, "The Interpretation Side of Child-Study," in *Transactions of the Illinois Society for Child Study* 2, no. 2 (1897): 17-27.

39. John Dewey, *The Way Out of Educational Confusion* (Cambridge: Harvard University Press, 1931), p. 16.

40. Ibid., p. 31.

41. John Dewey, "Can Education Share in Social Reconstruction?" *Social Frontier* 1 (October 1934): 12.

42. John Dewey, *Education and the Social Order* (New York: League for Industrial Democracy, 1934), p. 10.

Part Two
MODES OF KNOWING

CHAPTER II

Aesthetic Modes of Knowing

ELLIOT EISNER

So gorgeous was the spectacle on the May morning of 1910 when nine kings rode in the funeral of Edward VII of England that the crowd, waiting in hushed and blackclad awe, could not keep back gasps of admiration. In scarlet and blue and green and purple, three by three the sovereigns rode through the palace gates, with plumed helmets, gold braid, crimson sashes, jeweled orders flashing in the sun. After them came five heirs apparent, forty more imperial or royal highnesses, seven queens—four dowager and three regnant—and a scattering of special ambassadors from uncrowned countries. Together they represented seventy nations in the greatest assemblage of royalty and rank ever gathered in one place and, of its kind, the last. The muffled tongue of Big Ben tolled nine by the clock as the cortege left the palace, but on history's clock it was sunset, and the sun of the old world was setting in a dying blaze of splendor never to be seen again.

Barbara Tuchman
The Guns of August, p. 1.

An examination of the relationship between the form and content of the opening paragraph in Barbara Tuchman's *Guns of August* will help us understand what the phrase "aesthetic modes of knowing" alludes to. Before examining this relationship I wish to mention now a theme that I will return to later. The phrase, "aesthetic modes of knowing," presents something of a contradiction in our culture. We do not typically associate the aesthetic with knowing. The arts, with

I wish to acknowledge with gratitude the very useful critique of this chapter by my student, Lynda Stone.

which the aesthetic is most closely associated, is a matter of the heart. Science is thought to provide the most direct route to knowledge. Hence, "aesthetic modes of knowing" is a phrase that contradicts the conception of knowledge that is most widely accepted. I hope to show in this chapter that the widely accepted view is too narrow and that the roads to knowing are many. Let us return to Tuchman.

"So gorgeous was the spectacle on the May morning of 1910 when nine kings rode in the funeral of Edward VII of England that the crowd, waiting in hushed and black-clad awe, could not keep back gasps of admiration." What does Tuchman do in this, the opening line of her book? In the initial phrase, "So gorgeous was the spectacle on the May morning," Tuchman creates a rhythm, which is then punctuated by a staccato-like "when nine kings rode in the funeral of Edward VII." She then follows with contrasts between "gasps" and the soft sound of "hush." And then again, with the phrase "in scarlet *and* blue *and* green *and* purple, three by three the sovereigns rode through the palace gates," Tuchman creates a syncopation that recapitulates the sound of hoofs pounding the pavement as the horses pass by. Again, "with plumed helmets, gold braid, crimson sashes and jeweled orders flashing in the sun"—another series of short bursts filled with images as well as sound. And later in the paragraph, the "muffled tongue of Big Ben tolled nine by the clock." Here, the paired contradictions of "hushed gasps" and "muffled tones" appeal to our sense of metaphor. And for a finale Tuchman writes, "but on history's clock it was sunset, and the sun of the Old World was setting in a dying blaze of splendor never to be seen again." Like the coda of a classical symphony, Tuchman brings the paragraph to a slow declining close.

What occurs in the paragraph occurs throughout the book, and what occurs throughout the book is what makes literature literary. It is in the use of form, especially in the cadence and tempo of language, that patterns are established among the "parts" of the sentence and between the sentence and the paragraph that create their counterpart in the reader's experience. "After them came five heirs apparent, forty more imperial or royal highnesses, seven queens—four dowager and three regnant—and a scattering of special ambassadors from uncrowned countries." Like a partridge in a pear tree, the cadence of the sentence captivates and carries the reader off on a ride.

What also occurs in the paragraph is the generation in the reader's mind's eye of an array of visual images. The writing is vivid and it is vivid because it is designed to elicit images of scarlet and blue and purple and of the plumed helmets and the gold braid. The writing evokes the scene Tuchman wishes the reader to see. We are able to participate vicariously in events that occurred when we were not yet born.

Consider again her use of language: "the muffled tones of Big Ben" and "black-clad awe." The language is shaped to help us see and feel the day and hence to know it as participants. Its form and content transport us to another time, another place. The literary in literature resides in the aesthetic capacities of language to influence our experience.

The reader should not assume that the aesthetic treatment of form for purposes of vicarious participation in events not directly available is limited to literature. Poetry, dance, the visual arts, and drama all employ form for such purposes. The drama within drama is created through the tensions that writers, actors, stage designers, lighting experts, and directors produce. What happens on the stage is the result of a collective effort. What occurs in literary works and in the visual arts is usually the product of individuals. Whether collective or individual, the common function of the aesthetic is to modulate form so that it can, in turn, modulate our experience. The moving patterns of sound created by composers, in turn, create their counterparts in the competent listener. The physically static forms produced by visual artists create in the competent viewer a quality of life analogous to those in the forms beheld. In sum, the form of the work informs us. Our internal life is shaped by the forms we are able to experience.

The phrase "we are able to experience" is a critical one. If the forms that constitute the arts or the sciences spoke for themselves we would need no programs in the schools to help students to learn how "to read" them. What we are able to see or hear is a product of our cultivated abilities. The rewards and insights provided by aesthetically shaped forms are available only to those who can perceive them. Not only is competence a necessary condition for experiencing the form in works we have access to, but the particular quality of life generated by the forms encountered will, to some degree, differ from individual to individual. All experience is the product of both the features of the world and the biography of the individual. Our experience is influenced by our past as it interacts with our present.[1] Thus, not only must a certain kind of competence be acquired in order to perceive the qualities of form in the objects available to us, but the nature of our experience with these forms is influenced not only by the form itself but by our past.

I have thus far directed my remarks to the aesthetic functions of form as a source of experience and understanding in the fine arts and in literature. But I do not wish to suggest that the aesthetic is restricted to the fine arts and literature. All scientific inquiry culminates in the creation of form: taxonomies, theories, frameworks, conceptual systems. The scientist, like the artist, must transform the content of his or her imagination into some public, stable form, something that can be shared with others. The shape of this form—its coherence—is a critical feature concerning its acceptability. The adequacy of theory is not simply determined by experimental results. Experimental results can often be explained by competing theories. The attractiveness of a theory is a central factor in our judgment of it.

Viewed this way, both artist and scientist create forms through which the world is viewed. Both artist and scientist make qualitative judgments about the fit, the coherence, the economy, "the rightness" of the forms they create. Readers of these forms make similar judgments. It was his recognition of the universal character of form-making in every sphere of human life that prompted Sir Herbert Read to say that the aim of education was the creation of artists. What he meant was that all students should be enabled to produce good forms. He writes:

> Having established the relevance of aesthetics to the processes of perception and imagination, I shall then pass on to the less disputed ground of expression. Education is the fostering of growth, but apart from physical maturation, growth is only made apparent in expression—audible or visible signs and symbols. Education may therefore be defined as the cultivation of modes of expression—it is teaching children and adults how to make sounds, images, movements, tools and utensils. A man who can make such things well is a well educated man. If he can make good sounds, he is a good speaker, a good musician, a good poet; if he can make good images, he is a good painter or sculptor; if good movements, a good dancer or laborer; if good tools or utensils, a good craftsman. All faculties, of thought, logic, memory, sensibility and intellect, are involved in such processes, and no aspect of education is excluded in such processes. And they are all processes which involve art, for

art is nothing but the good making of sounds, images, etc. The aim of education is therefore the creation of artists—of people efficient in the various modes of expression.[2]

There is another sense in which form and the aesthetic experience it engenders can be considered. I have used the term "form" thus far to refer to the products made by both artists and scientists. Both, I have argued, create forms, and these forms have aesthetic features that appeal. But the term form can be conceived of not only as a noun, but as a verb. Following Read, we form groups, we form sentences, we form structures. "Form," in this sense, refers to something we do. Indeed, in Norway visual arts education is called "Forming." To form is to engage in an activity occurring over time, guided by attention to changing qualities whose end is to produce a structure, either temporal or spatial, that gives rise to feeling. To be able to produce such forms the qualities that constitute them must be appraised by their contribution to the life of feeling. The maker, in this case, must know what he has before him in order to make decisions that will yield the hoped for results. A satisfying end is achieved only if appropriate choices are made in process. To make such choices one must be aware of the qualities of form as well as the content as one proceeds. One must know the qualities of life that the qualitative components engender and how they will function within the whole when it is completed.

In this view the aesthetic is both a subject matter and a criterion for appraising the processes used to create works of science as well as art. The aesthetic is not simply the possession of completed works. The sense of rightness or fit that a scientist or artist experiences in the course of his or her work is crucial to the quality of the final work. But not only does the aesthetic function in this way. The ability to experience the aesthetic features of the process has been regarded as a prime motive for work. Alfred North Whitehead once commented, "Most people believe that scientists inquire in order to know. Just the opposite is the case. Scientists know in order to inquire." Scientists, Whitehead believed, are drawn to their work not by epistemological motives but by aesthetic ones. The joy of inquiry is the driving motive for their work. Scientists, like artists, formulate new and puzzling questions in order to enjoy the experience of creating answers to them.

The distinctions I have made concerning form and the aesthetic as a mode of knowing can be summed up thus far as follows. First, all things made, whether in art, science, or in practical life, possess form. When well made these forms have aesthetic properties. These aesthetic properties have the capacity to generate particular qualities of life in the competent percipient. In literature and in many of the arts such forms are used to reveal or represent aspects of the world that cannot be experienced directly. Second, form is not only an attribute or condition of things made; it is a process through which things are made. Knowing how forms will function within the finished final product is a necessary condition for creating products that themselves possess aesthetic qualities. Such knowing requires an active and intelligent maker. Third, the deeper motives for productive activity in both the arts and the sciences often emanate from the quality of life the process of creation makes possible. These satisfactions are related to the kinds of stimulation secured in the play process and from the aesthetic satisfactions derived from judgments made about emerging forms.

My comments thus far have been intended to free the aesthetic from the province of the arts alone and to recognize its presence in all human formative activity. All subjects have aesthetically significant features, from the process of making to the form the product finally takes. I have also argued that what we find satisfying in both art and science is a function of the coherence the things we make possess. The creation of coherence is a central aim in both art and science. The aesthetic as a mode of knowing therefore can be regarded in two senses. First, it is through aesthetic experience that we can participate vicariously in situations beyond our practical possibilities. The aesthetic in knowing, in this sense, performs a referential function; it points to some aspect of the world and helps us experience it.

Second, knowledge *of*, rather than knowledge *through*, the aesthetic is knowledge of the aesthetic qualities of form per se. We become increasingly able to know those qualities we call aesthetic by our developed ability to experience the subtleties of form. We come to know aspects of music and literature and science by being increasingly able to experience their nuances. The music of Mendelssohn and the paintings of Pollack contain certain unique features; they possess an "aesthetic." To know these features is to know aspects of the world. To achieve such knowledge the percipient must be aesthetically literate. He or she must be able to read their subtle and often complex aesthetic features. Knowledge within the aesthetic mode is therefore knowledge of two kinds. First, it is knowledge of the world toward which the aesthetic qualities of form point: we understand the emotional meaning of jealousy through the form that Shakespeare conferred upon *Othello*. Second, it is knowledge of the aesthetic in its own right, for no other purpose than to have or undergo experience. Such motives are often the driving force in the creation of both science and art.

One might well ask why the aesthetic should play such an important role in the arts and sciences. What is it that confers such a significant function upon what is often regarded as an ornamental and unnecessary aspect of life? One reason is related to man's biological nature. I speak here of the deep-seated need for stimulation. Humans have a low toleration for homeostasis. We seek to use our capacities, to activate our sensory systems, to vary our experience. When our life is without stimulation, as it is in sensory deprivation experiments, we hallucinate. When we are sated with one type of experience, we seek other kinds. Rather than being a stimulus-reducing organism, the human is stimulus-seeking. The aesthetic is one important source of stimulation. Secured within the process of coping with the problematic, its satisfactions arise as the problematic is explored and eventually resolved. The making of a form from the simplest sandcastle to the most advanced architectural achievement is a process in which aesthetic satisfactions are pervasive. Our need for variety and for stimulation is met, in part, through the aesthetics of human action.

The aesthetic is not only motivated by our need for stimulation; it is also motivated by our own need to give order to our world. To form is to confer order. To confer aesthetic order upon our world is to make that world hang together, to fit, to feel right, to put things in balance, to create harmony. Such harmonies are sought in all aspects of life. In science it is extraordinarily vivid: theory is the result of our desire to create a world we can understand. The scientist conceptualizes a theoretical structure, defines its parts, and arranges them in a configuration that appeals to our sensibilities so that the theoretical form helps us make sense of our world.

The need for coherence in things made is not, of course, limited to science or art; it manifests itself in all walks of life from the setting of a table to our social interactions.[3] The exquisite creation of either is a very high aesthetic achievement.

The aesthetic, then, is motivated by our need to lead a stimulating life. Related to the need to explore and play, the aesthetic is part and parcel of what these processes are intended to yield, not only practical outcomes related to premeditated goals, but the delights of exploration. The aesthetic is also inherent in our need to make sense of experience. This sense-making is located in the choices we make in our effort to create order. Both scientists and artists, to take paradigm cases, are makers of order—the former through the relationships created within theoretical material and the other through the ordering of the qualitative. Our sense of rightness, like our sense of justice, is rooted in that ineffable experience to which the word "aesthetic" is assigned.

I said at the outset that I would return later to a theme I introduced at that time. That theme was the contradiction in our culture between the terms aesthetic and knowing. The polarities we encounter between these terms hark back to Plato's conception of the hierarchies of knowledge. Plato believed that episteme—true and certain knowledge—could not be secured if one depended upon the information the senses provided.[4] The reasons, he thought, were clear enough. Sensory information is dependent upon the stuff of which our universe is made, namely, material things. Since material things are in a state of constant decay, any knowledge derived from them must, of necessity, be short-term at best and misleading at worst. Second, sensory information is not trustworthy. To illustrate how the senses mislead consider how a perfectly straight rod placed in a glass of water appears to be bent. Knowledge derived from what the senses provide, as such a case reveals, is misleading. The rod is straight, not bent, even though it *appears* bent. To secure knowledge that is dependable, Plato believed, one must move away from the empirical world that our senses come to know and move into the world of abstraction. The most secure and dependable form of knowledge is achieved not through empirical investigation or sensory information, but through the exercise of our rationality. Through our rational powers we can conceive of a perfect circle even though we will never see one in the world in which we live. Dependable knowledge is more likely as we move from the concrete to the abstract. The more we advance toward the abstract the more we achieve episteme.

Plato's views have had a profound effect not only upon our conception of knowledge, but upon our conception of intelligence. To be intelligent means in our culture—especially the culture of schooling—to be able to manipulate abstract ideas. One of the most vivid examples of this is to be found in the status of mathematics as a school subject. Mathematical ability is commonly regarded as a prime manifestation of intelligence. Ability in mathematics is considered prima facie evidence of one's suitability for the rigors of university work. Mathematics, the queen of the sciences, is the apotheosis of human intelligence.

Subjects that depend upon empirical information such as the natural and social sciences are a step lower in the intellectual hierarchy. Again, the reason is clear. Truth in mathematics does not require empirical evidence but rather rational comprehension. Claims to truth in the sciences look toward a decaying empirical world for evidence of validity.

When it comes to the arts and to things made, the level of intelligence employed is even lower in rank. And should emotion or feeling enter the picture, the likelihood of achieving dependable knowledge is smaller still. For Plato the life of feeling was, like the passions, an impediment to knowledge.[5] What one wanted was pure mind, unencumbered by emotion or by the misleading qualities of the empirical world.

This view of knowledge and intelligence did not terminate with Plato's passing. Our current view of knowledge is based largely upon it. Consider, for example, the distinction we often make between intelligence and talent: talent is displayed primarily in things related to the body, the arts and sports, for example. Intelligence is used to describe those who are good at abstraction. The highly intelligent enroll in college preparatory courses—the more abstract the better. Those who are talented are good at making and doing things. We are less apt to view these doings and makings as examples of intelligence at work.[6] Consider further the typical distinctions between the cognitive, the affective, and the psychomotor. We create tidy psychological domains, keep our categories clean, and assign the aesthetic to affect: its presence in human experience, we tacitly hold, is not a function of thinking.

Consider still further what our tests assess in the way of achievement. The *Scholastic Aptitude Test*, for example, focuses upon two areas of human performance, verbal and mathematical. Both of these areas are regarded as abstract rather than concrete in character. We assess a student's aptitude for the heady work of college by defining aptitude in terms of verbal and mathematical skills. To be sure, verbal and mathematical skills are relevant for college; my point is not that they are irrelevant. It is that these abilities are considered the primary surrogates of human intelligence and symbolize an entire constellation of assumptions about the mind, knowledge, and human ability. These assumptions are so pervasive in western culture and so dominant in our own professional culture that few of us have the psychological distance to regard them for what they are, human constructions, something made and, therefore, something that could be otherwise.

Given these assumptions, the aesthetic becomes a casualty in American education. It is embedded in a historical context that has underestimated the role it plays in man's effort to know. The aesthetic aspects of human experience are considered luxuries. And luxuries, as we all know, can be rather easily foregone in hard times.

The aesthetic is also diminished by our belief that we *search for* knowledge. Knowledge is considered by most in our culture as something that one discovers, not something that one makes.[7] Knowledge is out there waiting to be found, and the most useful tool for finding it is science. If there were greater appreciation for the extent to which knowledge is constructed—something made—there might be a greater likelihood that its aesthetic dimensions would be appreciated. To make knowledge is to cast the scientist in the role of an artist or a craftsperson, someone who shapes materials and ideas. The making of something is a techne, and for good techne one must be artistically engaged, and if artistically engaged, then aesthetic considerations and criteria must operate to some extent.

What does the argument I have provided imply for education? One implication pertains to the way in which we think about what we teach. The curriculum of the school performs a variety of important functions. One such function is to convey to students what we regard as important for them to learn. These values are expressed in what we choose to assess in school, in the amount of time we devote to various subjects, and in the location of the time that is assigned to what we teach. Our educational priorities are not expressed by our testimonials or our publicly prepared curriculum syllabi, but in our actions. By our works we are known.

If we believe that the aesthetic values of a subject are important for students to appreciate and experience, then we must, it seems to me, try to figure out how these values can be purposely introduced to them. We often recognize, in our conversations at least, that mathematics has an aesthetic dimension. What does this mean for designing curriculum and teaching? Are students aware of the aesthetic aspects of mathematics, and if not, what can we do about it?

Mathematics is, in some ways, far removed from what we usually regard as a subject having aesthetic dimensions, but clearly literature is not. Yet, how do we help students experience the aesthetic aspects of language? What kind of work would they be asked to do if we gave the aesthetic aspects of writing and reading a significant priority in the teaching of English? What kind of sensibilities would we cultivate—indeed must we cultivate—if writing and reading are to be more than simple encoding and decoding? One cannot write well if one has a tin ear. It is necessary to hear the melodies of language (as Barbara Tuchman obviously does) in order to use language in graceful and informative ways. While few students will become as skilled as Tuchman, all students can learn how to attend to the cadences of language. How do we help them do this?

Do students recognize the aesthetic features of inquiry in science and in the social studies, or do they separate the aesthetic from what they study in general and assign it to the realm of the arts alone? What would we need to teach in each of the fields students study to help them understand the role that the aesthetic plays in a particular field? How might we design tasks within a field of study so that inquiry in that field provided aesthetic satisfaction? Such questions point in a direction quite opposite to the direction in which curricula and teaching have been moving over the past ten years. Pedagogical practices in American schools have become increasingly fragmented. Because of pressures upon teachers to become "accountable," there has been a widespread tendency to break curricula into small units of instruction.[8] The result of this fragmentation is to make it increasingly difficult for students to see how each piece is a part of a larger whole. When the content taught for each small fragment is tested, the test is a signal to the student that he or she can forget what has been "learned" after the test has been taken. By using such teaching and testing procedures it is believed the teacher will secure an objective record of what a student knows and the student will have unambiguous feedback of how well he or she is doing. The educational liability of such teaching and learning procedures is that they emphasize short-term memory; it is difficult to remember small bits and pieces of information when there is no larger conception or armature upon which they can be placed. Indeed, this orientation to teaching and testing is formidable; it may make it difficult for students to achieve meaningful learning.

Another factor that undermines the aesthetic is that the rewards that are emphasized in class are rewards emanating from test performance. What far too many teachers and students care about almost solely is how well they do on tests.[9] Again, the focus is on the short-term and the instrumental. Yet the enduring outcomes of education are to be found in consummatory satisfactions—the joy of the ride, not simply arriving at the destination. If the major satisfactions in schools are high test scores, the value of what is learned tends to decline precipitously after the tests are taken. The only confident way to have a bull market in schooling is to turn students on to the satisfactions of inquiry in the fields into which they are initiated.

There is another implication of signal importance that pertains to the formation of curriculum and teaching in our schools. The implication I described earlier regarding the place of the aesthetic in the school curriculum is related to what we convey to students about what we value for them. The absence of a subject or its de facto neglect in the curriculum teaches students implicitly that we do not value that subject.

There is, finally, one more implication regarding the absence of a subject. This implication has to do with the fact that the curriculum is a mind-altering device. When we define the content and tasks that constitute the curriculum, we also define the kind of mental skills we choose to cultivate. The absence of attention to the aesthetic in the school curriculum is an absence of opportunities to cultivate the sensibilities. It is an absence of the refinement of our consciousness, for it is through our sensibilities that our consciousness is secured. If our educational program put a premium on the aesthetic as well as on the instrumental features of what is taught, students would have an opportunity to develop mental skills that for most students now lie fallow. Attention to the aesthetic aspects of the subjects taught would remind students that the ideas within subject areas, disciplines, and fields of study are human constructions, shaped by craft, employing technique, and mediated through some material. Works of science are, in this sense, also works of art.

Such an orientation to knowledge would reduce the tendency for students to regard the textbook as sacred and knowledge as fixed—not a bad outcome for a nation that prides itself on being a democracy. The more students conceive of their roles as scholars and critics, as makers and appraisers of things made, the less tendency they will have to regard the world as beyond their power to alter.

But for me the most important contributions of the aesthetic to education pertain to what I have called its referential and its consummatory functions. The referential function is performed as students acquire the ability to read the forms that aesthetic qualities convey: we can learn from aesthetically rendered lives what words, paradoxically, can never say. As Langer puts it:

> The arts, like language, abstract from experience certain aspects for our contemplation. But such abstractions are not concepts that have names. Discursive speech can fix definable concepts better and more exactly. Artistic expression abstracts aspects of the life of feeling which have no names, which have to be presented to sense and intuition rather than to a word-bound, note-taking consciousness.[10]

The consummatory function of the aesthetic provides delights in the inquiry itself. The durable outcomes of schooling are not to be found in short-term, instrumental tasks. Such outcomes must penetrate more deeply. When school programs neglect attention to the aesthetics of shaping form, they neglect the very satisfactions that reside at the core of education. If students are not moved by what they study, why would they want to pursue such studies on their own? But one has a hard time keeping them away from things that do provide them with deep satisfactions. Can we aspire for less in education?

The aesthetic in education has two major contributions to make, neither of which is yet a purposeful part of our educational agenda. First, it tells us about the world in ways specific to its nature. Second, it provides the experiential rewards of taking the journey itself. These potential contributions must surely be important to those who wish, as we do, to improve the quality of schooling for the young.

Footnotes

1. The concept that most succinctly captures this notion is John Dewey's term "interaction." See his *Experience and Education* (New York: Macmillan, 1938).

2. Herbert Read, *Education through Art* (New York: Pantheon Books, 1956), p. 10.

3. John Dewey, *Art as Experience* (New York: Minton Balch and Co., 1934), especially chap. 1.

4. Plato, *The Republic*, translated into English by B. Jowett (New York: Modern Library, 1941).

5. Ibid., Book Six.

6. It is telling, I believe, that the best overall prediction of intelligence test scores is the vocabulary section of group intelligence tests. The ability to know and use words is, in our culture, a mark of intelligence. This view is now being challenged by several psychologists. See, for example, Howard Gardner, *Frames of Mind* (New York: Basic Books, 1983).

7. Even some constructionist views of knowledge employ terms, in the books in which they appear, suggesting that knowledge is discovered. See, for example, Barney G. Glaser and Anselm Strauss, *The Discovery of Grounded Theory* (Chicago: Aldine Publishing Co., 1967) and Karl Popper, *The Logic of Scientific Discovery* (New York: Harper and Row, 1968).

8. Recent studies of classroom practices in secondary schools have revealed this tendency. See John I. Goodlad, *A Place Called School* (New York: McGraw-Hill, 1984).

9. Current studies of secondary schools undertaken at Stanford University suggest this quite clearly.

10. Suzanne Langer, *Problems of Art* (New York: Charles Scribners Sons, 1957), pp. 94-95.

CHAPTER III

On What Scientists Know, and How They Know It

D. C. PHILLIPS

In the opening speech of Shakespeare's *King Henry the Fifth,* the issue is raised of whether the stirring and heroic events of that monarch's reign could be adequately conveyed with the meager resources of the Globe Theater:

> Can this cockpit hold
> The vasty fields of France? Or may we cram
> Within this wooden O the very casques
> That did affright the air at Agincourt?

The answer, of course, was a qualified "yes." A parallel question—hopefully with the same answer—may be raised about the present enterprise: Can a single chapter, limited with respect to the number of pages available, present an adequate account of the contemporary debates about the nature of scientific knowledge? For there can be little doubt that momentous events have taken place here as well; there have been intellectual Agincourts aplenty that have laid waste to many long-standing beliefs about the nature of science. The literature is voluminous, and there are great subtlety and depth to many of the contributions. So, at the outset of any attempt to give an overview or an interpretation of what has been happening, it is wise to follow the bard's example and to seek pardon for daring to "bring forth so great an object."

The Centrality of Science

During the last few centuries of Western intellectual history,

I thank Harris Cooper, Robert Ennis, Rob Orton, Harvey Siegel, and Lynda Stone for their comments on the penultimate draft.

educated people typically have held an exalted view of science.[1] Together with mathematics, it has stood as the model of what a body of knowledge ought to be. In epistemological discussions in philosophy, it has been taken as an important case of "justified true belief." John Dewey wrote of science as "authorized conviction," and he said that "without initiation into the scientific spirit one is not in possession of the best tools which humanity has so far devised for effectively directed reflection."[2] Researchers in a variety of fields, ranging from history to psychology and sociology, have felt apologetic if their disciplines have fallen short of the ideals derived from physical science; they have engaged in the quest for laws and theories with vigor but without resounding success. In the field of education, curriculum theorists have often considered science to be one of the "basics," and since the time of Herbert Spencer it has been regarded as an important component of a liberal (or liberating) education. Plato, of course, thought of science as inferior to mathematics and philosophy because it dealt with the changing and hence unreal world of sense-experience, but Plato was not speaking for epistemologists of the nineteenth and twentieth centuries. The etymology of the word "science" reveals all; Jacob Bronowski writes that "we are a scientific civilization: that means, a civilization in which knowledge and its integrity are crucial. Science is only a Latin word for knowledge."[3]

During the last three decades this epistemological status of science has come into question. Not that there was a scarcity of serious questions earlier. In some ways John Dewey pointed the direction that later inquiry was to follow. For those who paid attention, he clearly raised the issue of how our various knowledge claims were warranted, and he suggested that there was no difference in principle between the warranting of scientific and other types of claims (including aesthetic and moral ones). But, for a variety of reasons, his work did not inspire more than a handful of those at the cutting edge of the philosophy of science during the 1950s and 1960s. For some, the landmark was the translation into English of Popper's *Logic of Scientific Discovery* in 1957. Here the message was clear—scientific knowledge claims can never be proven or fully justified, they can only be refuted. For others, the turning point was less sharply demarcated, and was constituted by the gradual erosion in the credibility of logical positivism—the position that seemed to be the foundation for the traditional view of the epistemology of science. Others were finally shaken by Kuhn's *The Structure of Scientific Revolutions* in 1962, or by the work of Lakatos or Feyerabend a little later. By the mid 1970s, the "rationality of science" had become a major issue, and the literature now has grown to mammoth proportions. Newton-Smith has summarized the situation well:

> The scientific community sees itself as the very paradigm of institutionalized rationality. It is taken to be in possession of something, the scientific method, which generates a "logic of justification.". . . For Feyerabend, Kuhn, and others, not only does scientific practice not live up to the image the community projects, it could not do so. For that image, it is said, embodies untenable assumptions concerning the objectivity of truth, the role of evidence and the invariance of meanings.[4]

Where do we stand today? How are scientific claims warranted? What rational grounds, if any, are there for a person to assent to the doctrines of modern science? Should workers in other disciplines strive to make them more like science? Or should people working in the sciences finally capitulate and acknowledge that, epistemologically speaking, their knowledge claims are no more secure than those put forward elsewhere?

Headway can be made with respect to these important questions by focusing on the insights that have been achieved over the past twenty years in philosophy of science. And the discussion of these insights can be grouped conveniently under the following headings: (a) Is observation in any sense foundational in science? (b) Are theories generated from, or determined by, evidence? (c) Is rational justification of knowledge claims possible? (d) Is justification necessarily relative to a framework? (e) Is there a difference in kind between natural and social science?

The Role of Observation

In the account of science given in textbooks for most of the century—an account supported to some degree by the philosophy of logical positivism—observation played a key role. There is little point in reviewing in detail the historical steps through which this "received view" decayed; it is sufficient to say that it is now widely regarded as untenable to hold that scientific theories are built up from a foundation of secure, unquestionable, objective, and theory-neutral observation.

Nor do any convincing grounds remain for believing that scientific theories, wherever they come from, can, after their production or invention, be reduced to a set of neutral "observation statements."

The two viewpoints that are rejected here are related, but they are not identical. The first view focuses upon the *production* of theories, while the second deals with the *logical status* of theories however they are produced. But taken together, the rejections of both theses have seemed to some writers to lead to a conundrum: science apparently is a body of knowledge about the sensible world, yet if observation plays no central role either in the production or in establishing the logical status of this knowledge, how can science be about the real world? In recent years there are many who have taken this slippery argument seriously; they have held that science has no objective basis whatsoever, it is merely one ideology or world view among many, but it has no special status or rationale warranting special respect. However, a good case can be made that the conundrum is overstated; it is not that observation plays no role at all, but that its role is not *foundational* in the sense (or senses) understood in earlier decades. Nor does it follow that science is ideological, or that it is a matter of whim. What, then, are the insights that have been attained about observation, and what is the new understanding of the role that can be ascribed to it?

To start with the rejection of the view that scientific theories are produced from an objective observational base, the work that immediately comes to mind here is that of N. R. Hanson. His discussion of the theory-laden nature of observation in his *Patterns of Discovery* (1958) has won the status of a classic.[5] He was not the first to say the things he did; several years earlier, in *Philosophical Investigations*, Wittgenstein even used one of the same diagrams to make the same point, and earlier still John Dewey realized that perception was not "neutral" but that knowledge and intelligence operated so as to influence it—"judgment is employed in the perception; otherwise the perception is mere sensory excitation. . . ."[6] But, for whatever reason, it was Hanson rather than these others who finally fixed the idea in contemporary consciousness.

Hanson's thesis may be stated in one sentence: "The theory, hypothesis, framework, or background knowledge held by an investigator can strongly influence what is observed." Or, in his own words, "there is more to seeing than meets the eyeball."[7] Thus, in a famous psychological experiment, slides were made from cards selected from a deck, and these were projected for very short periods onto a screen in front of various observers. The slides were all correctly identified, except for one that was a trick slide where the card was given the wrong color (for example, a black six of hearts). Most commonly the observers in the experiment saw this trick slide as a blur, or they misidentified the suit of the card. A Hansonian interpretation of this is that the observers' background knowledge (cards in the suit of hearts are red in color) influences their perception. There is some sort of interaction with the sensory data received from the slide, so that the final result is that the observers actually *see* a blur. There have been other psychological experiments in which people looking at slides of drawings saw different things depending on what particular theories they were armed with.

Until recently there has been little dispute about the truth of Hanson's thesis. Philosophers of science as diverse as Hempel, Popper, Scheffler, and Kuhn have accepted it. Recently, however, Jerry Fodor has begun to swim against the tide by arguing that indeed there are some observations, important for science, that are theory-neutral.[8] Putting this to one side, however, for some time there has been dispute about the *significance* of the thesis. A passage from Kuhn nicely expresses this; he is discussing several scientists who were looking at the same phenomenon but from the perspective of different background theories, and the Hansonian issue arises as to whether they therefore were seeing different things:

> Do we, however, really need to describe what separates Galileo from Aristotle, or Lavoisier from Priestley, as a transformation of vision? Did these men really *see* different things when *looking at* the same sorts of objects? . . . Those questions can no longer be postponed.[9]

One thing does seem clear: Hanson's thesis successfully undermines crude forms of empiricism and positivism, that is, those philosophical positions that suggest knowledge is built up from a neutral or objective observational base. For, according to Hanson, there is no such theory-neutral base. There has been no lack of writers, inspired by Hanson, who are willing to spell all this out. Thus, the neo-Marxist philosopher of education Kevin Harris, in his *Education and Knowledge* (1979), assumes all empiricists are crude, and he writes:

> The empiricist observes, collects, and infers. He goes out into the world and collects his data or his facts diligently, he puts them together and analyzes them, and then he draws out relations between them.[10]

It is, then, an easy matter for Harris to show (correctly) that "most of the problems with this approach come in the first step," for the observation and collection of "facts" are of course theory-laden.

At this point the discussion needs to turn, to focus upon the second role ascribed to observation. For what is overlooked by Harris, and by others who also wish to destroy the credibility of empiricism in a similar way, is that modern forms of empiricism do not talk of the *origins* of knowledge but of its *validation* or *justification*.[11] This is an entirely different matter, where the theory-ladenness of observation presents no problem. Indeed, it can be argued that here Hanson is a blessing; for in order to test or validate a theory one *must* use that theory's "way of seeing the world." For instance, when examining Freudian theory to see if it is warranted, one must use Freud's categories to deduce tests—it is illicit to use Skinnerian categories (except, of course, for a test of Skinner, or for a comparative test of the two theories, but in this latter case one would still have to use Freud as well). Neither does it follow from the truth of Hanson's thesis (if, indeed, it is true) that the very possibility has disappeared of running objective tests of a scientific theory. For no reason has been offered to support the view that because a theory is being worked with, and because, therefore, the observer will be influenced to see the world via the categories contained in the theory, then the world is thereby bound to *confirm* that theory. Israel Scheffler has put the point clearly:

> What is the upshot? There is no evidence for a general incapacity to learn from contrary observations, no proof of a preestablished harmony between what we believe and what we see. . . . Our categorizations and expectations guide by orienting us selectively toward the future; they set us, in particular, to perceive in certain ways and not in others. Yet they do not blind us to the unforeseen. They allow us to recognize what fails to match anticipation.[12]

There is a crucial difference between the thesis advanced here about the role of observation in testing, and a notorious view (referred to earlier) that was held by some of the logical positivists of past decades concerning "observation sentences" or "protocol sentences" (such as "red here now"). In holding that observation can still play an important role in the testing or justification of scientific knowledge claims, despite its theory-laden nature, it is not being held that scientific theories can be reduced to—that is, translated into—statements fully in observational terms. Indeed, a multitude of critics of logical positivism have driven home the point that the theoretical concepts of science have meanings that transcend definition in observational terms. Thus there are few today who would endorse the quest of yesteryear of Rudolf Carnap, who stated the theme of his first major book as follows: "The main problem concerns the possibility of the rational reconstruction of the concepts of all fields of knowledge on the basis of concepts that refer to the immediately given" (immediately given, that is, in experience such as observation).[13] Nor would many now endorse the program of P. W. Bridgman and the operationists, a program that had at its heart the belief that the meaning of any scientific construct or variable is given by the specification of the "activities or operations" necessary to measure it.[14]

But here another conundrum arises. On one hand it has just been argued that theory-laden observation can be efficacious in testing a scientist's knowledge claims. On the other hand, if these claims cannot be translated fully into observational terms, then it would seem to follow that any test that was conducted would not be absolutely authoritative. A theory that does not necessitate a precise set of observational consequences can never be decisively probed by any test, for there must always be some leeway or looseness that could allow the scientist to argue that the theory somehow was compatible with the test results (whatever they were). How, then, can it be argued that observation plays any worthwhile role in testing?

In effect, this query is a narrower version of a larger general question: In what ways are scientific theories related to evidence? It is to this that the discussion must turn.

Theory and Evidence

In the past few decades a whole host of problems concerning the relation between scientific theories and evidence have come to light. The overall effect of these has been to cement in place the view that theories are *underdetermined* by evidence. That is, whatever evidence is available, a variety of theories can exist that are compatible with it. Furthermore, as new evidence accumulates, there is a variety of ways in which every one of these competing theories could be adjusted in order to take account of the new material. No *specific* change in any theory is necessitated by new evidence; all that new evidence necessitates is that some accommodation be made somewhere. In the light of all this, there is little wonder that the rationality of science has become a topic of importance—what grounds are there for believing that any scientific theory is warranted, when the available evidence can also be used to support a host of rival theories? While this problem is a serious one, it will be argued that there are no grounds for despair.[15]

Because the developments that have led in this direction are numerous, and because they tend to overlap and partially reinforce each other, it is difficult to organize a clear discussion. The simplest procedure is to enumerate the points:

1. It has been recognized, at least since the time of David Hume in the eighteenth century, that there is a problem with the inductive support of scientific theories. A finite amount of evidence, for example, that all swans that have so far been observed are white does not, in logic, establish the claim that *all* swans are white. This is an inductive inference, and by definition the conclusion goes beyond the evidence provided—a finite number of observations on swans does not firmly establish anything about all swans. And although at first sight it seems reasonable to claim that the finite evidence makes the inductive inference probable, it is not clear how to calculate the precise degree of probability, nor is it clear that this does not beg the whole question. For the heart of the problem of induction lies in whether we have sound reason to believe that evidence about the past can throw any light at all on the future. (It would help if we could establish that nature was regular; but of course this principle itself would be a product of induction, so there is no succor here.) This "problem of induction" has been seen as a blot on the escutcheon of science (and of philosophy) for over two centuries.

2. With the questioning of the tenets of logical positivism over the past few decades,[16] it has been generally recognized, as discussed earlier, that the theoretical terms of science cannot have their meanings rigidly defined in observational or operational terms. Instead, theoretical terms gain their meaning from the network of relationships that tie them in with other terms in a theory. A scientific theory is a whole, it is an entity made up of interconnected parts, and as a whole it is

testable. Data can be fed in, providing that the net as a whole has some link with the observable or measurable realm—it was a mistake to believe that every individual theoretical term had to be so definable. Indeed, the image of a theory as net has gained great currency; even the partly reformed positivist Carl Hempel expressed it well:

> A scientific theory might therefore be likened to a complex spatial network: its terms are represented by the knots, while the threads connecting the latter correspond, in part, to the definitions and, in part, to the fundamental and derivative hypotheses included in the theory. The whole system floats, as it were, above the plane of observation and is anchored to it by rules of interpretation. These might be viewed as strings which are not part of the network but link certain points of the latter with specific places in the plane of observation.[17]

Now, the network analogy leads directly to the so-called Duhem-Quine thesis: evidence does not impinge on any particular individual item or theoretical element in science, it impinges on the whole net.[18] According to Duhem and Quine, it is the theory as a whole, as a single complex entity, that interfaces with evidence. The theoretical elements are not isolable, they always travel with the other items in the net. And so it is as an interrelated whole that they face up to the test of experience. Consequently, if a piece of recalcitrant evidence emerges, it can be accommodated by any of a variety of changes or modifications to various parts of the network; one scientist may want to change one part of the theoretical net, while another may advocate that changes be made elsewhere—it is always possible, by making sufficient changes in other parts, to preserve a favored portion of the net that might, at first, seem to have been thrown into question by the new evidence. Of course, the ease with which various parts of the network can be preserved may vary; in order to save one favored portion, quite severe changes may have to be made elsewhere—the tradeoffs involved might be quite difficult ones to make. But the point is that theoretical changes and developments in science are not *necessitated* by the evidence; scientists are free to use their judgment and their creativity. (The point being made here parallels the one made earlier during the discussion of the underdetermination of theories.) It would be a mistake to interpret this as indicating that scientific theories are a matter of mere whim or individual taste; to stress that individual judgment is required is not to throw away all standards, it is just to stress that decisions cannot be made in any mechanical way. However, contemporary philosophers of science generally recognize that not all "nonmechanical" decisions are equally sound, and one of the current unresolved issues is the precise delineation of the rational constraints that operate on scientific judgment.[19]

3. A number of issues have arisen which together make a similar point about testing. There is no mechanical procedure by which a given portion of a theoretical network in science can be put to decisive test. A scientist can use a theory, or part of a theory, to deduce a prediction that if X is done, then Y should result. But if this test is carried out, and Y does not result, there are many ways the new evidence can be accommodated; similarly, if Y does result, then there are various ways in which this can be accounted for. Again, a challenge for professional judgment.

For one thing, in striking contrast to older views of "scientific method," it is now accepted that it is legitimate to "save" or "repair" a theory that appears to have failed a test by introducing an *ad hoc* hypothesis. The "new" philosophers of science, led by Lakatos and Feyerabend, have provided many detailed historical case studies which give a quite realistic picture of how science has actually been carried out by successful scientists; and it is clear from this work that the use of *ad hoc* hypotheses is not uncommon and, furthermore, that often it has turned out to be fruitful. Feyerabend made the point strongly:

> The idea of a method that contains firm, unchanging, and absolutely binding principles for conducting the business of science gets into considerable difficulty when confronted with the results of historical research. We find, then, that there is not a single rule, however plausible, and however firmly grounded in epistemology, that is not violated at some time or other. It becomes evident that such violations are not accidental events. . . . On the contrary, we see they are necessary for progress. . . . More specifically, the following can be shown: considering any rule, however "fundamental," there are always circumstances when it is advisable not only to ignore the rule, but to adopt its opposite.[20]

Most philosophers of science regard Feyerabend's "anarchistic" position as too strong; and again an unresolved issue is the nature of the restraints on the use of *ad hoc* hypotheses.

Another insight concerns the use of "auxiliary" premises in the making of scientific predictions. The point here is that no test consequences follow from an isolated theory; in order to put a theory to a test some chain of reasoning has to be followed, and data and information from other branches of science—as well as from common sense, mathematics, and so forth—have to be used. (Typically measurements are made, using instruments that were designed on the basis of a host of other theories; and calculations are performed, using formulae drawn from many areas of science and mathematics.) Hempel has a striking example:[21] Semmelweis, the nineteenth-century physician who realized (before the development of the germ theory of disease) that "childbed fever" was a type of blood poisoning, deduced that if the physicians in his hospital washed their hands before attending to patients giving birth, then the patients would not get infected. He chose to use chlorinated lime as the cleansing fluid. And his test was successful—incidence of the usually fatal fever dropped dramatically. It is clear here that as well as the theory under test (that fever was caused by infection of the bloodstream of the patients), Semmelweis was making other (auxiliary) assumptions—that washing the hands of doctors would be efficacious, that chlorinated lime would do the job, and so forth. If the test had failed, if the patients still became infected, he might have rejected his theory as being incorrect when in fact it may have been one of the auxiliaries that was to blame (for example, the chlorinated lime might have been too weak). So, to generalize the point, if a test is failed it is a matter of judgment whether to blame the theory or to "pass the buck" to one of the everpresent auxiliary assumptions.

Another problem arises if the test has positive results. For as a point of logic, the positive result does not give unequivocal support to the theory or hypothesis under test; the form of inference involved is "affirming the consequent," which is fallacious.[22] If from some theory *T* it is deduced that some consequence *C* will follow under certain conditions, and if the test is carried out and *C* is found to occur, it cannot be concluded that therefore *T* is true:

$$\begin{array}{r} \text{If } T \text{ then } C \\ C \\ \hline \text{Therefore } T \end{array}$$

Which is not valid. (Consider "If it is raining then it is cloudy; it is cloudy; therefore it is raining.")[23]

Karl Popper concluded, after reflecting on these matters, that although a scientific theory or hypothesis cannot be proven, it *can* be decisively refuted—one negative result can show that a theory is untenable. The logical form involved here would be "modus tollens," which is valid:

If *T* then *C*
Not *C*

Therefore, not *T*

Thus, "If it is raining then it is cloudy; it is not cloudy; therefore it is not raining," which is logically unassailable. This Popperian "naive falsificationism," however, will not do as an account of the logic of scientific testing. (Popper has denied that he is "naive" in this sense.) For once it is recognized that, in carrying out the test, the scientist has made use of auxiliary premises or assumptions, then the negative test results can always be evaded by ascribing the blame onto one of these, or even by introducing some new *ad hoc* assumption. Schematically:

If *T* (and given auxiliary *A* etc.), then *C*
Not *C*

Therefore, either not *T* or not *A* (etc.)

Which again is perfectly valid. So, sadly, a scientific hypothesis or theory can neither be disproven, nor proven, by means of tests!

A final group of problems concerning testing has given substance to the suggestion that it cannot be judged, in isolation from the corpus of scientific theory as a whole, whether or not a piece of evidence offers support for a particular theory or hypothesis. It is not necessary to pursue at great length Hempel's "raven paradox" or Goodman's "grue and bleen paradox";[24] suffice it to state that because scientific theories are underdetermined by evidence, any single piece of evidence—any observation—may in principle support a range of theoretical statements, no matter how fanciful. (Goodman's example shows that the observation that emeralds are green may also be taken to support another theory that they are "grue," that is, green up to a certain date and blue after that!) In order to judge what the evidence can most reasonably be interpreted as supporting, it seems as if other theories must be drawn upon. (For instance, in Goodman's example, there are theories about the chemical constituents of emeralds, and theories about how the color is caused by these constituents, and it is these other theories that make the grue hypothesis unlikely—greenness is too well "embedded" a concept to be bypassed so frivolously.) But again, it is all a matter of judgment, and there is no routine or mechanical procedure a scientist can follow to link his or her evidence to the theories that are under investigation.

Rational Justification

Each of the points discussed above highlights, in its own way, the same fundamental issue: in what sense is the knowledge embodied in the sciences rationally justified or warranted? For scientific knowledge is not based, in any logically compelling sense, on observation; neither do tests absolutely confirm nor absolutely refute it. It seems that, on the basis of any body of evidence, a host of rival theories could be advanced, and the accumulation of further evidence does not compellingly disqualify any of these.

At first this situation seems shocking, but calm reflection puts the matter in a different light. It has long been realized that scientific knowledge is fallible; scientists seek the truth and often think they have found it, but when pushed they usually concede that one day they may be shown to be wrong—the tide of opinion, and of evidence, may turn against them. Thus, Newtonian physics prevailed for several centuries, but eventually it succumbed to Einstein;[25] in its turn, Einsteinian physics has started to develop flaws that some believe signal its imminent overthrow. Science moves, as the title of one of Popper's books so elegantly puts it, by "conjectures and refutations," with the caveat that refutations, as well as conjectures, are only tentative. Contemporary philosophy of science merely shows some of the logical and epistemological reasons why this must always be so.

But there is a point of deeper significance, a point which shows why philosophy of science has been a central area in philosophy in recent decades. The developments in philosophy of science that have been outlined have led to the abandonment (in many quarters) of justificationist or foundationalist epistemologies. These epistemologies—and all traditional schools of thought fit under these headings—worked on the supposition that we accept items of knowledge because they are soundly based. Thus, empiricists claimed that knowledge claims were soundly based if they were based on experience, while rationalists claimed that knowledge was soundly based when supported by the "light of reason." Knowledge, in other words, was identified with authority, either the authority of experience or that of reason.

The new epistemologies are nonjustificationist or nonfoundationalist in character, although the term "nonjustificationist" is somewhat misleading. People who adhere to this position still seek justified belief; the point is that they no longer hold that beliefs can be *absolutely* justified in the sense of being proven or being based upon unquestionable foundations. Walter Weimer has expressed it well:

> Knowledge claims must be defended, to be sure; however the defense of such a claim is not an attempt to prove it, but rather the marshalling of "good reasons" in its behalf. . . . The only way to defend fallible knowledge claims is by marshalling other fallible knowledge claims—such as the best contingent theories that we possess. There are no "ultimate" sources of knowledge or epistemological authorities.[26]

There is a metaphor that has been used by philosophers of science and by scientists for half a century that nicely captures this. The scientist is like an explorer crossing a wide expanse of water on a rotting ship. The worst plank is chosen and replaced by a little lumber found in the hold, but during the process the explorer has to place full weight on the other and hopefully less rotten planks; after one plank is replaced, it can bear the weight while another board is thrown away and replaced, but all the while the new planks are themselves rotting! An exciting situation; no wonder scientists have been regarded as paragons of intellectual virtue.

A further point can be illustrated using this metaphor. The rationality of the scientist's endeavors cannot be judged by examining what is happening at any instant (tearing out a plank in mid-ocean is not always a good idea); rather, what happens over time has to be considered (whether or not the ship is progressively made more seaworthy). Stephen Toulmin has endorsed the view that a person's rationality is displayed in how his or her beliefs change in the face of new evidence or experience.[27] Imre Lakatos also developed his "methodology of scientific research programs" to deal with this sort of situation; he stressed that there is no "instant rationality."[28] A scientist is free to make the best adjustments to a theory that he or she can—by abandoning an auxiliary assumption, by adding an *ad hoc* ingredient, or even by just ignoring temporarily the embarrassing evidence. The crucial thing is whether such changes make the theory or research program more progressive, in the sense that it is now able to predict and explain phenomena that previously it could not deal with. Lakatos wrote:

> . . . the idea of instant rationality can be seen to be utopian. But this utopian idea is the hallmark of most brands of epistemology. Justificationists wanted scientific theories to be proved even before they were published; probabilists hoped a machine could flash up instantly the value (degree of confirmation) of a theory, given the evidence; naive falsificationists hoped that elimination at least was the instant result of the verdict of *experiment*. I hope I have shown that *all these theories of instant rationality—and instant learning—fail*. . . . Rationality works much slower than most people tend to think, and, even then, fallibly.[29]

Unfortunately, rotting planks are not the only hazard facing the ship of science. The shoal of relativism will have to be traversed during the next stage of the journey.

Relativism and "Good Reasons"

The position that was advanced in the previous section seems reasonable: a scientist defends a knowledge claim by making the best case that is possible—by marshalling good arguments, relevant observations, solid experimental results, and so forth. And, where necessary, the scientist makes adjustments to the "web of science" (or to the "scientific research program") in the way that seems most appropriate and fruitful. But by what criteria are these things to be judged? On what grounds can it be decided that indeed the arguments are cogent, that the evidence is relevant, and that the results are solid? For we have seen that the case can be made that these things are not clear-cut—they are matters of professional judgment, and there can be disagreements. And it is here that the work of Thomas S. Kuhn becomes especially relevant.

Kuhn's book, *The Structure of Scientific Revolutions*, has meant many different things to many different people, but undoubtedly one of its chief "messages" has been the importance of the framework or paradigm in the context of which the scientist's work takes place. Even most of those who regard Kuhn's work as flawed, and who see his notion of "scientific paradigms" as being so vague as to be almost worthless, are forced to acknowledge that scientists do work within the context of sets of theories and assumptions that play an important role in shaping the direction and form that their work takes. Thus, a Freudian psychologist will work with the concepts and methods of that theoretical framework, and will tackle problems that appear to be important from that perspective. And the radical behaviorist will work within a different framework. Kuhn, of course, goes further than this, and he argues that rival paradigms are incommensurable—scientists in each will not be able to engage in rational dialogue across the boundary, for their concepts are different, their problems are different, and even the rules and criteria by which they make judgments are different. Scientists in different paradigms, according to Kuhn, live and work "in different worlds."[30]

Whether or not one goes the whole distance with Kuhn, there seems to be a problem here concerning the rational or at least the objective status of scientific knowledge. For if the pursuit of science involves the assessing of "best arguments," and if the scientist's criteria are greatly influenced by the framework in which he or she is housed, then it cannot be argued that the arguments advanced by a scientist from one frame are better (or "truer") than those put forward by someone from a different frame, for there are no framework-independent criteria (that is, no "absolute" or "external" criteria) by which to decide between the two cases. Once again, the claim of science to have solid knowledge seems to be overstated. The best that can be claimed, it appears, is that *relative to a given framework or paradigm*, a particular argument or a particular knowledge claim is well warranted. The argument has, indeed, led to the ship running aground on relativistic shores.[31]

Fortunately the whole train of argument is dubious, although a great deal of ink has been spilled over it in the past two decades. The crucial issue is whether Kuhn's incommensurability thesis is accepted; for if so—if two paradigms or frameworks are so disparate that rational discussion (and particularly the giving and receiving of sharp and cogent criticism) is impossible—then the relativistic conclusion is bound to be reached. If the thesis is rejected, and as will be indicated shortly there are good reasons to believe that it should be, then although it still has to be acknowledged that scientists work within frameworks it no longer follows that they cannot engage in rational discourse with each other. And if rational discourse is possible, then in principle there is no insurmountable obstacle to the making of defensible interparadigmatic judgments about which knowledge claims are the best-supported ones. There still is no mechanical procedure available for doing this, of course, but rationality has never been appropriately conceived as a mechanical process.

There have been many lines of attack on Kuhn's incommensurability thesis.[32] Scheffler has argued that because two scientists differ in the paradigms to which they adhere (and because, therefore, they differ with respect to their "first order" concepts and criteria and so on), it does not follow that they disagree at higher or deeper levels of abstraction (the "second order" level) about the basic criteria that are to be used in judging the merits of scientific work. There is, according to this view, no breakdown in communication at the really fundamental levels.[33] Toulmin has stressed that although two paradigms may differ with respect to many important items (witness Newtonian and Einsteinian physics), there will be many items that they possess in common (both Einstein and Newton accepted much of the corpus of physics, and of mathematics and logic). These common ingredients ensure that the paradigms overlap, rather than being incommensurable, and the channel for communication is left open.[34] Still other writers have attacked the theory of meaning that lies at the heart of much thinking about incommensurability and relativism—the theory, sometimes called semantic holism, that if a term (for example, energy) is embedded in several different theories or paradigms, then its meaning in all of these cases will be quite different because meaning is determined by the whole "web" in which the term is located. (It is interesting to note that this theory of meaning is one that has come down from the positivists and their view of scientific theories as networks; many contemporary relativists who accept this theory are fond of saying that there was nothing they admired about the positivists.)[35] Much of Newton-Smith's book, *The Rationality of Science*, to mention only one recent source, is devoted to a discussion of this theory of meaning, which he calls "radical meaning variance."

He points, *inter alia*, to a consequence of the theory that has been widely recognized: rival paradigms cannot be incompatible if the meanings of their terms are different. In other words, if paradigms are incommensurable, a person is free to accept every one of them.

> The meaning of a theoretical term was said to be determined by the entire set of sentences within the theory containing the term. Consequently any change in the postulates containing a given theoretical term was claimed to bring a change in the meaning of that term. Thus, if Einstein and Newton discourse about mass, force and all that, they fail to disagree. They are simply equivocating. On this account of the matter the assertion by the Newtonian "Mass is invariant" and the assertion by the Einsteinian "Mass is not invariant" are not logically incompatible, as the meaning of "mass" is not constant across the theories.[36]

This leads directly to another important point about relativism. In practice no one can consistently lead a life in strict adherence to the relativist position, for it is self-defeating. Relativists hold that their viewpoint is true, that is, true for everyone, and not just for them. And no relativistic professor would accept the argument from a student who had turned in an incorrect or faulty piece of work that "it is only faulty or incorrect for you, Professor, but for me, from my perspective, it is sound." It is apparent that the making of corrections, and the detection of error, disappear as options for the consistent relativist. Certainly there are few scientists who would be prepared to be so charitable to their rivals as to forego the right to offer criticisms in the course of day-to-day professional activity. On the contrary, on all sides in science there is commitment to truth as a *regulative ideal* (as Popper and others have termed it); scientists try to determine the truth and to hold true beliefs—their disputes are about whose views *are* true, or are *best regarded* as being true. Toulmin sums up a recent brief discussion of some of these issues pertaining to relativism with the words "It is hard to see how Kuhn can ultimately hold his critics at bay." [37]

Insights into Social Science

The points that have been made thus far pertain to the epistemology of science in general. Indeed, they may well apply to all forms of knowledge—that is, to all forms of belief that are justified or warranted by appeal to some kind of evidence (although, of course, to the nonjustificationist or nonfoundationalist there is no favored *kind* of evidence). It is to be supposed that the points also apply to the social sciences, and not just to the physical sciences that customarily provide the examples that philosophers are wont to ponder over. The social sciences, of course, have less remarkable achievements to point to than the physical sciences, and it is sometimes stated that developmentally they are on a par with physics just before the time of Newton and Boyle. Nevertheless, it can be said, epistemologically they are rather similar—the relationship between the evidence that is appealed to, and the knowledge claims that are made, is the same.

There is, however, one vital difference between these two areas of science. In physics, typically what is being studied is the behavior of some entity or system that is not sentient; a satisfactory explanation points to the causes that influence the behavior under investigation, and the resulting physical knowledge is codified in the form of laws and theories. In the social sciences the situation is different; humans are sentient—they act for reasons and motives, they react not to the features of their environments but to their interpretations or understandings of these features. While this viewpoint has never won dominance among social scientists in the United States, it has been fairly commonplace among philosophers and philosophically oriented social scientists on the Continent. Thus, late last century Wilhelm Dilthey wrote:

> We explain nature, but we understand mental life. . . . This means that the methods of studying mental life, history and society differ greatly from those used to acquire knowledge of nature.[38]

Later, Wittgenstein drew a distinction between behavior and action (roughly, human action is bodily movement or behavior "plus" some ingredient such as meaning). In recent times the philosopher Michael Simon has claimed that action is an "irreducible category";[39] and Macdonald and Pettit, echoing the sentiments of Peter Winch in his famous *The Idea of a Social Science*, have written (in a passage where they unfortunately use "human behavior" to refer to what others have called "human action"):

> Social science, insofar as its concern is the explanation of human behavior, begins to look like a discipline which belongs with the humanities rather than

the sciences. Social history, social anthropology, and social psychology, are attempts to do with art what is done crassly by common sense.[40]

It is not appropriate to pursue the details of this work, or the way in which philosophical "theory of action" has developed over the last few decades. Suffice it to say that a moral can be drawn that is similar to the one that was drawn at several places in the earlier discussion: pursuing an understanding of our fellow humans, like pursuing understanding of the physical universe, involves the making of reasoned judgments by researchers—there is no mechanical method or process by which such understanding can be generated, nor any mechanical process by which conclusions can be substantiated. There may well be constraints determining the range of reasoned judgments that are entertained, but this issue lies unresolved.

Conclusion, and Some Final Remarks on Education

The psychologist, educationist, and philosopher Donald Campbell has written a passage that captures well the themes that have been covered in the present essay:

> Nonlaboratory social science is precariously scientific at best. But even for the strongest sciences, the theories believed to be true are radically underjustified and have, at most, the status of "better than" rather than the status of "proven." All commonsense and scientific knowledge is presumptive. In any setting in which we seem to gain new knowledge, we do so at the expense of many presumptions. . . . Single presumptions or small subsets can in turn be probed, but the total set of presumptions is not of demonstrable validity, is radically underjustified. Such are the pessimistic conclusions of the most modern developments in the philosophy of science.[41]

All of which is true, and in the face of which some have lost heart. But Campbell has not lost his nerve, nor lapsed into despair or apathy or succumbed into the mire of relativism. And neither should the rest of us. To use Dewey's expression, who can doubt the importance of seeking "authorized conviction," even if the quest is less straightforward than it might have appeared in the heyday of positivism?

However, while the scientist need not lose heart, what about the science educator? If it is difficult, although possible, for the trained scientist to come to grips with the new epistemology—to learn that establishing a claim is a matter of building a strong case by making the best professional judgments one can—will it even be *possible* for the science student? Experience throughout the century has shown how nearly impossible it has been to teach the scientific method (whatever it was conceived to be), and to teach a deep understanding of science, to the general student. The post-Sputnik science curricula of the 1960s ran into trouble on this score, despite the many innovative exercises and examples that were woven into their materials. Earlier still, Dewey recognized the problem, but he also exposed the deficiencies in sticking to the easier path of just teaching the "facts of science" as they appear at the moment. There was little merit, he argued, in having students "copy at long range and secondhand the results which scientific men have reached"; this way students merely "learn a 'science' instead of learning the scientific way of treating the familiar material of ordinary experience." He poked gentle fun at the mindlessness of traditional science teaching: "There is sometimes a ritual of laboratory instruction as well as of heathen religion."[42] Of course, the new epistemology would have the scientist, at whatever level of expertise, avoid ritual and engage instead in *thinking*. Again, Dewey summarized it with words that have weathered the years well:

> The method of science engrained through education in habit means emancipation from rule of thumb and from the routine generated by rule of thumb procedure. . . . It means reason operates within experience, not beyond it, to give it an intelligent or reasonable quality. Science . . . changes the idea and the operation of reason.[43]

For Dewey, an epistemology had become an educational method. We could do worse than follow his lead.

Footnotes

1. This is not to deny that there has been a degree of social schizophrenia about science—after all, the deranged scientist has been a common cultural symbol. But few if any epistemologies have been based on this model.

2. John Dewey, *Democracy and Education* (New York: Free Press, 1966), p. 189.

3. Jacob Bronowski, *The Ascent of Man* (Boston: Little, Brown, and Co., 1973), p. 437.

4. W. H. Newton-Smith, *The Rationality of Science* (Boston and London: Routledge and Kegan Paul, 1981), pp. 1-2.

5. Norwood R. Hanson, *Patterns of Discovery* (Cambridge, England: Cambridge University Press, 1958).

6. Dewey, *Democracy and Education*, p. 143.

7. Hanson, *Patterns of Discovery*, p. 7.

8. Jerry Fodor, "Observation Reconsidered," *Philosophy of Science* 51, no. 1 (March 1984): 23-43.

9. Thomas S. Kuhn, *The Structure of Scientific Revolutions* (Chicago: University of Chicago Press, 1962), p. 119.

10. Kevin Harris, *Education and Knowledge* (London: Routledge and Kegan Paul, 1979), p. 5.

11. A variety of perspectives on modern empiricism is presented in Harold Morick, ed., *Challenges to Empiricism* (Indianapolis: Hackett Publishing, 1980).

12. Israel Scheffler, *Science and Subjectivity* (New York: Bobbs-Merrill, 1967), p. 44.

13. Rudolf Carnap, *The Logical Structure of the World* (Berkeley: University of California Press, 1969), Preface, p. v. This book was first published in 1928; Carnap later softened his views.

14. Percy W. Bridgman, *The Logic of Modern Physics* (New York: Macmillan, 1927), p. 34.

15. For discussion of some issues, and a suggested solution to the problems, see Clark N. Glymour, *Theory and Evidence* (Princeton, N.J.: Princeton University Press, 1980).

16. For a discussion of the strengths and weaknesses of positivism as an approach to science, see Denis C. Phillips, "After the Wake: Postpositivistic Educational Thought," *Educational Researcher* 12 (May 1983): 4-12.

17. Carl Hempel, *Fundamentals of Concept Formation in Empirical Science* (Chicago: University of Chicago Press, 1952), p. 36.

18. So named for the turn-of-the-century continental physicist-philosopher Pierre Duhem and the contemporary Harvard philosopher W. V. O. Quine, who both developed forms of this thesis.

19. For example, see Harvey Siegel, "Brown on Epistemology and the New Philosophy of Science," *Synthese* 56(1983): 61-89.

20. Paul Feyerabend, "Against Method," in *Analyses of Theories and Methods of Physics and Psychology*, ed. Michael Radner and Stephen Winokur, Minnesota Studies in the Philosophy of Science, vol. IV (Minneapolis: University of Minnesota Press, 1970), pp. 21-22.

21. Carl Hempel, *Philosophy of Natural Science* (Englewood Cliffs, N.J.: Prentice-Hall, 1966), chaps. 2, 3.

22. But see Glymour, *Theory and Evidence*, where he offers a "bootstrapping" theory of how evidence can be used to confirm a theory.

23. Jum Nunnally has a nice psychometrically oriented example involving a hypothetical theory relating anxiety and stress. See his *Psychometric Theory*, 2d ed. (New York: McGraw-Hill, 1978), p. 104.

24. A readable discussion of both of these can be found in Karel Lambert and Gordon Brittan, *An Introduction to the Philosophy of Science* (Englewood Cliffs, N.J.: Prentice-Hall, 1970), chap. 4.

25. Of course, Newtonian physics lives on as a very useful approximation, and the same fate may befall Einstein's work; "overthrow" in science does not always mean complete abandonment.

26. Walter B. Weimer, *Notes on the Methodology of Scientific Research* (Hillsdale, N.J.: Lawrence Erlbaum Associates, 1979), p. 41.

27. See the opening quotation in Stephen Toulmin, *Human Understanding* (Princeton, N.J.: Princeton University Press, 1972).

28. For discussion of Lakatos, and applications to education, see Denis C. Phillips, "Post-Kuhnian Reflections on Educational Research," in *Philosophy and Education*, ed. Jonas Soltis, Eightieth Yearbook of the National Society for the Study of Education, Part 1 (Chicago: University of Chicago Press, 1981).

29. Imre Lakatos and Alan Musgrave, eds., *Criticism and the Growth of Knowledge* (Cambridge, England: Cambridge University Press, 1972), p. 174.

30. Kuhn, *The Structure of Scientific Revolutions*, chap. 10. For further discussion of the issues raised here, see Denis C. Phillips, "Post-Kuhnian Reflections on Educational Research," and the papers in Lakatos and Musgrave, *Criticism and the Growth of Knowledge.*

31. Maurice Mandelbaum distinguishes three types of relativism in his Subjective, Objective, and Conceptual Relativisms," *The Monist* 62 (October 1979): 403-28.

32. For a good overall view, see Harvey Siegel, "Objectivity, Rationality, Incommensurability, and More," *British Journal for the Philosophy of Science* 31 (December 1980): 359-75.

33. Scheffler, *Science and Subjectivity*, pp. 81-83.

34. Toulmin, *Human Understanding*, pp. 123-24.

35. For examples of the mistakes made by critics of positivism, see Phillips, "After the Wake," and the reply by Elliot Eisner in the same issue of *Educational Researcher*.

36. Newton-Smith, *The Rationality of Science*, p. 11.

37. Stephen Toulmin, "From Form to Function: Philosophy and History of Science in the 1950s and Now," *Daedalus* 106 (Summer 1977): 156.

38. Wilhelm Dilthey, in *Dilthey: Selected Writings*, ed. Hans P. Rickman (Cambridge, England: Cambridge University Press, 1976), p. 89.

39. Michael A. Simon, *Understanding Human Action* (Albany, N. Y.: State University of New York Press, 1982).

40. Graham Macdonald and Philip Pettit, *Semantics and Social Science* (London: Routledge and Kegan Paul, 1981), p. 104.

41. Donald T. Campbell, "Qualitative Knowing and Action Research," in *The Social Contexts of Method*, ed. Michael Brenner, Peter Marsh, and Marylin Brenner (New York: St. Martin's Press, 1978), p. 185.

42. Dewey, *Democracy and Education*, pp. 220-22.

43. Ibid., p. 225.

CHAPTER IV

Interpersonal Modes of Knowing

ELLEN BERSCHEID

It is difficult to exaggerate the role other people play in determining what each individual "knows" about his or her world. To an extent far greater than most of us commonly recognize, what we know about our physical environment, our social environment, and ourselves is determined, either directly or indirectly, within our relationships with other people.

Much of this knowledge is, of course, transmitted by other people in formal education situations. They are "formal" in that the nature of the information to be conveyed, as well as the manner in which it is delivered to the recipient, usually has been carefully considered and designed in advance of the actual interaction between the "teacher" and "students." Further, and as this suggests, the message and the delivery are rarely custom-tailored to a single individual, although they often are to a group of individuals presumably homogeneous on dimensions considered relevant to the aims of the communication.

Much is known within the social and behavioral sciences about factors that influence whether the transmittal will be effective, including the characteristics of the communicator (for example, the teacher, the counselor, the author, the television announcer) that are associated with "successful" education, or results that satisfy the aims of the educator in modifying the current and future behaviors of the student. Within social psychology alone, for example, the problem of discovering the factors that influence the formation and change of an individual's beliefs and attitudes continues to account for the lion's share of theory and research.

It is not, then, the purpose of this chapter to review what is known of the role other people play in determining what an individual does or does not know, or even to document the assertion that most modes of knowing are, either directly or indirectly and to a greater or lesser extent, "interpersonal." Rather, the aims here are more limited and only three in number. The first aim simply is to highlight the importance to each individual, whether child or adult, of "knowing" the people who populate his or her world, for this is a prerequisite for interacting effectively with them. The second aim is to discuss briefly the fact that much of this knowledge, or "social intelligence," and most of these interaction skills, or "social competence," are obtained within the individual's actual ongoing personal relationships rather than through formal instruction. Third, since the formal educational system provides both the opportunities for, and the context of, many of the interpersonal relationships from which social intelligence and social competence are learned (if they are learned at all), I shall discuss the proposition that decisions about how best to impart impersonal knowledge and skills—decisions that may include curricula, class size and composition, teacher-training, computerized instruction, reward structure, and so on—all inevitably influence, in ways both known and currently unknown, the development of social intelligence and competence.

These aims derive from the apparent fact that "knowing and interacting effectively with people" is only rarely an explicitly stated objective of formal education, although it is a frequently recognized and valued by-product. Rather, the development of reading, writing, and arithmetic skills, and knowledge of biology, literature, and history, along with the attainment of other impersonal knowledge and skills, are typically the preeminent goals of formal educational systems. Such impersonal knowledge and skills, particularly those associated with disciplines in the humanities, are, of course, necessary to the development of social intelligence and competence, but they are no guarantee of it. People can, and not infrequently do, emerge from a rigorous and extensive formal education and yet know very little about the people who surround them or how to interact with them in ways that promote both their own interests and those of others. The figures of the learned ignoramus and of the brilliant social boob are too familiar within institutions of higher learning, not to mention corporate America, to doubt that even a doctorate in psychology provides uncertain certification that the possessor enjoys the ability to move happily and effectively in the world of people.

The attainment of interpersonal knowledge and skills, then, is usually an informal and a haphazard affair. Such knowledge and skills are learned in the "hard school of life," and some people do worse in this school than others. The divorce courts, the unemployment lines, and the mental health therapists' offices are filled with people who recently, and often painfully, flunked one of its courses. Contemporary American society as a whole, in fact, recently has been awarded poor grades in general social knowledge and skills by its leaders, governmental and otherwise, who typically hold the breakdown in interpersonal relationships, particularly family and other close relationships, as importantly responsible for the entire catalogue of current social ills—from decreasing productivity and increased welfare costs to increased crime and delinquency, soaring adolescent suicide rates, and astronomical costs of mental and physical health care. Thus, for example, recent Presidents Carter and Reagan have found it necessary to remind their constituents explicitly and periodically that stable and harmonious interpersonal relationships, especially familial relationships, are essential to the welfare of the nation.[1]

Few people need such reminders. Within American society, at least, most are acutely aware of the role their relationships with others play in their happiness and welfare.[2] What people *do* need and want, however, is the requisite interpersonal knowledge and skills that would enable them to interact effectively with others. Testimony to this fact is provided by the perpetual appearance on the best-seller lists of "self-help" books addressed to improving the reader's interpersonal relationships—with spouse, parents, children, coworkers, employers, employees, acquaintances and friends, and the list goes on to cover virtually all types of human relationships. It is also testified to by the proliferation of commercial organizations that offer formal instruction on interpersonal relationships to individuals and to employees within corporations—for example, through "assertiveness training," "encounter" and "sensitivity" groups—as well as by the burgeoning numbers of mental health counselors who offer "relationship therapy" to distressed individuals and families.[3] But perhaps the deep thirst for social knowledge and skills is best illustrated by the single fact that a slim volume entitled *How to Win Friends and Influence People*, published half a century ago, remains a best-seller and, along with the Bible, is considered a "perpetual classic."

It is clear, then, that many people emerge from the primary, secondary, and even higher education systems believing themselves to be deficient in social intelligence and competence and are willing to spend considerable time and money and effort outside those systems to improve themselves on these dimensions. Thus the question arises, if there is such a widespread desire for interpersonal knowledge and skills, why is more of a systematic effort not made within traditional educational settings to help people develop them?

Popular Rationales for the Benign Neglect of the Development of Social Knowledge and Skills within Traditional Educational Settings

The answers to this question are manifold, and one certainly is that educators are already overburdened with myriad aims and directives and responsibilities assigned them by society. Nevertheless, two other answers should be addressed here. The first is the notion that social intelligence and competence are not "basic" and thus may be safely ignored in the press to provide adequate impersonal knowledge and skills. The second is that, in any event, social intelligence and competence cannot be taught within the traditional educational setting.

The first answer, that social knowledge and skills are less "basic" than impersonal knowledge and skills, is a curious one, for there is in fact no knowledge and associated skill *more* basic to the individual's welfare and survival. Man's dependence upon others of the species for well-being and survival, for example, is frequently singled out as one of the two characteristics that distinguish us from other animals, the other being large brain size and capacity. It also has been argued that both characteristics, man's social nature and superior brain, were "wired into" the human at the same time and for the same reasons.[4] Specifically, the emergence of Homo sapiens appears to coincide with the time the primates left the forests for the plains of Africa where food was scarce and the lack of foliage made them easy prey for predators. In their struggle to survive in that harsh environment, those creatures had the same two resources their descendants living in an urban civilized society have today: their brains and each other. Those early humans who, for whatever reason, were incapable of forming and sustaining relationships with others of the species for defense, food gathering, and reproductive purposes did not survive. Nor did those who were indifferent to, or incapable of, making evaluative judgments about other people—of distinguishing between friend and foe—survive to contribute to the evolutionary development of humans.

The essential role others have always played in an individual's well-being and survival tends to be forgotten in a forgiving environment and rediscovered in a harsh one. Perhaps its most recent rediscovery by many people was during the severe recession of the early 1980s when the unemployment rate rose to its highest figure since the Great Depression. For example, the syndicated columnist John Mallory, who usually confines himself to advising his readers on how they can "dress for success," was moved at this time to mention his personal discovery of another factor people should keep in mind to protect their jobs in "tough times."[5] In a special "Note to Readers," he reported the results of an in-house survey conducted by one of the major corporations on the reasons why people in that corporation were fired. The *primary* reason was revealed to be the individual's inability to get along with superiors or coworkers. The second most frequent reason was an inability to do the job, and, ranking third and related to the first, was the individual's inability to "go along." Because the president of the corporation was astonished that inability to interact harmoniously with others was the main reason people lost their jobs, rather than the lack of impersonal knowledge and skills necessary to good job performance, a follow-up survey asked how many coworkers were good friends of the person fired. Not surprisingly, most of the people terminated had very few friends, which Mallory interpreted as indicating that if one is not liked by one's coworkers, one is more likely to be "canned."

That interpersonal knowledge and skills are "basic" is also easily forgotten in traditional educational settings. There, unlike any other sector of the world an individual is likely to encounter, it is possible for a person to be an overwhelming "success," to reap all the official rewards the classroom has to offer—an "A" or a diploma or a scholarship, for example—without knowing or interacting with anyone at any time, including the teacher, except in the most rudimentary ways. There, it is possible for the student to remain largely passive and silent, to absorb the material set before him or her, to reproduce that material in response to standardized written or oral questions, and yet to do very well. In any other setting, it is almost *never* possible for the individual to succeed without knowing and interacting effectively with those around him or her. For example, to secure even the opportunity to exercise hard-won impersonal knowledge and skills for his or her own benefit, as well as that of others, the brilliant engineer must, first, get a job. Then, he or she must keep it. These require effective interaction with a large number of people, beginning with the personnel consultant and the job interviewer and ranging through supervisors, coworkers, consumers, and clients, not to mention legions of supernumeraries. This fundamental difference between the prerequisites for success in the world of formal education and virtually everywhere else is perhaps one of the reasons students themselves often carefully distinguish between their educational setting and what they term "the real world."

With respect to the second answer, there are those who will readily concede that social intelligence and competence are "basic," but they argue: a) they are so basic that every person learns them readily and in sufficient degree that special concern with the matter is unnecessary; or b) while this type of knowledge and skill can be learned, it cannot be taught in a systematic way.

It is indeed true, as previously noted, that evolutionary time has produced an animal that appears to possess a superior capability and predisposition for making discriminative judgments among others of the species. This is particularly true along the evaluative—or friend versus foe—dimension. For example, even when people can say almost nothing else about a person, they *can* and will say whether they like or dislike him or her and will act accordingly.[6] Further, and remarkably, even in circumstances where exposure to a stimulus has been so brief that people cannot even report precisely what was seen or what the stimulus actually was, they *can* say whether they like or dislike it, and their evaluative reactions are in accord with the judgment that would have been expected from knowledge of the principles of interpersonal attraction had they had a longer exposure to the stimulus.[7]

Humans, thus, do appear to have a hair-trigger ability to sort out other people and objects along a "like—dislike" dimension. Further, they often "know" more than they can tell; that is, not only are they sometimes incapable of telling *how* they know (for example, that the other is a friend or a foe), but they also may be unable to report accurately *what* it is that has prompted their affective reaction.[8] Nevertheless, while most people seem to possess the requisite biological equipment for the development of social intelligence and competence, many, as previously discussed, apparently now believe that they have reached adulthood without developing these to the extent necessary to their welfare and happiness and so seek special instruction and training to do so.

There are many good reasons why social intelligence and competence may now be of heightened concern to individuals. Among these is the fact of increased interdependence within all elements of our industrialized, urbanized, and mobile society, and across the "global village" as well. To an extent never before in our history, it is understood that each individual's well-being and survival are dependent upon the good will and actions of others who may speak a different language, possess a different culture or subculture, and may even be located thousands of miles away in space. Thus, more is demanded of people than ever before in social acuity. At the same time, it is quite possible that people are more deficient than they used to be in social intelligence and competence. Developmental psychologists, for example, are discovering that stable and close parent-child relationships may be an important condition for the further development of these qualities in interaction with others.[9] If so, and since it is the case that disruption of the family unit, including physical separation from one parent, is increasingly the common lot of many children, then the possibility exists that social intelligence and competence are not so easily developed in nonhome settings as they once were.

Finally, and with respect to the other oft-heard reason for the benign neglect of the development of social intelligence and competence in formal educational settings—that they cannot be taught—the booming enterprise in "human relations" self-help books, courses, and programs itself suggests that many people believe otherwise and are willing to put their time and money where their beliefs are. The remainder of this chapter, then, discusses the concepts of social intelligence and competence and the properties of traditional educational settings that may be expected to influence their development.

The Development of Social Intelligence and Social Competence

Knowing other people and oneself, or social intelligence, is undoubtedly a necessary, although not sufficient, condition for social competence, or the ability to interact with others in ways that promote well-being. The process of coming to "know" another person is the process of learning the contingencies underlying his or her behavior so as to render that behavior predictable. If we know another person well, for example, we can accurately predict how that person will behave in a multitude of situations and circumstances. Such predictability is essential to the individual's control of his or her social environment. When an individual cannot predict that *this* action taken in interaction with another will produce *that* result, he or she is impotent to act in his or her own best interests vis á vis the other; if we cannot predict, we cannot control. We become helpless to act in ways that protect and enhance our well-being, and, as investigators are continuing to document, such helplessness produced by exposure to unpredictable environments—physical or social—often leads to depression, sickness, and death.[10]

What the individual is learning as one comes to know another, then, is the other's dispositions to respond in a certain way in certain situations, or the stimulus-response contingencies that underlie the other's behavior. Thus, the "language" of social perception, or knowing others, is composed of dispositional statements—the attitudes (for example, "conservative") the others hold, their beliefs (for example, "Christian"), and their personality traits (for example, "generous"). Each of these, where they are known about another, describes the other's general disposition to behave in a particular way given certain circumstances. This knowledge, in turn, allows the individual to tailor his or her own actions in interaction with that other in ways that will produce the results the individual desires.

There are two major routes to interpersonal knowledge. One of these is "reputational." If one wants to know another, one can ask those who do to tell "what Joe is like." They will undoubtedly respond to the query with a recital of Joe's attitudes, beliefs, and traits as they know them. From the beginning, the individual is exposed to an endless stream of information—from parents, siblings, TV, books, and peers—about what specific others and groups of others "are like." Much of the subject material in the traditional classroom provides such information. Students read *War and Peace* to learn, at least in part, what people in general are like. They are taught in political science, history, and current events what Communists are like, what politicians are like, what girls and women are like, and so on. If the information is available, if it is accurate, and if it is learned, then the individual is more prepared than otherwise for actual interaction with those others. If it is available and learned but inaccurate, the individual will be especially handicapped in actual interaction with those others. This is, of course, one of the reasons stereotypes about groups of people propagated inadvertently in textbooks are so dangerous; that is, although the principal argument for scrutinizing texts and instructional materials for stereotypy is that these are often "unfair" to the group so stereotyped, they are equally unfair to the individual who is taught them. The person who has been taught directly or indirectly that women are "illogical," "submissive," and "nurturant"—all components of the female gender stereotype—will act on those beliefs and thus will be in a poor position to interact effectively with a woman supervisor, coworker, or plumber who possesses quite different dispositional attributes. Further, of course, general "social theories," which stereotypes are, are always to some extent inaccurate in the single case, and so "extra" information is usually required to interact effectively with a specific individual.

Thus, the second major route to "knowing" another is through actual observance of the specific other's behavior and the context in which it occurs in order to arrive at one's own dispositional conclusions. The processes by which people attribute dispositions to others have been the principal focus of theory and research in social psychology for the past decade,[11] and much is known about the principles that govern the manner in which people arrive at dispositional attributes about others from actual observance of their behavior.

Recent work in social perception, however, suggests that the cognitive processes characteristic of learning about people through actual or anticipated interaction with them may be different from learning about people through formal classroom instruction. For example, whether the information about people presented and subsequently tested for is embedded in a history, English, or political science course, the student's goal in the classroom is often verbatim memory and reproduction of the material. Traditional theory and research on learning and memory have focused upon identifying the factors that influence the student's ability to memorize and reproduce such material as nonsense syllables or lists of adjectives, and the fruits of such research often have been applied to all learning processes, including social learning. However, the picture these traditional "accuracy" studies have presented may be misleading with respect to what goes on in learning about other people reputationally or through actual interaction with them, for here the goals relative to that other rarely involve verbatim memory of the behaviors and/or dispositions of the other. Rather, these social interaction goals usually are idiosyncratic to the individual's needs at the moment and the way the other is perceived to engage those needs in that particular situation. Or, as Anderson discusses, memory for persons in these situations is usually concerned with *judgment and future action* rather than memory per se, and

> judgment and action are goal directed in ways that memorizing is not. Instead of learning the prescribed stimuli, subjects need to evaluate them with respect to some goal, deciding how much to believe the person, for example, or how to get the person to do something, and to integrate the valuations of the several stimuli to obtain a unified response.[12]

Anderson's "integration theory" and research, as well as the work of others,[13] suggest that what is stored in memory will depend on the goals prevailing when the stimulus information is processed. Since in actual interaction situations with others that goal is almost never verbatim memory, "book learning" about people and "practical" learning about them in specific interaction situations may be quite different. At the least, the same social stimuli may produce very different products depending upon the goals of the individual. Further, and as Anderson notes, nonverbal stimuli—such as posture, physical appearance, and voice tone—and the discernment of their meaning are of special importance in person memory. As these are most likely to present themselves in actual interaction with another, they are also especially sensitive to the goals the individual is pursuing in that specific interaction. The critical role that the individual's needs and goals play in attention to another[14] and in the processing, storage, and retrieval of that information has only been recently recognized and explored. It will therefore have to suffice here to note that indirect learning about others through academic instruction in a history course is embedded in a superordinate goal to pass the course and a subsidiary goal to reproduce material verbatim. Such indirect learning may be quite different from learning about people in direct interaction with them.

Social "intelligence" can be distinguished from social "competence," which refers to the ability to produce the desired responses in interaction with another. That is, effective interaction requires not only that one understands the other's needs and goals vis á vis oneself (and thus the contingencies that govern the other's behavior) and that one also knows oneself (or the outcomes of interaction with the other that would protect and enhance well-being). One also must be capable of performing those actions that would direct the interaction along the desired channel. The individual may "know," for example, that the other would like to be reassured and consoled over a recent loss; the individual might also wish to console, but he or she may not have any notion of how, specifically, to go about it. Or, to take another example, two children may want to play a game of tennis with each other, but, although they accurately perceive each other's goal for their interaction and wish to facilitate it, they do not possess the requisite skills to hit the ball back and forth over the net. Further, no amount of passively watching people on TV playing tennis, or reading books about tennis, is going to produce that skill; only practice in interaction with a responsive partner will do it.

That both social intelligence and competence are required for effective interaction can be seen when one considers the necessary ingredients for initiating and maintaining a relationship with another. The essence of the concept of interpersonal relationship is "interdependence,"[15] and thus two people are in a relationship with one another only to the extent that they have impact upon each other's behavior—their thoughts and their actions. People can be conceived to be in a "close" relationship if their impact upon each other is frequent, if it is strong, and if their mutual influence extends to many different kinds of behavior and activities. Influence thus is observed in interaction where one person acts and the other reacts.

In most relationships, especially close relationships, much of the interaction is composed of relatively long "meshed" interaction sequences, where the other person's reaction serves as an important stimulus for the individual's next response, which in turn serves as a stimulus for the other's subsequent response and so on, in a chain of interconnected events. As we have noted, to interact with another effectively requires that the individual know his own needs and goals and how the other's behavior may affect the achievement of these goals, know the other's needs and goals and how the individual impinges on those, know the responses the other is likely to exhibit in reaction to the individual's own behavior, and, then, possess the capability of performing the responses necessary to bring about the desired effect. This last also requires the ability to interpret feedback from the other instantly—often in the form of highly ambiguous verbal and nonverbal cues—to make the necessary corrections to keep the interaction moving along the desired channel.

"Responsivity" to the other, then, which includes attending to the other's behavior and making the appropriate responses at the appropriate time, is critical to effective interaction.[16] There is reason to believe that many of these general responsivity skills must be learned and, further, that much of this learning occurs in the individual's early interactions with peers. Recent investigations by developmental psychologists, for example, demonstrate that peer relations contribute uniquely to the capacity to relate to others and to the development of social controls.[17]

Peer interaction, of course, affects behavioral development in conjunction with experience occurring in the child's other social relationships, particularly family relationships. In fact, as Hartup concludes from his review of the available evidence: "Secure family relations are the basis for entry into the peer system and success within it. Family breakdown tends to interfere with adaptation to the peer culture, and good family relations are needed throughout childhood and adolescence as the basis for peer relations."[18] As noted earlier, however, many children are now experiencing disrupted family relationships and are left without a secure base from which to develop social intelligence and competence. Thus, as they have in so many other cases of default in socialization by the family and community, many now look to the formal educational system to help compensate.

The Traditional Classroom and Its Implications for the Development of Social Intelligence and Competence

They do so, however, at a time when there is a feeling that there is something wrong with the education American children are receiving—and at a time when the old familiar remedy, a "return to basics," is once again offered. In a speech to the National Association of Secondary School Principals in February of 1984, for example, President Reagan associated the "decline" in the schools with a general decline in American military and economic strength and offered his solution—a "return to basics and a restoration of school discipline."[19] The "basics" to which he and others refer probably do not, as we have discussed, include increased attention to the development of social intelligence and competence. To the contrary, and in accord with the claims of science and high technology that are being pressed in all quarters, the "return to basics" slogan carries stronger than ever emphasis upon the development of specialized impersonal knowledge and skills within the traditional classroom setting. It also carries with it, of course, the implication that it is important to cut out the superfluous "frills" that have come to adorn the corpus of education, especially "extra" curricular activities.

Thus, the "return to basics" philosophy within the traditional classroom setting conjures up a familiar picture of thirty or so students seated quietly at their desks, passively absorbing the instructional lecture, speaking when spoken to, diligently reading and writing about the material put before them, and reproducing that material to exhibit its mastery. This picture of the traditional classroom, structured to focus primarily upon the transmission of impersonal knowledge and skills, can be expected to influence the development of social intelligence and competence in at least two ways: first, in the extent to which it permits or encourages peer interaction, and, second, in setting the context in which that interaction takes place.

With respect to the first of these, the extent to which peer interaction is encouraged in the classroom, it was noted earlier that the academic classroom is one of the few settings in which an individual can perform successfully with minimal social interaction. In an important part, this is because the traditional classroom usually has an "individualistic" and/or "competitive" rather than a "cooperative" task and reward structure. Not only does such a structure discourage peer interaction, but the competitive element helps ensure that when it does occur, it will not be in a context that is optimal for the development of harmonious peer relationships. Recent evidence comparing the products of cooperative versus traditional learning situations, for example, indicates that "cooperative goal structures, as compared to competitive or individualistic ones, induce friendlier and more facilitative interaction, more positive attitudes toward self and others, and greater productivity—in most circumstances."[20]

Perhaps the consequences of the traditional classroom task and reward structure might best be sketched with respect to the decline in American economic strength for which the schools are being held partially responsible. One result of the American decline in productivity has been national interest in the techniques used by Japanese business, especially the use of cooperative problem-solving groups in the business context.[21] Attempts by American business to imitate these techniques have not been entirely successful, however. The experience of a major international high technology corporation based in Minneapolis, which had recently placed many of its engineers in cooperative work groups, is a case in point. It quickly became apparent that the experiment was a disaster. As the corporation's representative put it: "These engineers just don't know how to work together effectively." Thus, he asked (and not unpredictably) the Department of Psychology to offer a special course for the engineers, a course that would outline principles of group dynamics, as well as current theory and research.

This hoped-for remedy for the corporation's problem carried a number of assumptions, few of them valid. For example, it was tacitly assumed that exposing the engineers to yet another body of impersonal knowledge (that is, theory and research in group dynamics) would translate into the interpersonal knowledge and skills necessary for successful cooperative job performance. The work habits of a lifetime, extending to the engineer's earliest educational experience, it was supposed, could be quickly overcome with requiring the traditional verbatim reproduction of the principles of group dynamics. Second, it was assumed that by merely changing the task structure to a cooperative one, the engineers would use such interpersonal knowledge and skills as they possessed for effective group problem solving even though the reward structure in the corporation remained much the same—an individualistic and competitive "zero-sum" game, in terms of salary and promotion. As the corporation came to realize, something more than a course in group dynamics for its employees was necessary to achieve corporate aims.

Reward structure is only one contextual element that can be expected to influence the nature of social interaction that takes place within a setting and what the participants learn about themselves and others from it. In his review of research investigating the factors influencing peer relationships, Hartup comments:

> One of the major themes . . . is the pervasive role played by contextual factors in determining the nature of peer relations in childhood. Even when cultural variations are set aside, few aspects of peer interaction are free from situational constraints—for example, group composition, physical space, the task at hand, and other circumstantial variations.[22]

Thus, few of the properties of the traditional classroom can be expected *not* to influence the development of social intelligence and competence. Class size, for example, is undoubtedly a factor, not only in terms of the likelihood that one's peers will be known and familiar but also in the extent to which interaction with the teacher on anything other than a stereotyped and superficial basis is possible. The homogeneity of the peer group is surely another, for it is clear from a variety of sources that similar groups, other things being equal, promote the likelihood of interaction and attraction.[23] That all of these contextual elements will interact with each other is also apparent, and class size and homogeneity are instances. For example, it might be deemed desirable that children learn to know and interact with others very different from themselves—in background, intelligence, education, age, race, and so on. Since dissimilarity is an inhibitor to interaction, a large heterogeneous classroom might spell disaster, for interaction with others might be expected to be sporadic and destructive when it occurs, whereas a small heterogeneous group might achieve the aim.

Because the role of peer relationships in child development in general, and the development of social intelligence and competence in particular, has only recently been the subject of a systematic investigation, and since the ways in which this type of knowledge and associated skills influence the learning of impersonal knowledge and skills within educational settings are only now beginning to emerge, it will have to suffice here to conclude this brief discussion with the caution that the oft-heard panacea to problems with the educational system—to return to "basics"—requires careful consideration of just what is *truly* basic to the individual's welfare and to the larger society, as well as of the role formal education does or does not currently play, wittingly or unwittingly, in securing that knowledge and skill.

We conclude, then, with noting just one of the many ironies presented by the return to basics philosophy. That is, when one asks "Where, within most education settings, *do* children currently have the opportunity for spontaneous and uninhibited peer interaction in a cooperative task and reward structure?" the answer is likely to be, "In extracurricular activities," those frills that are prime candidates for the axe in a rush to return to the teaching of basics through even more impersonal, often computerized, modes of instruction. No one ever put on a class play all by one's self, issued a school newspaper without coordinated social interaction, or developed a winning football team by one's own efforts. These activities are "extra," however, and, as this implies, voluntary—often thought to be provided largely for the entertainment and amusement of students and parents. Further, their supervision by teachers is often on an "overload" or "extra-pay" basis. It would thus be surprising if it were not the case that the students who are most likely to take advantage of these experiences, and to benefit by them in terms of enhanced social intelligence and competence, were not those *least* in need of it. And it would be surprising, too, if teachers were not assigned to these extracurricular activities on bases other than their experience and training in the development of human relations skills.

Footnotes

1. Ellen Berscheid and L. A. Peplau, "The Emerging Science of Relationships," in *Close Relationships*, ed. Harold H. Kelley et al. (San Francisco: W. H. Freeman, 1983).

2. Ibid.

3. Ellen Berscheid, D. Kulakowski, and S. W. Gangestad, "Emotion in Close Relationships: Implications for Relationship Counseling," in *Handbook of Counseling Psychology*, ed. S. D. Brown and R. W. Lent (New York: Wiley, 1984).

4. Robert Plutchik, *Emotion: A Psychoevolutionary Synthesis* (New York: Harper and Row, 1980).

5. *St. Paul Dispatch*, 21 November 1983.

6. Ellen Berscheid, "Interpersonal Attraction," in *Handbook of Social Psychology*, 3d ed., ed. Gardner Lindzey and Elliot Aronson (Reading, Mass.: Addison-Wesley, forthcoming).

7. See, for example, R. B. Zajonc, "Feeling and Thinking: Preferences Need No References," *American Psychologist* 35 (February 1980): 151-75.

8. Richard E. Nisbett and Timothy D. Wilson, "Telling More Than We Can Know: Verbal Reports on Mental Processes," *Psychological Review* 84 (May 1977): 231-59.

9. Willard G. Hartup, "Peer Relations," in *Handbook of Child Psychology*, vol. 4, 4th ed., ed. Paul H. Mussen (New York: Wiley, 1983).

10. M. E. P. Seligman, *Helplessness: On Depression, Development, and Death* (San Francisco: W. H. Freeman, 1975).

11. For a review, see Harold H. Kelley and J. L. Michela, "Attribution Theory and Research," in *Annual Review of Psychology*, vol. 31, ed. Mark R. Rosenzweig and Lyman W. Porter (Palo Alto, Calif.: Annual Reviews, Inc., 1980), pp. 457-502.

12. N. H. Anderson, "Schemas in Person Cognition," Report no. 118 (La Jolla, Calif.: Center for Human Information Processing, Department of Psychology, University of California, San Diego, 1983), p. 4.

13. For example, see R. S. Wyer, Jr. and T. K. Srull, "The Processing of Social Stimulus Information: A Conceptual Integration," in *Person Memory: The Cognitive Basis of Social Perception*, ed. Reid Hastie, T. M. Ostrom, E. B. Ebbeson, R. S. Wyer, Jr., D. L. Hamilton, and D. E. Carlston (Hillsdale, N.J.: Lawrence Erlbaum Associates, 1980).

14. Ellen Berscheid, William Graziano, Thomas Monson, and Marshall Dermer, "Outcome Dependency: Attention, Attribution, and Attraction," *Journal of Personality and Social Psychology* 34 (November 1976): 978-89.

15. For example, see Kelley et al., eds., *Close Relationships*.

16. For example, see Deborah Davis, "Determinants of Responsiveness in Dyadic Interaction," in *Personality, Roles, and Social Behavior*, ed. William Ickes and E. S. Knowles (New York: Springer-Verlag, 1982).

17. See William Damon, *Social and Personality Development: Infancy through Adolescence* (New York: Norton, 1983).

18. Hartup, "Peer Relations," p. 172.

19. *St. Paul Dispatch*, 7 February 1984.

20. Hartup, "Peer Relations," p. 157.

21. See, for example, the best seller by Richard T. Pascale and Anthony G. Athos, *The Art of Japanese Management: Applications for American Executives* (New York: Simon and Schuster, 1981).

22. Hartup, "Peer Relations," pp. 172-73.

23. Berscheid, "Interpersonal Attraction."

CHAPTER V

The Double-edged Mind: Intuition and the Intellect

RUDOLF ARNHEIM

I have it on good authority that there are educators who neglect or even despise intuition. They are certain that the only way of acquiring solid and useful knowledge is that of the intellect, and that the only mental arena in which the intellect can be trained and applied is that of verbal and mathematical language. Furthermore, they are convinced that the principal disciplines of learning are based exclusively on intellectual thought operations, whereas intuition is reserved for the visual and performing arts, poetry, or music. Intuition is considered a mysterious gift, bestowed on an occasional individual by the gods or by heredity and therefore hardly teachable. For the same reason intuitive work is not expected to require serious mental effort. In consequence, in the planning of school curricula "solid" programs are distinguished from the lightweight ones, which give undue space to the arts.[1]

On the following pages I shall attempt to demonstrate why, to the best of my understanding, this view of learning is psychologically incorrect and educationally harmful. I will show that intuition is not a freakish speciality of clairvoyants and artists but one of the two fundamental and indispensable branches of cognition. The two sustain all operations of productive learning in all disciplines of knowledge, and they are crippled without one another's help. Those of my readers who feel more assured when they can assign a habitation in the physical world to a mental ability may want to locate intuition in the right hemisphere of the brain, installed in quarters as roomy and respectable as those of the intellect in the left brain.

Intuition and the intellect are the two cognitive procedures. By cognition I shall mean here the acquisition of knowledge in the most comprehensive sense of the term. Cognition, thus understood, reaches from the most elementary recording of sensations to the most refined accounting for human experience—from the mere awareness of a fragrance in the air or the flash of a passing bird to a historical study of the causes of the French Revolution or a physiological analysis of the endocrine system in the mammalian body, or perhaps a painter's or musician's conception of discord striving toward harmony.

Traditionally, the acquisition of knowledge has been believed to come about through the cooperation of two mental powers: the gathering of raw information by the senses and the processing of that information by the more central mechanisms of the brain. In this view, perceiving was limited to doing the lowly spadework for the more highly positioned executives of thought. Even so, it was clear from the beginning that the gathering of perceptual material could not be entirely mechanical. Thinking did not possess the kind of monopoly attributed to it. In my book *Visual Thinking* I have shown that perception and thinking cannot function separately.[2] The abilities commonly credited to thinking—distinguishing, comparing, singling out, and so forth—operate in elementary perception, and all thinking requires a sensory basis. Thus I shall work in the following with a continuum of cognition, which reaches from direct perception to the most theoretical constructs. Once this is agreed upon I can take the step to which this paper is devoted. I can specify the two procedures that are available to the mind for the acquisition of knowledge, and I can indicate how intimately they depend upon each other.

Intuition and intellect are somewhat complexly related to perception and thinking. Intuition is best defined as one particular property of perception, namely, its ability to apprehend directly the effect of interaction taking place in a field or gestalt situation. Intuition is also limited to perception because perception alone operates by field processes in cognition. Since, however, perception is nowhere separate from thinking, intuition has a share in every cognitive act, be it more typically perceptual or more like reasoning. And the intellect as well operates at all levels of cognition.

Our two concepts are by no means new. They pervade the entire history of philosophical psychology and are variously defined and evaluated. The basic distinction between them, however, has prevailed throughout. In the seventeenth century, René Descartes, in his *Rules for the Directions of the Mind*, states that we arrive at an understanding of things by means of two kinds of operation, which he calls intuition and deduction or, in less technical words, perspicacity and sagacity. "By *intuition* I understand not the fluctuating testimony of the senses nor the misleading judgment that proceeds from the blundering constructions of imagination but the conception which an unclouded and attentive mind gives us so readily and distinctly that we are wholly freed from doubt about that which we understand." Thus, Descartes thinks of intuition not as the less reliable but as the more reliable faculty of the mind. He calls intuition simpler than deduction and therefore more certain. "Thus each individual can mentally have intuition of the fact that he exists and that he thinks; that the triangle is bounded by three lines only, the sphere by a single surface, and so on. Facts of such a kind are far more numerous than many people think, disdaining as they do to direct their attention upon such simple matters." By *deduction*, on the other hand, "we understand all necessary inference from other facts that are known with certainty," that is, acquired by intuitively gained knowledge.[3]

In our direct experience we are better acquainted with the intellect, for the good reason that intellectual operations tend to consist of chains of logical inferences whose links are often observable in the light of consciousness and clearly distinguishable from one another. The steps of a mathematical proof are an obvious example. Intellectual skill is clearly teachable. Its services can be obtained somewhat like those of a machine; in fact, intellectual operations of high complexity are carried out nowadays by digital computers.[4]

Intuition is much less easily understood because we know it mostly by its achievements whereas its mode of operation tends to elude awareness. It is like a gift from nowhere and therefore has sometimes been attributed to superhuman inspiration or, more recently, to inborn instinct. For Plato intuition was the highest level of human wisdom, as it afforded a direct view of the transcendental essences to which all the things of our experience owe their presence. Again in our own century the direct vision of essences (Wesensschau) was proclaimed by the phenomenologists of the Husserl School as the royal road to truth.[5]

Depending on the style of the times, intellect and intuition were considered collaborators, in need of one another, or rivals, who interfered with each other's effectiveness. This latter conviction, a child of Romanticism, was already forcefully proclaimed by Giambattista Vico, whose views have been lucidly summarized in Benedetto Croce's history of aesthetics.[6] Identifying the intellect with philosophy and intuition with poetry, Vico stated that "metaphysics and poetry are naturally opposed to each other." The former resists the judgment of the senses, the latter makes it its principal directive—a view that leads to the characteristic statement: "La Fantasia tanto è più robusta, quanto è più debole il Raziocinio," that is, the power of poetry grows stronger, the weaker reasoning becomes.[7]

In the nineteenth century the Romantic split between intuition and intellect led to a conflict between the worshipers of intuition, who viewed the intellectual disciplines of the scientists and logicians with contempt, and the adherents of reason, who called the nonrational character of intuition "irrational," in the negative sense of the term. This harmful controversy between two one-sided conceptions of human cognition is still fully with us. In educational practice, as I mentioned in the beginning, intuition has been considered an untrainable specialty of the arts, a luxury, and a recreational respite from the useful skills, which are considered purely intellectual.

It is high time to rescue intuition from its mysterious aura of "poetical" inspiration and to assign it to a precise psychological phenomenon that is badly in need of a name. As I mentioned before, intuition is a cognitive capacity reserved to the activity of the senses because it operates by means of field processes, and only sensory perception can supply knowledge through field processes. Consider ordinary vision as an example. Vision starts physiologically with the optical stimuli projected upon the many millions of retinal receptors. Those many dot-sized recordings have to be organized in a unified image, which ultimately consists of visual objects of various shape, size, and color and located in space.[8] The rules that control such organization have been extensively studied by gestalt psychologists, with the principal finding that vision operates as a field process, meaning that the place and function of each component is determined by the structure as a whole.[9] Within this overall structure, which extends across space and time, all components depend upon one another, so that, for example, the color of a certain object depends on the colors of its neighbors. By intuition, then, I mean the field or gestalt aspect of perception.

As a rule, the articulation of a perceptual image comes about rapidly and below the level of consciousness. We open our eyes and find the world already given. Only special circumstances make us realize that it takes an intricate process to form an image. When the stimulus situation is complex, unclear, or ambiguous, we consciously struggle for a stable organization, which defines each part and each relation to establish a state of finality. The need for such stable organization is less obvious in daily, practical orientation, for which we commonly need little more than a rough inventory of the relevant features of the environment: Where is the door, and is it open or closed? A much better defined image is demanded, for example, when we try to see a painting as a work of art. This requires a thorough examination of all the relations constituting the whole, because the components of a work of art are not just labels for identification ("This is a horse!") but characterize the work's meaning through all their visual properties. Faced with such a task, the viewer, be he the artist himself or a beholder, explores the perceptual qualities of weight and directed tension that characterize the various components of the work. He thereby experiences the image as a system of forces, which behave like the constituents of any field of forces, namely, they strive toward a state of equilibrium.[10] What concerns us here is that this state of equilibrium is tested, evaluated, and corrected entirely by direct perceptual experience, the way one keeps in balance on a bicycle by responding to the kinesthetic sensations in one's body.

Needless to say, aesthetic perception is a very special case. I am referring here to the arts only because they offer us the experience of watching intuition at work. In musical composition and performance, too, a striving for balanced order is directly perceived, and the kinesthetic control of the bicycle rider repeats itself in the ways in which dancers, actors, or acrobats direct the action of their bodies. For that matter, the struggle of the infant in learning to stay upright and walk is an early impressive demonstration of intuitive motor control.

The more elementary visual product of intuitive cognition is the world of defined objects, the distinction between figure and background, the relations between components, and other aspects of perceptual organization. The world as given to us, the world we are taking for granted, is not simply a ready-made gift, delivered by courtesy of the physical environment. It is the product of complex operations, which take place in the nervous system of the observer below the threshold of awareness.

Genetically, then, all knowledge of the environment and all orientation within the environment begin with the intuitive exploration of the perceptually given. This is true for what happens at the beginning of life, and it repeats itself in every act of cognition that takes off from the apprehension of the facts delivered by the senses. To do justice to the complexity of this task, we must add that mental activity is not limited to processing the information received from the outside. Cognition comes about biologically as the means by which the organism pursues its goals. Cognition distinguishes desirable from hostile targets and focuses on what is vitally relevant. It singles out what is important and thereby restructures the image in the service of the perceiver's needs. A hunter's world looks different from that of a botanist or a poet. The input of these various determining forces, cognitive as well as motivational, is forged into a unified perceptual image by the mental power we call intuition. Thus intuition is the basis of it all; and it therefore deserves all the respect we can offer.

Intuition alone, however, would not get us far enough. It supplies us with the overall structure of a situation and determines the place and function of every component within the whole. But this fundamental gain is received at a price. If every given entity risks looking different every time it appears in a different context, generalization becomes difficult or even impossible. Generalization, however, is a mainstay of cognition. It lets us recognize what we have perceived in the past and therefore enables us to apply to the present what we have learned before. It makes for classification, that is, for the grouping of variations under a common heading. It creates generalized concepts; and without such concepts there can be no fruitful cognition. Such operations, based on standardized mental contents, are the domain of the intellect.[11]

There exists, then, a permanent tug-of-war between two basic tendencies in cognition, namely, that of seeing every given situation as a unified whole of interacting forces and that of constituting a world of stable entities, whose properties can be known and recognized over time. Each of the two tendencies would be hopelessly one-sided without the other. If, for example, we considered the "personality" of some individual as constant, unaffected by the forces acting upon him or her in a given setting, we would operate with an impoverished template that would not account for the actual behavior of the person in any one situation. If, on the other hand, we could not extricate the image of the person from the context of any particular situation, we would be left with a sampling of aspects, each different from the other and none supplying us with the underlying identity of what we are trying to grasp. We all know the experience of children who do not recognize their teacher when they meet her in the grocery store.

In consequence, the two approaches to cognition must cooperate from the beginning and forever. What is primarily given is the totality of the perceptual field, in which interaction is maximal. This field is by no means homogeneous. Normally it is made up of variously connected units, constituting an organization, which, however, modifies the role and character of each unit whenever the context changes. Projected upon this field is the need to identify relevant elements of the field, to isolate them from the context and give them the stability that will let them persist through the kaleidoscopic changes of the setting. To repeat our example: the figure of the teacher, which in the mind of the younger child was inextricably tied to a particular setting, namely, that of the school room, is eventually conceived as a self-contained entity, defined by certain enduring properties and detachable from the particular setting. This segregation allows the child not only to identify the figure of the teacher independently of the context but also to group various teachers variously met under the common conceptual heading "teacher." Solidified conceptual units of this kind are the material needed for the operations of the intellect.

The foregoing description of the cognitive process is easily misunderstood. It calls for a few explanatory notes. I. The stabilized entities which I am saying are needed for generalization may be confused with the "schemata" that, according to some psychologists, are the necessary premise for the perception of visual objects. I am not talking here of primary schemata that make perception possible but of a secondary hardening by which perceptual entities are detached from their intuitive context.[12] II. I am *not* saying that the intellect supplies operations of a higher rank, which during the development of the mind supersede the more elementary intuitive perception. Rather, in order to avoid the one-sidedness to which I referred before, the parts of the total field must be perceived both as inseparable components of the whole context and as persistent standardized elements. III. I am *not* saying that the hardening of field components into segregated units removes the cognitive process from the realm of intuition and makes knowledge exclusively a matter of the intellect. On the contrary, the formation of such self-contained units is in itself quite typically an intuitive process, by which various aspects and appearances of an entity and various examples of one and the same class of things are forged into one representative structure. The generalized concept *cat* can come about through the intuitive conformation of many aspects of one and the same cat and of a multitude of cats met in the course of experience. Such intuitive concept formation, which reorganizes and compounds the overall structure of individual instances, differs in principle from the intellectual procedure of traditional logic, which classifies by extirpating common elements.[13]

We are now in a position to clarify the distinction between intuitive and intellectual cognition. The intellect handles connections between standardized units. It is therefore limited to linear relationships. Intellectually, the statement a + b = c is a linear chain of three elements connected by two relations, of which one is a summation, the other an equation. It can be read in either direction, as a statement about the parts or as one about the whole, but in both cases it is sequential. Nor can more than one such statement be dealt with at one and the same time.[14] Of course, all pertinent statements can be assembled and arranged in a diagram as to their relative locations, crossings, successions, etc. Such an assembly represents what I have called an intellectual network.[15] Although the relations making up such a network can be shown together, they cannot be dealt with together intellectually but only one after the other. Hence the basically insoluble problem of describing a field process intellectually: how is one to account in sequence (diachronically) for the components of a totality (gestalt) that operate simultaneously (synchronically)? How, for example, can a historian manage to describe the constellation of the happenings that led to World War II? How can an art theorist describe intellectually the way in which the components of a painting interact to create the composition of the whole? Propositional language, which consists of linear chains of standardized units, has come about as a product of the intellect; but while language suits the needs of the intellect perfectly, it has a desperate time dealing with field processes, with images, with physical or social constellations, with the weather or a human personality, with works of art, poetry, or music.[16]

How does verbal language tackle the problem of dealing with synoptic structures by means of a linear medium? The problem can be solved because language, though verbally linear, evokes sets of referents that can be images and are therefore subject to intuitive synthesis. A line of poetry, picked at random, will make the point:

> "Though the names of their weed-grown stones are
> rained away."[17]

As the mind of the reader or listener is led along the chain of words, the words evoke their referents, which organize the unitary image of the mossy gravestones with their eroded names. Through the translation of words into images the intellectual chain of items is returned to the intuitive conception that inspired the verbal statement in the first place. Needless to say, this translation of words into images is no privilege of poetry, but is equally indispensable when someone wishes to understand, by means of a verbal description, the flow chart of a business organization or the endocrine system of the human body. The words do their best to supply the pieces of an appropriate image, and the image supplies an intuitive synopsis of the overall structure.

Synopsis is not the only indispensable condition for the understanding of an organized whole. Equally important is structural hierarchy. We must be able to see where in such a whole any particular component is located. Does it stand on top or at the bottom, in the center or on the periphery? Is it unique or coordinated with many others?[18] The intellect can arrive at the answer to such questions by ascertaining the linear interrelations between the single items, adding them up, patching all the connections together to a comprehensive network, and finally drawing the conclusion. Intuition complements this process by grasping the whole structure in simultaneity and seeing each component in its place in the total hierarchy. A simple example will illustrate the difference. A quick glance at Fig. 1 reveals the hierarchy of the row of squares synoptically: one of the squares is at the top, another at the bottom, while the others dwell, each at its place, in between. The unaided intellect would have to proceed link by link, defining the height of each element with regard to that of its neighbors. From the sum of these linear connections the intellect could derive the pattern as a whole, the way a blind man explores the shape of an object with a stick. That would be the price to be paid if productive thinking were to neglect the help of intuition.

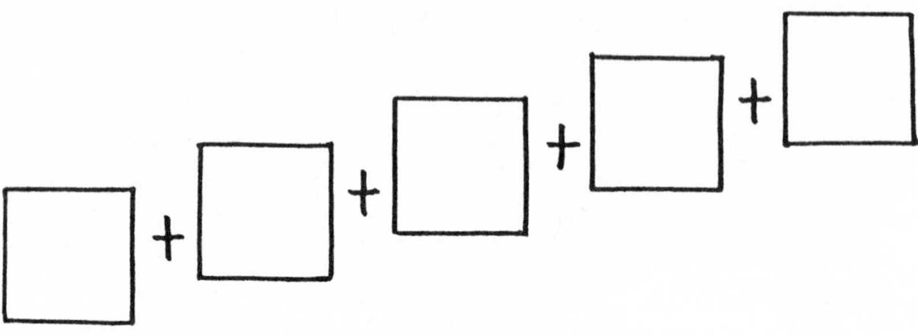

Figure 1.

At this point of our study some practical examples will serve to illustrate the indispensable cooperation of intuition and intellect. Let us assume that a high school class studies the geography and history of Sicily. The teacher and the textbook furnish a number of hard, solid facts. Sicily, an island in the Mediterranean, belongs to the republic of Italy, from whose mainland it is separated by the Straits of Messina. A map shows where the island can be discovered by the eyes. The pupils learn about its size, its population, its agriculture, its volcanoes. They receive a list of the political powers that occupied it in succession: the Greeks, the Romans, the Saracens, the Normans, the Germans, the French. These facts, interesting or not, are unlikely to stay in the student's memory unless they are linked to a guiding theme, which unites and organizes them and which yields the live experience of a dynamic presence. Such a theme is best provided by an image, in our example by the puzzlesome contradiction between two images. One of them derives from a map of Italy, showing the sturdy boot of the long promontory, to whose toe the island of Sicily is lightly attached like an appendix, a mere afterthought. It does not seem to belong. Farthest away from Central Europe, to which Italy is tied culturally, politically, and economically, the island on this map supplies the students' intuition with an unforgettable image, readily related to the neglect and isolation to which Sicily has been exposed by the "real" Italy and its government.

But there is another image. This one focuses on the Mediterranean, the breeding ground of Western culture, the busy basin formed by the East and the West, Islam and Christendom, the European North and the African South. This second map, too, shows Sicily but this time not as a negligible appendix. Rather it is now located close to the center of the cultural context. When the students turn from the first map to the second, they experience what in the psychology of problem solving is called the restructuring of a visual situation. The island moves from its inferior position at the outskirts of the European continent to the very center of the entire Western world, geographically suited to be the seat of its ruler. And under the impact of this intuitive revelation teacher and students are now made to remember that for a few momentous years of the occidental history around 1200 Palermo was in fact the capital of the West, the throne of Emperor Frederick II, that cosmopolitan genius who spoke all the languages and united in his mind the spirit of the North and the South, Christianity and Islam. No reasonably sensitive learner will fail to realize the tragic contrast in Sicily's history between what the island seemed predestined to be and what it became when the center of the Western world shifted from the Mediterranean to Northern Europe. This intuitive apprehension of geographic structure will make history come alive with an immediacy that could hardly be matched by a mere combinative listing of individual facts and relations.[19]

Not all geographical maps are so accommodating as to reflect relevant political or cultural situations through visual symbolism; but in any field of study and for any purpose images are available that offer an intuitive grasp of the cognitive situation, be they diagrams or metaphors, photographs, cartoons, or rituals; and it is easy to show in every practical case that such intuitive apprehension of the total situation is not just an enjoyable illustration but an essential foundation for the total cognitive process.

I will now cite an example from a field that is considered the very prototype of knowledge acquired through the intellectual method of sequential progression, namely, the mathematical proof. The mathematician starts from a problem situation and proceeds by uncovering partial relationships, each accredited by intuitive evidence or by previously supplied proof and each leading logically to the next link of the chain, until the last one provides the *demonstrandum.* Every proof traces its authority directly or indirectly back to the axioms, and at least in the original Euclidian sense the axioms are facts of self-evident intuition. We are reminded of Descartes' assertion that "mankind has no road towards certain knowledge open to us, save those of self-evident intuition and necessary deduction."[20]

Descartes also maintained that any intuited proposition "must be grasped in its totality at the same time and not successively." This points to a serious difficulty arising in sequential demonstration. Each link of the chain, although intuitively evident in itself, is self-contained and structurally separate from its neighbors, so that the sequence looks more like a freight train than a melody. The student manages to understand each single fact in and by itself but finds it connected to the next by a mere coupler. The rationale of the sequence passes him by, and it is for that reason that Schopenhauer compared the Euclidian proofs with conjurers' tricks. "Almost always truth enters by the backdoor in deriving *per accidens* from some secondary circumstance." He refers specifically to the auxiliary lines commonly used to prove the Pythagorean theorem.[21]

The familiar Pythagorean figure is beautiful in the sense that it clearly presents the eyes with the relation to be explored: the triangle in the center, with the three squares attached to its sides (Fig. 2a). This figure, which represents the problem-solving situation, must be kept present in the mind of the student and must remain directly related to each step of the operation if the student is to stay in touch with what is going on. Instead the very opposite takes place. The three commonly used auxiliary lines smash the structure of the problem situation like a brick thrown through a window; or perhaps it would be more appropriate to say that they scratch out the pattern on which the student is supposed to work (Fig. 2b). Through the introduction of the auxiliary lines each edge of the right-angled triangle is perversely united with one edge of a square to form the roof of a new triangle, which works against the grain of the Pythagorean pattern. Under the influence of these new, paradoxical shapes the original pattern vanishes from the scene, only to reemerge from the conjurer's bag unexpectedly at the end of the demonstration. The proof is ingenious but ugly.

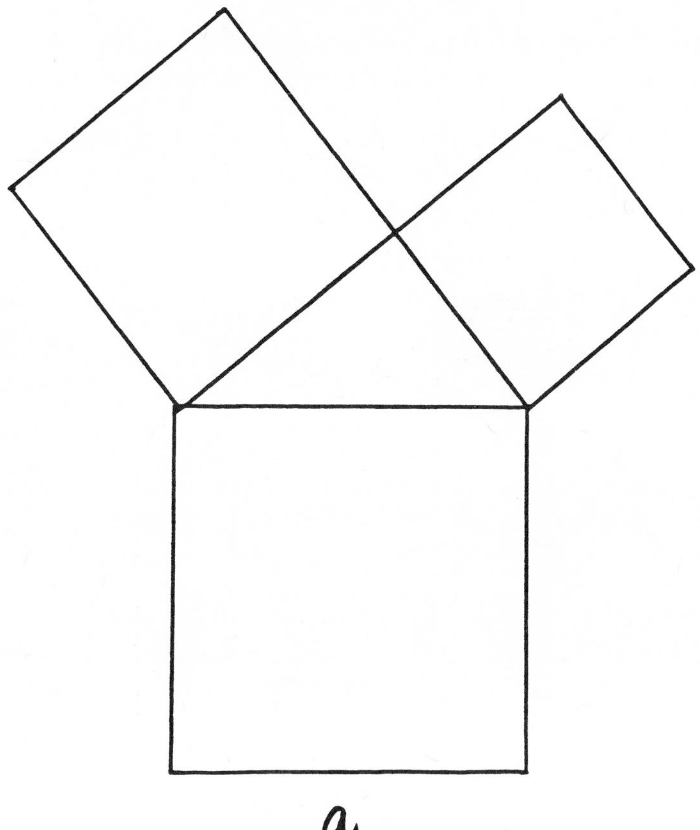

Figure 2a.

This violation of the conditions that favor intuition may be unavoidable, but the teacher should be aware of the educational price that is paid by a one-sided reliance on intellectual sequence. Actually there are ways of demonstrating the Pythagorean theorem by means of a single coherent switch of the configuration. Let us arrange four equal triangles in the square of Fig. 3a. The large square thereby created in the center is the one described on the hypotenuse. By cutting the four triangles out of cardboard we can easily rearrange them as shown in Fig. 3b. The two squares that are now left over by our four triangles are obviously the ones described on the other two sides of the triangle; and it is also clear that the space occupied by the two smaller

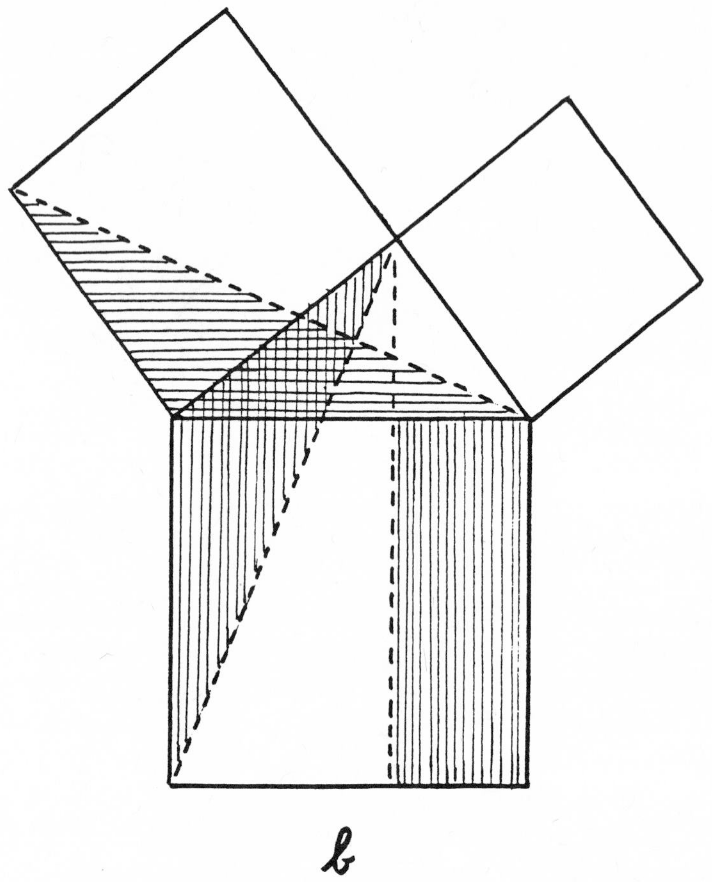

b

Figure 2b.

squares is equivalent to the one of the larger square. The Pythagorean theorem has been made directly plausible to the eyes.

Here, too, a restructuring has transformed the initial problem situation, but the rearrangement refers to the structure as a whole and keeps the original pattern directly discernible in the new one so that the comparison between them can be accomplished by direct intuition. This is what mathematicians call a "beautiful" proof. ("The mathematician's patterns, like the painter's or the poet's, must be *beautiful*," writes G. H. Hardy; "the ideas, like the colors or the words, must fit

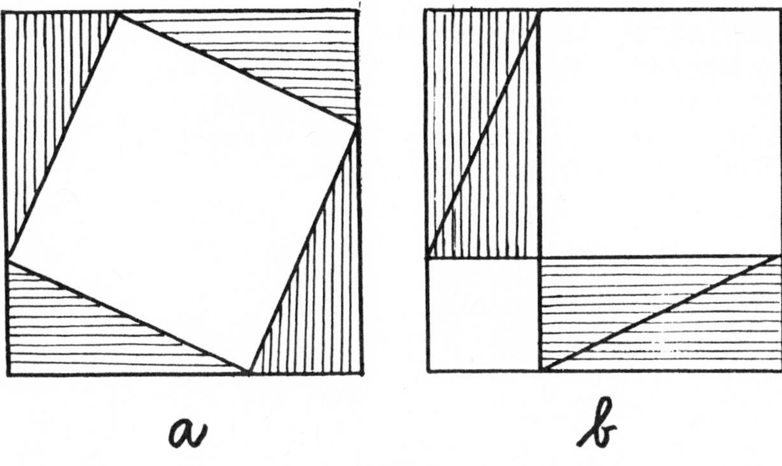

Figure 3.

together in a harmonious way. Beauty is the first test; there is no permanent place in the world for ugly mathematics.")[22]

One reason why intuition has been treated with suspicion by those who believe that knowledge should be acquired only by intellectual means is, as I observed earlier, the way in which the results of intuition seem to fall from the skies like a gift of the gods or of inspiration. Add to this now the misleading belief that when a situation is apprehended as a whole it comes across as an indivisible unity, a holistic totality, an all or nothing like a flash of light or a mere feeling. According to this belief, intuitive insight is not accessible to analysis, nor does it require it. Thus, Leibniz in his *Nouveaux Essais* offers the example of a polygon with a thousand edges.[23] Intellectually one can discover in such a figure all sorts of properties; but intuitively one cannot distinguish it from a polygon with 999 edges. Leibniz calls this sort of image *confused*, in the original Latin sense of the term; that is, all elements are fused and mingled together in an indivisible whole. Even so, he refers to porters or carriers who can tell the weight of a load to the exact pound. This ability is practically useful, and it is based on a *clear* image. But such an image although clear, says Leibniz, is *confused* rather than *distinct* because it reveals "neither the nature nor the properties" of the object. Obviously, intuition would be of little cognitive value if it did suffer from this limitation.

But does it? Kant, in his *Anthropology*, objected to Leibniz's assertion that perception (Sinnlichkeit) is distinguished from the intellect merely by a deficiency, namely, a lack of distinctness in the apprehension of the parts.[24] He retorts that perception "is something thoroughly positive and an indispensable addition to the intellect, if insight is to be obtained." To be sure, certain acts of recognition or description are based on nothing but the most generic characteristics of the object. We tell from a distance: This is a helicopter, a goldfinch, a painting by Matisse! And an artist can render a human figure by the simplest of shapes. Such a lack of detailed structure, however, is not due to a deficiency of intuitive cognition but to the principle of parsimony that governs recognition and representation. It is a virtue rather than a fault that cognition refuses to record a perceptual situation with the mechanical completeness of a photograph. The structural level of the image is geared intelligently to the purpose of the cognitive act. For the mere distinction between two objects it is helpful to limit the observation to the pertinent characteristics—a principle that, needless to say, holds for the intellect as much as for intuition. When, however, the task requires it, intuitive perception can be every bit as detailed and rigorous as that of the intellect.

No unprejudiced observer will overlook the articulate structure of intuited images if he as much as looks at the world around him. What could be richer and more precise, what more clearly distinct than the array of visual objects that faces us at any moment? Therefore, the psychologist W.R. Garner is easily misunderstood when in a recent article "The Analysis of Unanalyzed Perceptions" he writes:

> Thus I want to accept the fact that a great deal of perception involves a complete lack of analysis by the perceiving organism, that forms are perceived as unitary wholes, that attributes may be perceived as integral under some circumstances, and that such stimulus properties as good figure, symmetry, rhythm, and even motion are perceived in a totally nonanalytic way. At the same time I want to argue that for us as scientists, each of these holistic or unanalyzed phenomena is capable of the kind of careful and constructive analysis that allows us to come to understand the true nature of the phenomena under study.[25]

When Garner describes intuitive images as unanalyzable he may seem to commit the traditional error of denying that integrated wholes possess structure whereas all he wants to do is to distinguish the intuitive perception of structural organization from the specifically intellectual procedure of isolating the components of a whole and the relations between them.

The distinction is clear and useful, but it seems to me most important to avoid the suggestion that the perceptions of what Garner calls the "ordinary person" are entirely intuitive whereas the scientist's procedure relies solely on intellectual analysis. If this were true, the configural factors, which determine the character of any field situation, would be ignored by the scientist when he constructs his network of conceptual elements—a procedure whose insufficiency has been so strikingly demonstrated by the gestalt psychologists. Actually, every successful scientific investigation of a field process begins with the intuitive grasp of the configuration to be accounted for, and the intellectual network of elements and relations must endeavor, by constant matching, to approach as closely as possible the structure of that configuration. On the other hand, ordinary perception is so thoroughly composed of well-defined parts that one can hardly indicate the moment at which some such elements are segregated from the context and subjected to intellectual analysis. As a simple example take our conception of causality. "When we infer effects from causes," writes David Hume, "we must establish the existence of these causes; which we have only two ways of doing, either by an immediate perception of our memory or senses, or by an inference from other causes."[26] Take a red billiard ball hitting a blue one and setting it in motion. Intuitively we observe two clearly distinct units, inseparably conjoined by a transfer of power from the red component of the process to the blue.[27] When this phenomenon is accounted for by intellectual analysis, it is reduced to two units in temporal conjunction; and perhaps a force transferring energy is added as a connecting link, a third element, introduced to take care of the intuitively perceived act of causation.[28]

What are we to make of all this? We recognize that practically all the mental and physical topics we wish to study, to teach, to learn about are field or gestalt processes. This is true for biology, physiology, psychology, and the arts, for the social sciences and a good deal of natural science as well. These processes range all the way from the theoretical extreme of total interaction to the opposite limiting case of totally independent sums of parts. Typically the configural context is interspersed with "petrified" elements, which act as constraints because they are not influenced by the structure of the whole. Examples of such "one-way causation," as Konrad Lorenz calls it, would be, within limits, the effect of skeletal bones upon the dynamics of muscles and tendons or the constraints of the legal articles of the constitution upon the pushes and pulls of our nation's history.[29] A game of chess is understood as an intuitive configuration within which the properties of each piece are invariable. Similarly the relations between subwholes range from the extreme of total absence of subdivision to almost total lack of interaction.

To take care of this variety of structures the human mind is equipped with two cognitive procedures, intuitive perception and intellectual analysis. These two abilities are equally valuable and equally indispensable. They are not special to particular human activities but common to all of them. Intuition is privileged to perceive the overall structure of configurations. Intellectual analysis serves to abstract the character of entities and events from individual contexts and defines them "as such." Intuition and intellect do not operate separately but require each other's cooperation in almost every case. In education, to neglect the one in favor of the other or to keep them apart cannot but cripple the minds we are trying to assist in their growth.

Footnotes

1. Elliot W. Eisner, *Cognition and Curriculum* (New York: Longman, 1982), chap. 1.

2. Rudolf Arnheim, *Visual Thinking* (Berkeley and Los Angeles: University of California Press, 1969).

3. René Descartes, "Rules for the Direction of the Mind," in *The Philosophical Works of Descartes* (New York: Dover, 1955), Rule III, p. 7.

4. The controversy on whether or not machines can think intelligently would profit from the realization that our present computers can perform the kind of operation needed for intellectual cognition but not those required for intuition. Hence the limitation of their services for the thinking mind.

5. Pierre Thévenaz, *What Is Phenomenology?* (Chicago: Quadrangle Books, 1962).

6. Benedetto Croce, *Aesthetic as Science of Expression and General Linguistic* (New York: Noonday, 1953).

7. Giambattista Vico, *The New Science* (Ithaca: Cornell University Press, 1948) Book 1, Elements XXXVI.

8. There is no need here to discuss the form detectors, those hereditary shortcuts that simplify certain basic types of form perception at the retinal or cerebral level. The fundamental task of visual organization is not taken care of by these special mechanisms.

9. Wolfgang Köhler, *Gestalt Psychology* (New York: Liveright, 1947); see also Michael Kubovy and James R. Pomerantz, eds., *Perceptual Organization* (Hillsdale, N.J.: Lawrence Erlbaum Associates, 1981).

10. Rudolf Arnheim, *Art and Visual Perception* (Berkeley and Los Angeles: University of California Press, 1974), chap. 9, "Dynamics."

11. At the most elementary biological level these invariant cognitive entities are represented by the sensory stimuli which act as releasers for reflex reactions of animals. Konrad Lorenz describes them as "simplified diagrams of the adequate situation." Cf. his paper "The Role of Gestalt Perception in Animal and Human Behavior" in *Aspects of Form*, ed. Lancelot L. Whyte (Bloomington, Ind.: Indiana University Press, 1951).

12. Ulric Neisser, *Cognition and Reality* (San Francisco: Freeman, 1976), pp. 20, 23, 63.

13. The psychologist Max Wertheimer gave much thought to a gestalt logic in which he intended, for example, to develop a theory of concept formation based on structural organization rather than shared elements.

14. I am not referring here to the ability to perform two or more unrelated activities at the same time but to carrying out two or more related intellectual part activities simultaneously. Cf. Ulric Neisser, "The Multiplicity of Thought," *British Journal of Psychology* 54 (1963): 1-14

15. Arnheim, *Visual Thinking*, pp. 233 ff.

16. Rudolf Arnheim, "Perceptual Analysis of a Symbol of Interaction," in Rudolf Arnheim, *Toward a Psychology of Art* (Berkeley and Los Angeles: University of California Press, 1967).

17. Dylan Thomas, "In the White Giant's Thigh," in Dylan Thomas, *In Country Sleep* (New York: New Directions, 1952), p. 23.

18. Max Wertheimer, "A Girl Describes Her Office," in Max Wertheimer, *Productive Thinking* (Chicago: University of Chicago Press, 1982).

19. Allan K. Henrikson has shown in important papers that the visual organization of world maps in the minds of policymakers can have a fundamental influence on political strategy. It makes all the difference, for example, whether the North Atlantic is viewed as a lake that unifies America and Europe or as a divider that confines the Western Hemisphere to a map of its own, separate from the map of Europe. Cf., for example, "America's Changing Place in the World: From Periphery to Center," in *Center and Periphery: Spatial Variation in Politics*, ed. Jean Gottman (Beverly Hills, Calif.: Sage Publications, 1980).

20. Descartes, "Rules for the Direction of the Mind," Rule XII.

21. Arthur Schopenhauer, *The World as Will and Idea* (New York: Scribner, 1948-50), Book 1, section 15.

22. G. H. Hardy, *A Mathematician's Apology* (Cambridge, England: Cambridge University Press, 1967), p. 85.

23. Gottfried Wilhelm Leibniz, *New Essays Concerning Human Understanding* (New York: Cambridge University Press), Book 2, chap. 29.

24. Immanuel Kant, *Anthropology from a Pragmatic Point of View*, trans. Mary J. Gregor (The Hague: Nijhoff, 1974), Book 1, chap. 1.

25. W. R. Garner, "The Analysis of Unanalyzed Perceptions," in Kubovy and Pomerantz, eds., *Perceptual Organization*, p. 120.

26. David Hume, *A Treatise of Human Nature* (London: Longmans, Green, and Co., 1890), Part I, section IV.

27. Albert Michotte, *The Perception of Causality* (New York: Basic Books, 1963).

28. I cannot concern myself here with the truth value of propositions and perceptions. Intuitive perception can tell the truth about the physical situations about which it reports or, as in optical illusions, it may be unreliable. Similarly, intellectual analysis may do more or less justice to the psychological or physical facts to which it refers.

29. Lorenz, "The Role of Gestalt Perception in Animal and Human Behavior," p. 158.

CHAPTER VI

Narrative and Paradigmatic Modes of Thought

JEROME BRUNER

Let me begin by setting out my argument as baldly as possible and then go on to examine its basis and its consequences. It is this. There are two irreducible modes of cognitive functioning—or more simply, two modes of thought—each meriting the status of a "natural kind." Each provides a way of ordering experience, of constructing reality, and the two (though amenable to complementary use) are irreducible to one another. Each also provides ways of organizing representation in memory and of filtering the perceptual world. Efforts to reduce one mode to the other or to ignore one at the expense of the other inevitably fail to capture the rich ways in which people "know" and describe events around them.

Each of the ways of knowing, moreover, has operating principles of its own and its own criteria of well-formedness. But they differ radically in their procedures for establishing truth. One verifies by appeal to formal verification procedures and empirical proof. The other establishes *not* truth but truth-likeness or verisimilitude. It has been claimed that the one is a refinement of or an abstraction from the other. But this must either be false or true only in the most trivial way, for in their full development, the one seeks explications that are context free and universal, and the other seeks explications that are context sensitive and particular. Moreover, there is no direct way in which a statement derived from one mode can contradict or even

This paper was given as an Invited Address, Division 1, American Psychological Association, Toronto, August 25, 1984.

corroborate a statement derived from the other. As Rorty has recently put it, one mode is centered around the narrow epistemological question of how to know the truth; the other around the broader and more inclusive question of the meaning of experience.[1]

Lest all this sound like intellectual teasing, let me quickly and loosely characterize the two modes so that we can continue more precisely with the enterprise. One mode, of course, is the paradigmatic or logico-scientific one. At its most developed, it fulfills the ideal of a formal, mathematical system of description and explanation. It is based upon categorization or conceptualization and the operations by which categories are established, instantiated, idealized, and related one to the other to form a system. In terms of these relations of connection, its armamentarium includes on the formal side such ideas as conjunction and disjunction, hyperonymy and hyponymy, and presupposition, and the devices by which general propositions are extracted from statements in their particular contexts. At a gross level, the logico-scientific mode (I shall call it paradigmatic hereafter) deals in general causes, and in their establishment, and makes use by constraining principles to assure verifiable reference and to test for empirical truth. Its language is regulated by requirements of consistency and noncontradiction. Its domain is defined not only by observables to which its basic statements relate, but also by the set of possible worlds that can be logically generated and tested against observables, that is, it is driven by principled hypotheses.

We know a very great deal about the paradigmatic mode of thinking, and have developed over the millennia a powerful set of prosthetic devices for helping us carry on: logic, mathematics, sciences, and automata for operating in these fields as painlessly and swiftly as possible. We also know a fair amount about how children who are weak initially at the paradigmatic mode grow up to be fairly good at it—or good enough to get on in the literal world and a few interpretive ones as well. The imaginative application of the paradigmatic mode leads to good theory, tight analysis, logical proof, and empirical discovery guided by reasoned hypothesis.

The imaginative application of the narrative mode leads instead to good stories, gripping drama, believable historical accounts. It deals in human or human-like intention and action and the vicissitudes and consequences that mark their course. It is essentially temporal rather than timeless (as with the paradigmatic mode, however much that mode may use temporal parameters or variables in its operations). And we know much less about it.

It operates by constructing two landscapes simultaneously. One is the landscape of action, where the constituents are the arguments of action: agent, intention or goal, situation, instrument. Its other landscape is the landscape of consciousness: what those involved in the action know, think, or feel. The two landscapes are essential and distinct: it is the difference between Oedipus sharing Jocasta's bed before and after he learns from the messenger that she is his mother. Whereas truth in the paradigmatic mode is a clear matter that depends upon tests in some possible world to determine whether an explanation captures the relevant facts, the "truth" of a narrative is in principle problematic. To be sure, as Nelson Goodman constantly reminds us,[2] the "facts" against which the truth of a scientific explanation is tested are determined by the explanation or theory. But the tests to be applied to the facts are, given the condition, straightforward. Narrative accounts, on the other hand, can be lifelike and exhibit verisimilitude even when they contain demonstrable falsehoods. The property of narrative rightness remains invariant across outcomes of truth tests performed on "factual" components of the narrative. Science "progresses" in a way that storytelling and drama do not. However much Goodman may argue that science-making and narrative-making are, after all, both only examples of constructing world,[3] the fact remains that we collect treasuries of the world's stories, but do not give pride of place to disproved scientific theories or to erroneous logical derivations. There is nothing in science and logic that corresponds to narrative or poetic license. Popper proposes that falsifiability is the cornerstone of the scientific method.[4] But believability is the hallmark of well-formed narrative. When we apply criteria of falsifiability to a narrative, we replace the narrative by a paradigmatic structure. Historical films are notable for the historians they hire as consultants who are then ignored when the story requires it.

We hear increasingly from psychoanalytic theorists that human adaptation to life itself depends upon the success of the patient (or Everyman) in generating a believable narrative, one that in some robust fashion weaves in but does not necessarily mirror the historical truth.

The prosthetic devices available for guiding the creation of narrative are far more like templates than they are like generating principles. That is to say, our cultural history has provided us with standard myths, with genres, with depictions of human situations that inspire and guide variants of them. It is in this sense, of course, that Oscar Wilde could say that life imitates art. But it is also true that there are narrative and generative principles of discourse, tale-telling, and drama that are also part of any culture's tool kit, and we will explore some of them later.

As already noted, narrative is concerned with the explication of human intentions in the context of action. Surprisingly, however, literary research reveals that there are a rather limited number of narrative forms by which such contextualizing of intention in action has been depicted. This limitation suggests that the narrative mode is not as unconstrainedly imaginative as it might seem to the Romantic. For example, most narratives that create an aura of believable lifelikeness involve a recounting of an initial canonical steady state, its breach, an ensuing crisis, and a redress, with limited accompanying states of awareness in the protagonists. This has led various literary theorists to suggest that there is a highly constrained deep structure to narrative, analogous to the deep structure, say, of a grammar, and that good stories are well-formed surface realizations of this underlying structure.[5] But this is a matter for much more research.

It is often claimed that the narrative mode is implicitly deontic, that it implies criteria of value—as represented by the canonical state-breach-crisis-redress cycle in which "good" or "evil" prevails. We shall want to examine this claim more seriously later. In any case, narrative is often said to be value-laden in contrast to logic's value-freedom.

We know very little about how narrative thinking *develops* in childhood. What we *do* know, of course, is that the ability to comprehend stories develops or is present very early. This is sometimes offered as support for the deep structure argument. But childlike storytelling, with its linear ordering "reflecting" the order of occurrence of events depicted, is a far cry from the conventions of skilled narrative with its flashback, soliloquies, metaphors, and other tropes. And the childlike emphasis on event sequences, with omission of a second level of epistemic information, is as remarkable as the child's capacities to tell or comprehend stories at all. Indeed, the relationship between the time course and order of events "in the world" and their representation in narrative time and narrative order has been shown to be rather more variable across cultures than might be expected given claims about narrative universals.[6] But, however these issues are finally resolved, it is apparent that there is a discernible developmental course that characterizes narrative telling and the thought processes that underlie it.[7] More to illustrate it than to attempt any delineation of it, let me mention one in particular. Hickmann has shown that young children have great difficulty, when recounting what happened in a film, in dealing conjunctively with what happened in the action and what the protagonists were thinking or saying.[8] If this is not due simply to an inability to deal with more than a limited amount of information cognitively or linguistically, at any time there may be a genuine initial difficulty either in taking the subjective perspective or in wedding the objective and subjective. Indeed, some work by Beveridge and Dunn[9] suggests that the distinction between what is intended and what is actually done is a difficult one for young children to make—a distinction often grasped when the young child has a younger sibling who forces her to face the dilemma of reconciling the two. And Olson and Astington's demonstration of the young child's difficulty in grasping the semantics of factive verbs,[10] particularly those dealing with intention, suggests that the linguistic tools for that reconciliation are absent. In any case, these are the kinds of matters that must surely affect the young child's capacity to grasp narrative structures of varying complexity. The distinguished French literary theorist, Greimas, has suggested that tales of deceit, involving a disjunction between action and intention, are among the most primitive of those that wed the subjective and objective.[11] Do young children readily grasp them? Would that we had a tenth of the number of studies on children's conception of deceit that we have on class inclusion or invariance transformation!

* * *

This is hardly the first time that the distinction between the two modes of thought has been noted. A century ago, Dilthey even went so far as to argue that all efforts to codify human knowledge could be divided into *Naturwissenschaften* and the *Geisteswissenschaften*, the sciences of nature and of humanity, the first seeking generality and the second uniqueness, one guided by the methods of science and logic, the other by a search for the meaning of historical and personal events in their full, comprehensible richness.[12] And Rorty, as stated, has raised the issue in the last years in more modern dress.[13] It is curious, however, that psychologists have never looked at the matter more closely. In the main, we have relegated narrative thought to others. Propp, Levi-Strauss, Ricoeur, Greimas, Todorov, Burke, Jakobson, and others have gone a long way in the last half century toward clarifying the structure of narrative with no assist from psychology.[14] And where we have looked at story production, as with Murray's work on the Thematic Apperception Test,[15] it has been to explore the nature of personality and its projection in a story rather than to explore story making and its functions.

By a curious twist of history, the psychology of thought has concentrated on one mode, the paradigmatic, at the expense of the other. Like its parent, philosophy, it has been concerned with the epistemological question: how mind comes to know the world, to represent it, to reach right conclusions about it, to avoid errors, to achieve generality and abstraction. With the advent of cognitive psychology, we redoubled our efforts to understand the information processing that serves these paradigmatic functions, and the problem of representation has become the keystone in the arch—representation that maps the world, a classically epistemological objective. Strategies, heuristics, and modes of categorization have been explored with zeal and with increasingly narrow scope. Even when "storying" has been investigated, it has been in the spirit of abstract story grammars, or of the generic properties of scenarios.

And in our studies of reasoning and inference, when subjects fail to conform to Bayesian rules and ignore known base-rate probabilities in judging the likelihood of single events, as in the rich research of Kahnemann, Slovic, and Tversky,[16] we still treat these departures as "errors in thought," forms of human folly. And, indeed, so they are—given the tasks set by the investigators. Or when subjects fail to process the information contained in instances of a concept presented to them, as in the old Bruner, Goodnow, and Austin studies,[17] why should it be treated as anything other than a fall from rational grace? Yet, as I shall try to show presently, these so-called errors can also be taken as switchovers (even if inappropriate) to quite a different way of thinking, as a search for a narrative rather than logical structure.

I think the curious twist of history that produced this odd posture in psychology is probably located in our longed-for proximity to the natural sciences: it was more important to study how the scientist came to his right conclusions than how Ibsen produced *The Doll's House* or how Macedonian tale-tellers captivated their audiences with their modularly constructed recitals.[18] Piaget, for all his genius, saw the growth of mind as paralleling the growth of science—or vice versa. There is no reasoned way in his system of characterizing the difference between the prattling of the Department gossip and a Homer, a Joyce, or a Hardy. For some reason, the nature and the growth of thought that are necessary for the elaboration of great stories, great histories, great myths—or even ordinary ones—have not seemed very attractive or challenging to most of us. So we have left the job to the literary scholars and linguists, to the folklorists and anthropologists. And they have studied not the process, but the product, the tales rather than the tellers.

* * *

I began with the bold claim that our two modes of thought were natural kinds. En route to backing up that claim, let me first say what I mean by a natural kind. It is *not* an appeal to naturalism in philosophy in the spirit of Morris Cohen and John Dewey.[19] Rather, it is the more modest (and perhaps more serious) claim that under minimal contextual constraint, each type of thought comes spontaneously into existence in the functioning of human beings, can be recognized by common sense without specialized discovery procedure as the one or the other, is remarked upon as missing in those rare instances when absent, and (most important of all) can be shown to be analyzable into constituent operations that derive from the overall process they constitute. The significance of constituent processes lies in the role they play in narrative construction and paradigmatic reasoning respectively. Even though stories may require for their believability conformity to some of the same rules used in a logical argument (for example, the rule of simple contradiction), the two forms do not do so for the same reason or in the same way. Contradiction affects believability in narrative differently from the way it negates a logical proof. There is no way that contradiction can be made defensible in a logical proof, but modern novelists and playwrights use it and exploit it by special means as in the plays of Pirandello where, for example, characters both exist and do not exist. Without the use of appropriate literary means, however, a play or novel containing contradiction would seem unbelievable.

* * *

So let us examine some of the constituents or components that go into the construction of paradigmatic and narrative thought. Two features distinguish the modes' uses of language and interpretations of action. The first and obvious matter to be examined is, of course, language. Jakobson has distinguished two axes in terms of which language use is organized: a vertical axis of selection, and a horizontal axis of combination.[20] The first has to do with the possible substitution of lexical and other meaning units for each other, a substitution that (within limits) is meaning-preserving: boy, immature male, lad, and so on. But what about substituting phrases or other larger expressions for each other? Here the matter becomes more telltale in differentiating the two modes. Is "I should have been a pair of ragged claws scuttling across floors of silent seas" captured by the expression, "I am depressed?" Is this kind of asymmetry similar to what happens when we substitute the expression, "the biggest city in North America" for "the harbor at the mouth of the Hudson?" One pair easily preserves reference; the other does not, and it is not enough simply to invoke metaphor as the reason.

The horizontal axis of combination derives from the generative design feature of human grammar, its capacity to substitute varied elements within grammatical frames:

He has a secret
He has a bicycle
He has a burning ambition
He has a bee in his bonnet

The distinction is familiar in psychology as the paradigmatic and syntagmatic, used for distinguishing word associations of the kinds "banana: fruit" versus "banana: El Salvador," showing the latter having been found to occur earlier in children and therefore thought to be more primitive. But let us take this with a grain of salt, for it must surely be absurd to assume that two words that can fit into a sentence (the syntagmatic) are more primitively joined than two that bear a relation of synonymy, antinomy, hyponymy, or hyperonymy. They are simply different and testify only to the fact that classification systems develop later than sententiality as a basis for relating words.

The two modes of thinking, for their expression and (I wish to argue) for their cognitive realization, must obviously use the two forms of linguistic organization, one for word selection, the vertical, and the other for sentential combination, the horizontal. But each uses a different criterion. Vertical organization is given two very different functions in the narrative and paradigmatic modes. The narrative mode operates vertically with a view toward maximizing sense at the expense of definite reference, to use Frege's distinction;[21] or to put it more loosely, sacrifices denotation to connotation. It is for this reason that the metaphoric richness of a story or a line of poetry is as important as the events to which it refers and, why, for example, a story cannot be reduced to a set of atomic propositions derived from its particular set of statements. The paradigmatic mode emphasizes reference at the expense of sense. It aspires to the astringent goal of singular, definite, referring expressions with severe restrictions on alternative senses. It is this that makes it possible to ban ambiguity. Its aim is formal description employing terms whose status within a hierarchical system of terms is evident. The sense of any particular term derives from its position within a system of terms. Keil's description of hierarchical semantic trees,[22] as Susan Carey has shown,[23] characterizes paradigmatic usage only, and then only at its most formal reach.

As for the horizontal axis of combination, the criteria guiding usage in the two modes are again radically different. Some years ago, I tried to characterize three bases for the formation of concepts or categories: affective (I would now say "factive"), functional, and formal. We can illustrate the factive by "kind of people I like to spend my spare time with," and the functional by "elements that can be characterized as between atomic weight 6.0 and 6.7 in the Mendeleev Table." The narrative mode concentrates on the construction of sentences that are factive and functional and on their relation, the paradigmatic on the functional and formal and their relation. A simpler way of saying it is that stories are about events in the real world, the functional, and the reactions of people to them, the factive; theories are about events in the real world, the functional, and abstractions that capture some more structured aspect of them that gives them order, the formal. Good narrative is full of human factivity—wanting, opining, decrying—and the writing of scientists and logicians is sparse in this respect.

* * *

This brings us to a second distinguishing feature for the two modes: the two ways in which action can be interpreted. One is in terms of the working out of human intentions in a real or possible world; the other is through the operations of causes, structural requiredness, reasoned correlation.

Arguments (if I may use that term for what is produced in the paradigmatic mode) and stories, if they are to emphasize respectively *cause* and *intention*, require forms of language (or symbol use) that are markedly different. Both, to be sure, must adhere to syntactical requirements, though the poetic extensions of narrative may use certain forms of tense and aspect marking and styles of semigrammaticality not found in descriptive prose. Where real differences begin to be apparent is in the forms of meaning employed by the two modes. One view of meaning, the verificationist theory, is that the meaning of a word or expression is the set of true propositions that can be stated in respect to it. Recall that meaning encompasses two features: reference and sense, what a term or expression "stands for" in some world, and how it relates to other words or expressions. Verificationist meaning places high emphasis on reference. But there are also ideas of meaning that are based on *use*, ideas that stem mainly from Wittgenstein.[24] Use-based meaning relates to the context in which an expression is used and, crucially, to the intention of the speaker in making a particular utterance in a particular context.

Use-based meanings, in addition to referring (however ambiguously they may do so), must, because of the need to match context and to fulfill speaker intentions, fulfill conditions on their performance, to use the jargon. Utterances must be right for the context and convey intention well enough to assure a hearer's uptake of the locution and of its illocutionary force. This implies immediately that there are conventions that govern speaking or, more precisely, communicating by language. Here we are dealing with the domain—real as life, and as murky—of pragmatics. And before we return to our central issue, let me sketch out a few pragmatic devices that must concern us. One is speech acts; a second, conversational implicatures; the third, the "triggering" of presuppositions by the use of certain linguistic devices.

As John Austin first noted,[25] meaningful utterances cannot be captured in the two categories of analytic and empirical propositions: analytic ones like "Man is an animal" or empirical ones like "Most men can speak." The greater part of human talk is made up of warnings, encouragements, greetings, promises, expressions of want, and the like, involving a performative: an act that can be carried out by speaking alone, say, by the act of promising. Or as John Searle put it, speech consists of locutions (what is said) and a conventionally governed illocutionary force (what is intended), uptake of which by an interlocutor depends upon his sharing the convention.[26] And so the famous, "Would you be so kind as to pass the salt?" is not a question about the limits of the hearer's compassion, but a request taking account of the hearer's nonobliged status. Grice has extended and refined this analysis by adding the notion of implicature.[27] Not only are there conventions governing speech acts (felicity conditions on their utterance to be fulfilled, like preparation, essentiality and sincerity), but there is also a highly general Conversational Principle (CP) in operation. This CP contains maxims concerning the quantity to be said, the quality and relevance of the utterance, its sincerity, and so forth. These maxims provide a guide to banality: be brief, perspicuous, as truthful as possible, relevant. Their existence, Grice argues, provides us, by opportunities for patterned violation, with the means for meaning far more than we say, or meaning something quite different from what we say, as in:

> Where's Jack?
> Well, I saw a yellow VW out front of Susan's.

In short, violation of maxims (in this case perspicuousness and relevance) is intended to recruit presuppositions about what is going on in the ongoing narrative. Which brings us to the third issue, presupposition.

Presupposition is an ancient and complex topic in logic and linguistics, and deserves closer study by psychologists. A presupposition, formally defined, is an implied proposition whose force remains invariant whether the explicit proposition in which it is imbedded is true or false, the classic folk example of which is, of course:

Do you still beat your wife?

This is obviously not the occasion to discuss the logic of presuppositions that remain invariant across negation. Fortunately that has been done brilliantly by Karttunen and Peters[28] and by Gazdar[29] whose penetrating discussion of presuppositional triggers, filters, plugs, and holes is richly suggestive for the psychologist. All of these matters relate to what are called heritage expressions, the manner in which a presupposition is built up over discourse in order to project itself into later statements. Triggers are forms of expression that have the force of projection, and four simple examples will serve to illustrate their manner of operating.

As trigger:

Definite descriptions:	*John saw/didn't see the chimera.* There exists a chimera.
Factive verbs:	*John realized/didn't realize he was broke.* John was broke.
Implicative verbs:	*John managed/didn't manage to open the door.* John tried to open the door.
Iteratives:	*You can't get buggy whips anymore.* You used to be able to get buggy whips.

And there are many other triggers. I think it is plain (though the details are not easy) that triggering presuppositions, like intentionality violating conversational maxims, provides a powerful way of "meaning more than you are saying," or going beyond surface text, or packing the text with meaning.

It will seem on first glance that such maneuvers must depend mightily on the presence of mutual knowledge between speaker and hearer: that S knows that H knows and that K knows that H knows that S knows, *ad infinitum*, but this turns out to be far too strict a constraint for what may turn out to be a deep psychological reason. As Sperber and Wilson have noted,[30] it is a characteristic of conversation that interlocutors assume that what somebody said makes sense and will, if in doubt about *what* sense, search for or dream up an appropriate context to assign an utterance that will *give* it sense. Example on a London street (after Sperber and Wilson):

> *Will you buy a raffle ticket for the RNLB Institution?*
> *No thanks, I spend summers near Manchester.*
> *Ah yes, of course.*

Now let me return to my point. Narrative discourse, because it is built around the vicissitudes of human intentions being acted out, uses the full range of speech acts as its keyboard: expressives, declaratives, commissaries, and so forth. Paradigmatic discourse narrows increasingly as it develops toward pure expression of analytically and empirically verifiable propositions of the conventional type; that is, it aspires to be as verifactionist in its meanings as it possibly can, or in John Searle's classification,[31] specializes in *representatives*, the only speech acts that commit the speaker to the truth of what he expresses. Paradigmatic discourse, moreover, avoids all conversational implicatures if it can, and when it cannot, it employs only those that have heritage expressions that permit unambiguous unpacking of utterances back to the canonical or maxim-governed forms. In logic and in science you attempt to mean what you say. In narrative, to be successful, you mean more than you say and treat a text or utterance as open to interpretation rather than literally fixed with, so to speak, the "truth in the text."

Or to put it in terms of the theory of presuppositions, the storyteller depends for the power of his exposition on triggering presuppositions: it is the only way in which narrative time is made to be shorter than the events and psychic states that it is narrating. It permits, as well, using different orderings in the story than that which happened in life. Paradigmatic discourse, on the other hand, eschews or blocks the triggering of presuppositions or renders them as transparent as possible. It substitutes entailments in place of presuppositions—an entailment being an implied proposition that is rendered false if the explicit proposition in which it is embedded is negated.

Stories, to achieve the condensation and the tropes that render them something other than the mere recountal of events, depend upon establishing a high level of sharable presupposition; they rest upon what Joseph Campbell many years ago called a "mythologically instructed community" who will know how to assign appropriate presuppositional interpretations to what is being said.[32] Indeed, as some literary theorists have argued,[33] the birth of literary tropes and other devices depends upon the invention of violations of the banality prescribed by standard conversational maxims, such violations as irony, hyperbole, synecdoche, and the rest. These violations become possible only when discourse is freed from the exclusive demands of verification.

I have couched much of the foregoing discussion in terms of *language* in which paradigmatic and narrative thought is expressed, but I do not intend that *expression* should be the basis for their distinctness. Rather, the point I would make is that each of the two modes of thought each *requires* for its realization both internally in cognition and externally in speech different uses of language. And as one becomes socialized in a communicative sense, the cognitive modes further differentiate in the sense that the rules of the medium of expression dictate increasingly the compositional rules of thought that find expression in different media. Or, to paraphrase McLuhan's famous catch phrase: the medium compels the message, which then compels the generative thought form for composing it.[34]

* * *

Let me bring the discussion to a close by sampling some of the implications of what has been said for research on the thought processes. Perhaps the best way to do so is to illustrate with research now in progress that demonstrates the one-sidedness of which I initially complained. I prefer to start with some research of my own where I am freer to be savage. Take concept attainment of the kind reported in Bruner, Goodnow, and Austin's *A Study of Thinking*.[35] Forgiveably, perhaps, those authors were out to demonstrate that inference is a product of how we process information in various strategic ways—of using information about instances to construct paradigmatic categories governed by certain rules of combining attributes. The instances these authors presented were, in the main, picture cards of geometric figures in different numbers, with different colors, and with differing numbers of borders. Fortunately, some of the experiments involved "narratable" material: picture cards of adults and children in day dress or nightdress, giving or withholding gifts, and so forth. With the narratable material the authors report (rather wistfully) that the efficiency in information utilization dropped, that subjects hung on to their hypotheses, even when they were contradicted by negative instances, and were somehow less rational all round. There is a hint that subjects were doing something else besides processing information for categorical inference, but the authors did not deign to find out *what* they were doing. Now, more than twenty-five years later, I *have* found out. To put it in Nelson Goodman's expression, they were involved in a different kind of world making, ignoring instruction from the experimenter about how the instances were composed of attributes of different values, and so forth. One of our subjects (my collaborator in this research is Alison McClure) was, for example, operating on the hypothesis that the category might be "a parent and child in a good relationship." As cards were presented to her, she was busily involved in trying to figure out what the experimenter might have had in mind by a good relationship, and if an instance that seemed to negate her hypothesis came along, she would continue to rebuild the kinds of "stories" that might count as "good." Each instance was an occasion for expanding or modifying the story, involving agents, actions, goals, scenes, and instruments in the manner of Kenneth Burke's pentad.[36] In the end, she came out with a rather interesting if cockeyed story—her version of a world in which the instances could live, including such matters as "misunderstandings," "doing things for the good of the child," and so forth. On paradigmatic grounds, she committed errors galore, required staggeringly redundant input, and so on down the list of paradigmatic sins. But her story was an interesting and believable one. She was, after all, a therapist concerned with the family dilemma. If her protocol had been analyzed by Paul Ricoeur or Greimas[37] or by Roy Schafer or Donald Spence,[38] all of them would have commented upon the narrative rationality of the "fiction" she was creating.

Or take the old experiment of Solomon Asch's on trait names, how *intelligent* changes meaning when paired with *cold* or with *warm*.[39] It is a brilliant, trail-blazing study that served Asch well in illustrating the Gestalt-theoretic manner in which an overall impression alters the meaning of the component parts. Henri Zukier and I have been redoing the study, using a wide variety of trait lists, varying in their surface compatibility. Give your subjects an initial opportunity to create a general superordinate impression by inclusion of some compatible traits, like *spiritual, introverted, religious* (yielding such descriptions as "saintly kind of person") and then add *practical* and *money-minded*, and narrative organization takes over: "He's saintly alright, but he's only trying to earn a living in a cut-throat business," or "Yes, of course, he's probably one of those Amish or Mennonite farmers who's great within his own group, but drives a very hard bargain outside." Again the Burke pentad, and now the matter of intentions and consciousness about what the contexts might be and how the person acts in each. The language of subjects changes—factive and implicative verbs increase, modal auxiliaries enter indicating stance, the tell-tale "just-even-only" constructions enter ("He's only trying to earn a living"), the presuppositional load increases dramatically, intention and awareness come in, the account becomes firmly situated in time and in space and in context.

Or take the equally trail-blazing studies of Kahnemann and Tversky.[40] They have shown that strategies for making inferences about individual events, given base-rate information about the probabilities that govern outcome in classes of similar events, do not follow standard Bayesian models. Recall, you tell your subjects that you are presenting them sketches chosen at random from sketches of a hundred people, seventy of whom became salesmen, thirty librarians. Now read them a sketch about somebody who is "shy and withdrawn, . . . a meek and tidy soul, . . . a need for order and structure and a passion for detail . . . ." In spite of the 70-30 base-rate, subjects will say, "Librarian"—though if the information in the sketch is indifferent, they *will* go the Bayesian way. In a finely reasoned paper, Zukier and Pepitone show that the way subjects go depends upon their orientation: whether it is scientific and propositionally oriented, or "clinical" and geared to particulars.[41] The scientific produces Bayesianism, the clinical, an account far more based on a narrative world one can construct for the particular case. They conclude, "The results are consistent with the proposition that different judgmental contexts may activate different representations of the problem, and different judgmental objectives, which require different inferential strategies." And again I would argue that the two strategies are not only different but are drawn from two fundamentally different modes of putting together knowledge.

Let me in conclusion comment upon a remark made earlier in passing, to the effect that outcomes produced by the two modes of thought could neither contradict nor corroborate the other. It is a very radical claim, and also very easily misunderstood. Let me say, at the outset, that it is possible to do a logical analysis of a story—or as an undergraduate once told me, Hamlet was not very cost-effective and needed three deaths to get his culprit. Conversely, you can tell good stories about scientific discoveries—Pasteur, Einstein, the Curies, even Freud have all sat for their narrative portraits. My economist friend, Robert Heilbroner, recently said to me, "When an economic theory fails to work easily, we begin telling stories about the Japanese imports or the slowness of the Zuric 'snake'." Yet, when the Japanese imports get included as parameters within the theory, the story does not go away: it can still be told, still judged for its verisimilitude—like the causes of war, the reasons for the decline of the Labor Party in Britain or the Empire in Rome. Moreover, a story can be shown to be false, and still have a compelling believability about it. For stories per se are not proved false, only some of their component propositions. What I must reiterate is that narrative is a form and the narrative thinking that brings it into being a process that, in the end, preclude verification as the basis for their "reality" or "meaning." And by the same token, logical science and the paradigmatic thinking that supports it rest upon an eventual verification and logical proof that prevail regardless of their counterintuitiveness, their lack of dramatic verisimilitude. Perhaps this is the only sense in which the adage, "Truth is stranger than fiction," is true. Each is a version of the world, and to ask which depicts the real world is to ask a question that even modern metaphysicians believe to be undecidable.

Footnotes

1. Richard Rorty, *Philosophy and the Mirror of Nature* (Princeton, N.J.: Princeton University Press, 1979).

2. Nelson Goodman, *Of Minds and Other Matters* (Cambridge, Mass.: Harvard University Press, 1984).

3. Nelson Goodman, *Ways of World Making* (Indianapolis and Cambridge: Hackett Publishing Co., 1978); idem, *Of Minds and Other Matters.*

4. Karl Popper, *The Logic of Scientific Discovery* (New York: Harper and Row, 1968).

5. Victor Turner, *From Ritual to Theater: The Human Seriousness of Play* (New York: Performing Arts Journal Publications, 1982): Tzvetan Todorov, *The Poetics of Prose* (Ithaca, N.Y.: Cornell University Press, 1977).

6. Nelson Goodman, "Twisted Tales: Or, Story, Study, Symphony," in *On Narrative*, ed. W. J. T. Mitchell (Chicago: University of Chicago Press, 1981).

7. Brian Sutton-Smith, *The Folkstories of Children* (Philadelphia: University of Pennsylvania Press, 1981).

8. Maya Hickman, "The Implication of Discourse Skills in Vygotsky's Developmental Theory," in *Culture, Communication, and Cognition: Vygotskian Perspectives*, ed. James V. Wertsch (New York: Academic Press, 1983).

9. Michael Beveridge and Judy Dunn, "Communication and the Development of Reflective Thinking" (Paper presented at the Annual Conference of the Developmental Section of the British Psychological Society, University of Edinburgh, 1980).

10. David Olson and Janet Astington, personal communication, 1984.

11. A. J. Greimas and J. Courtes, "The Cognitive Dimension of Narrative Discourse," *New Literary History* 7 (Spring 1976): 433-47.

12. Wilhelm Dilthey, *Pattern and Meaning in History: Thoughts on History and Society*, edited and introduced by Hans P. Rickman (New York: Harper, 1962). For a briefer account, see Hans P. Rickman's essay on Dilthey in the *Encyclopedia of Philosophy* (New York: McMillan, 1967).

13. Rorty, *Philosophy and the Mirror of Nature.*

14. Vladimir Propp, *Morphology of the Folk Tale* (Austin, Tex.: Texas University Press, 1968); Claude Levi-Strauss, *Structural Anthropology* (New York: Basic Books, 1963); Paul Ricoeur, *Hermeneutics and the Human Sciences* (Cambridge: Cambridge University Press, 1981); Greimas and Courtes, "The Cognitive Dimension of Narrative Discourse"; Todorov, *The Poetics of Prose*; Kenneth Burke, *A Grammar of Motives* (New York: Prentice-Hall, 1945); Roman Jakobson, "Linguistics and Poetics," in *Style in Language*, ed. Thomas A. Sebeok (Cambridge, Mass.: MIT Press, 1960).

15. Henry A. Murray, *Explorations in Personality* (Oxford: Oxford University Press, 1938).

16. See, for example, Daniel Kahnemann, Paul Slovic, and Amos Tversky, *Judgment under Uncertainty: Heuristics and Biases* (Cambridge University Press, 1982).

17. Jerome Bruner, Jacqueline Goodnow, and George Austin, *A Study of Thinking* (New York: John Wiley and Sons, 1956).

18. Albert Bates Lord, *Singer of Tales* (Cambridge, Mass.: Harvard University Press, 1960).

19. Morris Cohen, *Reason and Nature: An Essay on the Meaning of Scientific Method* (New York: Harcourt Brace, 1931); John Dewey, *Experience and Nature,* 2d ed. (Chicago and London: Open Court Publishing Co., 1925).

20. Jakobson, "Linguistics and Poetics."

21. Gottlob Frege, "On Sense and Reference," in *Translations from the Philosophical Writings of Gottlob Frege*, ed. Peter T. Geach and Max Black (Oxford: Blackwell, 1952).

22. Frank C. Keil, *Semantic and Conceptual Development: An Ontological Perspective* (Cambridge, Mass.: Harvard University Press, 1979).

23. Susan Carey, "The Child as Word Learner," in *Linguistic Theory and Psychological Reality*, ed. Morris Halle, Joan Bresan, and George A. Miller (Cambridge, Mass.: MIT Press, 1978).

24. Ludwig Wittgenstein, *Philosophical Investigations* (Oxford: Blackwell, 1953).

25. John Austin, *How to Do Things with Words* (Oxford: Oxford University Press, 1962).

26. John R. Searle, *Speech Acts: An Essay in the Philosophy of Language* (Cambridge: Cambridge University Press, 1969).

27. H. P. Grice, "Logic and Conversation," in *Syntax and Semantics*, vol. 3, *Speech Acts*, ed. Peter Cole and Jerry L. Morgan (New York: Academic Press, 1975).

28. Lauri Karttunen and R. S. Peters, "Requiem for Presupposition," in *Proceedings* of the Third Annual Meeting of the Berkeley Linguistics Society (1977), pp. 360-71.

29. Gerald Gazdar, *Pragmatics: Implicature, Presupposition, and Logical Form* (New York: Academic Press, 1979).

30. Dan Sperber and Deirdre Wilson, "Mutual Knowledge and Relevance in Theories of Comprehension," in *Mutual Knowledge*, ed. N. V. Smith (London and New York: Academic Press, 1982).

31. John R. Searle, *Experience and Meaning: Studies in the Theory of Speech Acts* (Cambridge: Cambridge University Press, 1979).

32. Joseph Campbell, *The Hero with a Thousand Faces* (New York: Meridien Books, 1956).

33. See, for example, S. Fish, "Normal Circumstances, Literal Language, Direct Speech Acts, the Ordinary, the Obvious, What Goes on Without Saying, and Other Special Cases," in *Interpretative Social Science: A Reader*, ed. Paul Rabinow and William M. Sullivan (Berkeley, Calif.: University of California Press, 1979).

34. Marshall McLuhan, *Understanding Media* (New York: McGraw-Hill, 1964).

35. Bruner, Goodnow, and Austin, *A Study of Thinking*.

36. Burke, *A Grammar of Motives*.

37. Ricouer, *Hermeneutics and the Human Sciences*; Greimas and Courtes, "The Cognitive Dimension of Narrative Discourse."

38. Roy Schafer, "Narration in the Psychoanalytic Dialogue," in *On Narrative*, ed. W. J. T. Mitchell (Chicago: University of Chicago Press); Donald Spence, *Narrative Truth and Historical Truth* (New York: W. W. Norton, 1982).

39. Solomon E. Asch, "Forming Impressions of Personality," *Journal of Abnormal Social Psychology* 41 (1946): 258-90.

40. Daniel Kahnemann and Amos Tversky, "On the Psychology of Prediction," *Psychological Review* 80 (July 1973): 237-51.

41. Henry Zukier and A. Pepitone, "Social Roles and Strategies in Prediction: Some Determinants of the Use of Base Rate Information," *Journal of Personality and Social Psychology*, in press.

CHAPTER VII

Formal Modes of Knowing

NEL NODDINGS

"Mathematics," said Benjamin Peirce, "is the science which draws necessary conclusions."[1] Mathematical knowledge, from this point of view, is formal knowledge, that is, knowledge produced through the faultless execution of precisely defined procedures. Learning mathematics, therefore, requires both gaining competence in the use of formal procedures and accumulating a catalog of results already produced.

Peirce's son, the philosopher-logician Charles Sanders Peirce, admired and accepted his father's definition in part but noted that there was more to mathematics than drawing necessary conclusions. Indeed, he said that such a definition "makes or seems to make the deduction of the consequences of hypotheses the sole business of the mathematician as such."[2] He went on to remark that the framing of general hypotheses often requires "immense genius" and that "even the framing of particular hypotheses of special problems almost always calls for good judgment and knowledge, and sometimes for great intellectual power."[3] Further, he noted that things must "be DONE" in mathematics[4]—schemata are built—and hence both construction and observation are called into play.

What we see here is a conflict over the basic nature of mathematical activity. If it is agreed that mathematics itself is a body of formal knowledge (and even that is in some doubt), it does not necessarily follow that mathematical activity takes place entirely in a formal mode of knowing. *Is* there such a thing as a formal mode of knowing, or must

I wish to thank D. C. Phillips for his careful reading of the first draft of this chapter and for his suggestions.

we enter other modes in order to construct formal objects and to understand formal results?

In order to explore these questions, I will discuss three domains of mathematical activity: the domain of informal, naive, or concrete experience; the domain of formal procedures (Benjamin Peirce's mathematics); and the metadomain in which we critique and discuss the domain of formal procedures. My main point will be that "doing mathematics" involves work in several modes of knowing across all three domains of activity. In particular, we shall see that, in order to achieve meaning and understanding, mathematicians rely heavily on scientific, intuitive, and aesthetic modes of knowing and that much of their activity takes place outside the domain of formal procedures.

Pedagogical questions of great importance arise in this discussion: On which domain should mathematics educators concentrate? In which should instruction begin? How should movement across the domains be organized?

The Domains of Mathematical Activity

In this century, more than any other, there has been vigorous debate over the nature of mathematics. Faced with paradoxes at the very foundations of mathematics, mathematicians and philosophers have attempted to resolve the difficulties in various ways, of which the most prominent are known as logicism, formalism, and intuitionism. Logicists attempt to assimilate mathematics to logic so that mathematical reasoning can be freed of any contamination that arises from distinctly mathematical objects; formalists attempt to axiomatize or formalize all of mathematics so that its procedures are absolutely explicit and its objects are freed of real-world interpretation; and intuitionists attempt to develop all of mathematics constructively from completely transparent, self-evident beginnings.[5] All of these positions try to establish the infallibility of mathematics by separating mathematics from the empirical world. More recently, however, there has been a revival of interest in empiricism in mathematics. Imre Lakatos, for example, has suggested that the methods actually used by working mathematicians strongly resemble scientific methods and that the development of mathematics itself is very like that of science.[6] From this point of view, claims for the infallibility of mathematics are mistaken.

Debate at the foundations of mathematics centers on the ultimate nature of both mathematical objects and procedures. For mathematics educators, however, foundational controversies give rise to debates over emphasis. As educators we need not be centrally concerned with the ultimate nature of mathematics nor with the actual problems of strengthening the foundations, but we must be concerned with the variety of legitimate activities emphasized by competing mathematical philosophies. We must be concerned with this variety precisely *because* we are educators, and it is our task to introduce students to the universe of mathematical content and thinking. By choosing to construct our curricula and teaching methods under the guidance of only one perspective (as we came very close to doing with the "new math"), we risk closing off from our students the very possibilities that gave rise to the legitimate differences, and we make it far more difficult for them to take the critical stance that we are always quick to posit as one of our main aims.

I noted at the start of this discussion that most mathematicians acknowledge at least a kernel of truth in the elder Peirce's claim that mathematics consists of deductive procedures. While it is generally agreed that mathematics cannot be entirely formalized, it is indisputable that formal knowledge consists of rule-produced configurations (theorems in mathematics, strings in linguistics and computer science, sequences in music, patterns in art); it is also clear, however, that the creation of formal knowledge usually involves something other than the mindless application of rules. Given appropriate objects and rules, machines can produce theorems or strings faultlessly; they "draw necessary conclusions." But it is generally acknowledged that mathematicians are not simply theorem-proving or string-producing machines. Indeed, Lakatos claims that working mathematicians find such exercises "uninteresting" and even that mathematics itself is best represented heuristically or genetically and not formally. Certainly, he advises, it should not be *presented* formally. "According to formalists," he says, "mathematics is identical with formalized mathematics. But what can one *discover* in a formalized theory?"[7] Clearly, Lakatos is thinking here about both learners and producers of mathematics.

In a similar, though milder critique, Rudy Rucker says: "In the initial stages of research, mathematicians do not seem to function like theorem-producing machines. Instead, they use some sort of mathematical intuition to "see" the universe of mathematics and determine by a sort of empirical process what is true."[8]

The "seeing" to which Rucker refers (and to which C. S. Peirce also referred) occurs in an intuitive mode and is not confined to the domain of formal objects in which we are restricted to highly abstract basic objects, a few precisely defined, given configurations, and those complex configurations we can produce by a set of specific inference or production rules. Rather, when we seek meaning—hypotheses, ideas, understanding—we often move into a domain of informal or naive experience where we work for a while with concrete objects. Children, we may note, usually begin mathematical activity on actual objects. As they select candies for a group of people, for example, they may say "Mommy, Daddy, Jimmy, Me," carefully matching candies to persons. In performing this activity of one-to-one correspondence, they are engaged in primitive mathematical activity on real-world objects. Later, they learn that discrete objects of any kind can be counted using the universal symbols, "one, two, three, four, ..." Now, these symbols themselves become an object set, and children become acquainted with verbal manipulations of the sort, "two and one make three." Still later, they are introduced to numerals and written symbols for operating on them. It is symbols of this new sort that constitute the usual objects of a mathematical system.

Not only do we perform our very first mathematical acts in the domain of informal experience, but we continually return to this domain as our mathematical competence grows, and the domain itself changes with respect to content. The college student's domain of naive experience is very different from that of the kindergartner. But however the objects may change in sophistication, the fundamental procedures of constructing schemata with concrete objects and looking at the results remain the same. Hermann Weyl, an intuitionist mathematician, captured this emphasis in a maxim for aspiring mathematicians: "Think concretely."[9] Further, he spoke in direct opposition to the elder Peirce when he said: "The business of the constructive mathematician is *not* to draw logical conclusions. Indeed his arguments and propositions are merely an accompaniment of his actions, his carrying out of constructions."[10]

Not only do we find a difference of opinion among mathematicians concerning the ultimate nature of mathematics, the importance of thinking concretely, and the relation of mathematics to the real world, but we find these differences underscored in recommendations for the precollegiate mathematics curriculum. Speaking on the possibility of reform, Morris Kline recommended that the direction of reform "should be diametrically opposite to that taken by the new mathematics."[11] Whereas the new mathematics had emphasized activity in what I shall call the "metadomain," Kline wanted the emphasis to be shifted to that of applications—to the domain of informal experience. It is important to understand that work in the domain of real-world experience, although it is properly characterized as informal, naive (mathematically), and concrete, is not necessarily unsophisticated. On the contrary, the progress of civilization takes place in this domain, and we return to it over and over in the pursuit of both understanding and application. Speaking from this view, Kline said:

> What we should be fashioning and teaching, then, beyond mathematics proper, are the relationships of mathematics to other human interests—in other words, a broad cultural mathematics curriculum which achieves an intimate communion with the main currents of thought and our cultural heritage. Some of these relationships can serve as motivation; others would be applications; and still others would supply interesting reading and discussion material that would vary and enliven the content of our mathematics courses.[12]

If we were to move in the direction Kline has suggested, we would emphasize interaction between the domain of formal procedures (mathematics proper) and that of informal experience. But there is another compelling view. Is it not important that students understand not only how mathematics can be used but also why its procedures work as they do? Should we not teach something about the structure of mathematics?

Discussion of why things work as they do in a formal domain takes place in what we usually call a "metadomain." The language of this domain—like that in the informal domain—is natural language (for example, English), but it is sophisticated natural language. It is a metalanguage[13]—natural language tailored to describe and explain what is happening in the formal domain or object language. Just as we turn to the domain of informal experience when we want to interpret or bring commonsense meanings to what we are doing in the formal domain, so we turn to the metadomain when we have questions about the procedures themselves. Is what we are doing "legal"? What underlies this legality and ensures it? What principles undergird all systems of this sort? As we shall see, there are disputes concerning the nature of metamathematics also. (Formalists were especially interested in this domain, and their work came to be identified with "metamathematics.") At this point in the discussion, I am using "meta" terms in a basic and general way to refer to domains in which we "talk about" formal domains.

The makers of the new mathematics emphasized questions of the kind just noted. Their emphasis, then, was on activities in the metadomain. While they are often accused of putting inordinate emphasis on formal procedures, particularly on deductive proof, they actually intended to promote understanding of those procedures through knowledge of the underlying structure of mathematics. In this they were greatly encouraged by parallel emphasis on the structure of knowledge in both psychology and education. Jerome Bruner, in his influential *Process of Education*, proposed as a hypothesis that an understanding of structure would make mathematics generally more intelligible,[14] and Joseph Schwab drew attention to the structure of disciplines in general, suggesting that these structures should form the bedrock of curriculum content.[15] Thus the promoters of the new math were not alone in seeking and recommending curricular forms that would transcend mere collections of information and the rote performance of basic skills.

Both proponents and opponents of the new mathematics wanted students to understand and enjoy mathematics. Proponents wanted understanding to precede action so that mathematical manipulation would not be mindless—a mere shuffling of symbols. Opponents argued that the sort of understanding sought by the vast majority of users of mathematics is a functional sort: understanding of how procedures are done, where they may be applied, and with what effect. Must we choose between these two? And what of the formal domain itself? Has it no value in its own right? For some thinkers, as we have seen, activity in the formal domain *is* mathematics.

Division of mathematical activity into informal, formal, and metadomains is a fairly recent development. For centuries, most disciplines—even mathematics—were conducted in ordinary language. Douglas Hofstadter remarks:

Since mathematical reasoning had always been done in "natural language" (e.g., French or Latin or some language for normal communication), there was always a lot of possible ambiguity. Words had different meanings to different people, conjured up different images, and so forth. It seemed reasonable and even important to establish a single uniform notation in which all mathematical work could be done, and with the aid of which any two mathematicians could resolve disputes over whether a suggested proof was valid or not.[16]

Mathematical exposition, then, came to be conducted in a rule-governed language of well-defined objects (the formal domain), and discussion about this mathematical system shifted to a metadomain. But as we have already noted, the objects of the formal system, which are the first or original objects for the metathinker, are *not* the first objects encountered experientially. There is a genetic story left out in most accounts of formal systems and metasystems, and this genetic story is absolutely central for any serious educational thinking. Both the initial experiential domain and the highly sophisticated metastructures use a form of natural language, but only the latter is a metalanguage in the technical sense; the language used in the initial experiential encounter, as we have seen, *precedes* the identification of mathematical objects. A great deal of mathematics is done in the informal domain.

As we have become more sophisticated in our views of mathematics, and of formal systems in particular, it has become paradoxically more difficult to decide just which sort of activity—activity in which domain—is "real mathematical" activity. The domain of formal procedures (defined, albeit, somewhat informally for initiates) is the one we usually associate with school mathematics. It is the domain dearly loved by "back to basics" advocates, and it consists largely of algorithmic procedures—procedures which, if applied correctly and executed faultlessly, guarantee their results. Most mathematics educators counsel against great emphasis on these activities, arguing that mathematics instruction should be "meaningful." This advice implies, of course, a shift of emphasis to either the domain of applications and informal mathematics or to the metadomain of structures. One may, however, argue convincingly that activities in all three domains are important to mathematical understanding and that, instead of pressing for an emphasis on one, we should analyze the characteristic activities in each domain to see how they contribute to the learning of mathematics.

Learning, Understanding, and Doing Mathematics

When we consider mathematical activity in three domains, it is natural to ask in which domain instruction should begin and how movement across the domains should be organized. My main thesis in this section will be that we should abandon efforts to characterize mathematical learning as "top-down" or "bottom-up" and instead consider all questions concerning movement through the domains as context- or topic-bound. What I am referring to here is the common and disconcerting tendency of mathematics educators to insist on an emphasis of order among the domains: either structure first, then procedures, then applications or else potential applications (problems) first, then procedures, then structural understanding. Emphasis on the learning context and how the topic is embedded in it points to a very different mode of working. We would not, from this point of view, reject out of hand suggestions to start instruction on some topics with rote use of algorithms, nor would we insist that no topic should be introduced through the painstaking elucidation of its underlying structure. Instead, we would probe persistently to find out what the history and nature of a particular topic reveal about the activities characteristic in its treatment.

It is easy to poke fun at the mindless sort of manipulation that often occurs when students confine their activity to the formal domain—especially when they transfer the rules of one mathematical game thoughtlessly to another. Lewis Carroll has delighted us with examples; this one, from the trial of the knave in *Alice in Wonderland*, is typical:

> The first witness was the Hatter. He came in with a teacup in one hand and a piece of bread-and-butter in the other. "I beg your pardon, your Majesty," he began, "for bringing these in; but I hadn't quite finished my tea when I was sent for."
>
> "You ought to have finished," said the King. "When did you begin?"
>
> The Hatter looked at the March Hare, who had followed him into the court, arm-in-arm with the Dormouse. "Fourteenth of March, I *think* it was," he said.
>
> "Fifteenth," said the March Hare.
>
> "Sixteenth," said the Dormouse.
>
> "Write that down," the King said to the jury; and the jury eagerly wrote down all three dates on their slates, and then added them up, and reduced the answer to shillings and pence.[17]

In trying to find methods proof against this amusing (but mathematically deplorable) behavior, mathematics educators have periodically insisted that understanding should precede manipulation. In programs so oriented, children often spend months on exercises requiring the use of structure-revealing devices such as expanded notation rather than on rote practice of computation. Now, I am certainly not suggesting that we give up efforts to teach children something about the structure of mathematics, but I am arguing that an understanding of structure need not always precede the mastery of algorithmic forms. Indeed, starting instruction in the middle domain of formal procedures is often entirely reasonable: it gives a foothold from which to move to either of the other domains with some security. Insecure students sometimes choose the wrong procedure in attempting to apply their mathematics, that is, in trying to solve word problems, because they are not confident in handling the correct procedure. A fourth grader, for example, first responded, "Divide," during a thinking-aloud protocol on word problems. He then said, "No, I guess I'll multiply." When the researcher asked why he switched procedures, he said, "Because I don't remember how to divide these numbers."

The fact that behavior such as this really does occur does not give us sufficient reason to keep children endlessly at drill and practice. Rather, common sense suggests two promising directions: first, skills acquired straightforwardly should be quickly and appropriately applied; second, the necessary drill and practice should be made into fun and games whenever possible. (We might recall here that even Plato, in *The Republic*, counseled that children be taught by games.) Further, it simply is not true that most children hate rule-bound activity. Many learn the rigid conventions of basic programming, for example, quite easily and on their own. The key seems to be that they get *to do things that they want to do* with their newly learned conventions. This raises a warning for curriculum makers who will be asked to write increasingly standardized curricula for computer science courses. It is vital not to become bogged down in drill for its own sake, but it is also important not to present the whole field as "computer science"—the theoretical study of why things work as they do with computers. The fascination that youngsters have shown with computers is a sure sign that people like to *use* the skills that they acquire *toward their own ends*.

This is a good point at which to say something further about the domain of applications. To be pedagogically sound, the opportunities we offer for applications should not be drawn entirely from the stock of applications that are assessed as important by experts in various fields; rather, they should be genuine opportunities for students to use the mathematics they have learned toward achieving ends they themselves desire. For young children, all sorts of games represent such genuine opportunities to apply the basic arithmetic skills they have learned. There is no sound pedagogical reason why elementary school children should not be involved in all sorts of games in their classrooms—card games, board games, dice games. Educators and interested lay persons are often alarmed when they see children so engaged during school hours; they are uneasy because they are unsure of what is being learned and because they feel that education (like life) cannot always be fun. But just as budgets, house plans, timetables, and checking accounts are appropriate domains of application for young adults, so games are the fundamentally appropriate domain for children.

There *is* something to worry about, however, in this recommendation. Teachers need to know what can be learned by way of mathematics in these games and what each phase of learning suggests for the next. In order for teachers to use games effectively, researchers need to tear themselves away from school-bound and test-bound research and engage in the careful analysis of materials and what can be learned from them. The kind of research envisioned is the sort suggested by David Hawkins in a series of articles several years ago.[18] The information gained through materials-in-action research and research on "preparation" could be used by teachers in planning sequences of games and activities that fit integrally into the curriculum of concepts and skills. It is hard to overestimate either the need for or the value of such research. Promising curricula—Elementary Science Study (ESS) comes to mind here—have often been underused and even abandoned because teachers were unsure of what children were learning through the materials. What is required, then, is a rigorous and imaginative examination of the natural domains of mathematical applications for students of various ages and aptitudes and of how activity in these domains can be used to enhance the learning of mathematics.

Not only can we move more confidently into the informal domain of applications when algorithmic procedures have been mastered, but we can also move into the metadomain with informed curiosity. Usually we think of this domain as the field in which we study and critique the formal structures of mathematics, and such study is, of course, a paramount concern of metamathematicians. But emphases may differ in this domain, also. Lakatos criticized the formalists for turning metamathematics into mathematical logic—the axiomatization or formalization of all mathematics. What had formerly been "philosophy of mathematics" now became "metamathematics" narrowly construed.[19]

As I have been using the term, "metamathematics" refers to any relatively sophisticated, critical, and organized examination of the products and processes of working mathematics. It is the domain in which we talk about the objects and procedures of the formal domain. From this point of view, students can be invited fairly early on to engage in metamathematical thinking, and the lines between the domains become indistinct. High school students can engage, for example, in a *search* for algorithms. Clearly, this activity is different from undergoing instruction on why a given, standard algorithm works, but it still involves an implicit understanding of structure and is far more challenging. Students are taught to handle complex fractions by standard division, for example, but bright youngsters can certainly invent short cuts and, in doing so, they are led to explore the structural underpinnings of their inventions. They should be aware, as they undertake this sort of task, that some of the world's great mathematicians have been unashamedly "algorists." E. T. Bell says of Euler, an outstanding algorist:

> As an algorist Euler has never been surpassed, and probably never even closely approached, unless by Jacobi. An algorist is a mathematician who devises "algorithms" (or "algorisms") for the solution of problems of special kinds. . . .
>
> It is fashionable today to despise the "mere algorist" yet, when a truly great one like the Hindu Ramanujan arrives unexpectedly out of nowhere, even expert analysts hail him as a gift from Heaven: his all but supernatural insight into apparently unrelated formulas reveals hidden trails leading from one territory to another, and the analysts have new tasks provided for them in clearing the trails. An algorist is a "formalist" who loves beautiful formulas for their own sake.[20]

But the "formalist" to whom Bell refers is a different sort from the metamathematical formalist identified earlier. This "formalist" is not concentrating on the legality of formal procedures but, rather, on their usefulness and beauty; he or she is captivated by the subject while in an intuitive mode—he or she *sees* something beautiful that has not yet been led across into the generally observable world. Further, the actual work of invention is conducted in all three domains. The algorist may ask: What will convince others that this lovely thing functions as I believe it does? Why does it work? In what cases does it fail? To what objects does it apply? How far can I extend it? Can it be made even more simple and beautiful?

We find algorists in fields other than mathematics as well. The composer, Johann Sebastian Bach, might well be called an "algorist." He found marvelous ways of stringing together standard forms so as to produce exquisite new patterns. Cross and Ewen note:

> He invented no new forms and created no new style or idiom. But to the old forms and styles and idioms he brought an emotional expressiveness, a nobility of thinking, a majesty of concept, a spaciousness of design which were unique. So completely had he exhausted both the technical and aesthetic possibilities of polyphony that by necessity the composers who followed him had to set off in an altogether new direction.[21]

Yet Bach was considered by many of his contemporaries to be stuffy and old-fashioned. In a similarly ill-considered judgment, mathematics educators have despised "mere computation" and concentrated on structural explanations of why mathematical algorithms work. It is indeed odd that, even at a time when interest in "discovery" ran high, we gave little attention to the discovery of procedures and so much to the discovery of dusty generalizations.[22] Yet even young children can discover shortcuts and streamlined procedures and, in doing so, learn a great deal about heuristic activity in mathematics.

We could fill volumes in a discussion of algorists and their work: M. C. Escher in art,[23] Sam Loyd in puzzles,[24] Lewis Carroll in "nonsense" poetry.[25] But there is a more compelling reason to emphasize activity in the formal domain today. Algorithms, codes, and meaningful patterns pervade all areas of thinking, and the search for naturally occurring coded information is as important today as ongoing attempts to encode information in ever more concise and elegant forms. It is no longer supposed that order of the grammatical sort is something entirely invented by human beings. Jeremy Campbell remarks, "The theory of information suggests instead that order is entirely natural: grammatical man inhabits a grammatical universe."[26] Geneticists, astronomers, linguists, musicologists, artists, and mathematicians are not merely trying to decode or decipher configurations that obviously contain messages, but, rather, they are engaged in a deliberate search for coded messages. The universe itself is thought to be composed of matter, energy, and *information.* Further, even though so many people regard rules as constraining and somewhat boring, rules are in fact, in the context of information, generative; that is, they may be used to generate enormous varieties of new and interesting configurations.[27]

It would seem reasonable to give more attention to the generative capacity of rules in our early mathematics lessons. Ten year olds, for example, often love to generate large numbers by systematically adding zeros: "ten, one hundred, one thousand, . . . , one billion, . . . , one skillion!" Instead of encouraging children to use their algorithmic skills to generate numbers, however, we usually require them to produce answers to pre-set computational puzzles. The need for practice could be met as well, for example, by asking children to produce all the numbers they can by multiplying by 4: Start with the digits 0, 1, 2, . . . , 9; multiply any one of them by 4; keep going. At the end of an exercise like this, children might examine each other's sequences for interesting patterns. The pedagogical difficulty here is, of course, that there is no easy means for the teacher to check everyone's paper or to be sure that every interesting pattern is detected or that everyone achieves exactly the same objective as everyone else. We encountered a similar difficulty in connection with learning mathematics through games; as we noted in that discussion, teachers often do not know what mathematics can be learned from particular games, what games "to choose next," or how to evaluate the chain of activities. Similarly, researchers find such activities uncongenial to the usual mode of treatment and assessment of outcomes. The only defensible response to objections of this sort has to be this: if the present structure of schooling and research gets in the way of significant learning and inspired teaching, then *it* must be changed. We must not warp our best methods in the service of maintaining recalcitrant structures.

I set out in this section to explore pedagogical questions about the three domains of mathematical activity. It is clear, I think, that genuine mathematical activity occurs in all three domains and that mathematical thinkers work in a variety of modes of knowing in all three domains. Even in the purely formal domain, the intuitive mode is functional; one can see or hear or feel that something is not quite right before detecting the actual error. The scientific mode is valuable, also, because we may have to ask repeatedly whether a particular production rule is the one we should be using, given the goal we have in mind: if this does not work, what else might we try? And when we finally have our result, we may turn an aesthetic eye upon it and ask: is there a more elegant way to attain it or in which to express it?

We have had opportunities to move toward this more complex view of mathematical activity in the past. Robert Davis, for example, suggested some years ago a teaching method called "torpedoing" in which students are led to form a conjecture, the teacher produces a counterexample, and the student seeks a new conjecture.[28] This instructional pattern is very like the mode of actual mathematical productivity as described by Lakatos ("proofs" and refutations). It is characterized by a continual movement across domains and a good deal of social interaction in the form of challenge and response. If we enter a new era of enthusiastic curriculum development, we should certainly reconsider instructional methods that conform to the reality of mathematical activity, but, in doing so, we should resist the temptation to use any one of them pervasively. Not everything is best taught by discovery, or by "torpedoing," or by rote, or by group discussion, or by meticulous elaboration of underlying structure.

Very little current research is directed at the rational analysis of mathematical topics, the plausible relations between presentational modes and the genesis of ideas, or the creation and selection of materials appropriate for such genetic presentations. While excellent work is being done on the conceptualization of problem solving,[29] on models of thinking processes,[30] on task analysis[31] (which is very different from topic analysis), and on error analysis,[32] research directly applicable to curriculum and instruction is scarce—the former much more scarce than the latter.[33] The sort of research suggested by my analysis would not be conclusion-oriented research. Rather, it (like mathematics itself) would be conjecture- and argument-oriented and, as such, would be directly applicable to practice; it would produce a body of materials and suggested presentational formats that would be "worth trying." Further, since the materials would be presented in conjectural form (not as *the* way to reform school mathematics), evaluation and refinement would be built into the research/instruction enterprise, and we would not suffer the embarrassment of failing to conduct convincing evaluations of major curriculum projects.

To shift research and instructional emphases from the linear, deductivist approaches currently so popular to modes more in tune with heuristic methods in teaching and learning will require changes in the preparation of both teachers and researchers. It will not be easily accomplished. As Lakatos noted: "The change from the deductivist to the heuristic approach will certainly be difficult, but some of the teachers of modern mathematics already realize the need for it."[34]

In spite of the obvious difficulties involved, the possibilities for genuine reform—reform that will enliven mathematics teaching and learning—make a program of heuristic and genetic curriculum development attractive. Such a program, by its very nature, does not involve a sequence of authoring, field-testing, training, and evaluation but, rather, integrated development subject to continuous refinement.

Summary

I started this discussion by asking whether there is such a thing as a formal mode of knowing. By analyzing questions and tasks characteristic of three domains of mathematical activity, I concluded that formal operations play a crucial role not only in mathematics but in a host of disciplines dependent upon "information." Hence we should not despise formal procedures nor fear doing them by rote. But these formal operations do not in themselves constitute either mathematical knowledge or formal knowing. *To know* requires informal activity in intuitive, scientific, and aesthetic modes as well as skillful operation in the formal domain. Mathematics, far from being infallible formal knowledge, is a human enterprise characterized by heuristic activity.

Building on the analysis of mathematical activity, I suggested that teaching and learning might profitably be brought into congruence with this heuristic view of mathematics: that linear top-down and bottom-up approaches both be abandoned in favor of methods derived from topical analysis, that genetic methods be explored, that domains of "natural" application be investigated, and that research should be reoriented toward the conjectural. All of these suggestions are compatible with a heuristic description of mathematical activity, and they may be especially useful now at a time of renewed interest in the reform of mathematical education.

Footnotes

1. Quoted in Charles S. Peirce, "The Essence of Mathematics," in *The World of Mathematics*, ed. James R. Newman (New York: Simon and Schuster, 1956), p. 1773.

2. Ibid., p. 1779.

3. Ibid.

4. Ibid., p. 1776.

5. For a full discussion of the three great philosophical schools, see Howard Eves and Carroll V. Newsom, *An Introduction to the Foundations of Mathematics* (New York: Holt, Rinehart and Winston, 1958); Max Black, *The Nature of Mathematics* (Totowa, N.J.: Littlefield, Adams, 1965); Philip J. Davis and Reuben Hersh, *The Mathematical Experience* (Boston: Birkhauser, 1981).

6. Imre Lakatos, *Proofs and Refutations: The Logic of Mathematical Discovery*, ed. John Worrall and Elie Zahar (Cambridge, England: Cambridge University Press, 1976).

7. Ibid., pp. 3, 4.

8. Rudy Rucker, *Infinity and the Mind* (Boston: Birkauser, 1982), p. 208.

9. Hermann Weyl, "The Mathematical Way of Thinking," in *The World of Mathematics*, ed. Newman, p. 1836.

10. Ibid., p. 1845.

11. Morris Kline, *Why Johnny Can't Add* (New York: Vintage Books, 1974), p. 173.

12. Ibid., p. 175.

13. There is much confusion in current educational research concerning so-called "meta" terms. See R. Murray Thomas, "Mapping Meta-Territory," *Educational Researcher* 13 (January 1984): 16-18.

14. Jerome Bruner, *The Process of Education* (Cambridge, Mass.: Harvard University Press, 1960).

15. Joseph Schwab, "The Concept of the Structure of a Discipline," *Educational Record* 43 (July 1962): 197-205.

16. Douglas Hofstadter, *Godel, Escher, Bach: An Eternal Golden Braid* (New York: Basic Books, 1979), p. 23.

17. Martin Gardner, *The Annotated Alice*, Introduction and notes on *Alice's Adventures in Wonderland* and *Through the Looking Glass* by Lewis Carroll (New York: World, 1963), p. 146.

18. See his essays in *The Open Classroom Reader*, ed. Charles E. Silberman (New York: Random House, 1973): "The Triangular Relationship of Teacher, Student, and Materials," pp. 364-73; "How to Plan for Spontaneity," pp. 486-503; "The Importance of Unguided Exploration," pp. 703-11. See also, David Hawkins, "Teaching the Unteachable," in *Learning by Discovery*, ed. Lee S. Shulman and Evan R. Keislar (Chicago: Rand McNally, 1966), pp. 3-12.

19. Lakatos, *Proofs and Refutations*.

20. Eric T. Bell, *Men of Mathematics* (New York: Simon and Schuster, 1937), p. 140.

21. Milton Cross and David Ewen, *Milton Cross's Encyclopedia of the Great Composers and Their Music*, vol. 1 (Garden City, N.Y.: Doubleday, 1953), p. 22.

22. Some mathematics educators did, of course, pay attention to the sort of discovery discussed here. See, for example, Robert B. Davis, "Discovery in the Teaching of Mathematics," in *Learning by Discovery*, ed. Shulman and Keislar, pp. 115-28.

23. See Hofstadter, *Godel, Escher, Bach.*

24. See the account of Loyd's activities in Martin Gardner, *Mathematical Puzzles and Diversions* (New York: Simon and Schuster, 1959).

25. "Jabberwocky" uses the usual rules of syntax together with odd lexical items to generate a marvelous variety of ideas and meanings. See Gardner, *The Annotated Alice*, pp. 191-97.

26. Jeremy Campbell, *Grammatical Man* (New York: Simon and Schuster, 1982), p. 12.

27. Ibid., pp. 127-36.

28. Davis himself points to the genetic quality of this procedure. See "Discovery in the Teaching of Mathematics," pp. 117-19.

29. See Frank K. Lester, Jr. and Joe Garofalo, eds., *Mathematical Problem Solving* (Philadelphia: Franklin Institute Press, 1982). See also, Edward A. Silver, ed., *Teaching and Learning Mathematical Problem Solving: Multiple Research Perspectives* (Philadelphia: Franklin Institute Press, in press).

30. See the summary in Lauren B. Resnick and Wendy W. Ford, *The Psychology of Mathematics for Instruction* (Hillsdale, N.J.: Lawrence Erlbaum Associates, 1981), pp. 196-237.

31. See the discussions of cognitive, rational, and empirical analysis in Resnick and Ford, *The Psychology of Mathematics for Instruction.*

32. See, for example, John S. Brown and Richard R. Burton, "Diagnostic Models for Procedural Bugs in Mathematical Skills," *Cognitive Science* 2 (April-June 1978): 155-92. For types of error analysis in problem solving, see Nel Noddings, "Word Problems Made Painless," *Creative Computing* (September 1980): 108-13.

33. There are some promising efforts in this direction. The reader will note, however, that far more of this material pertains to instruction than to curriculum. See, for example, the chapters by Richard Lesh (real world applications), Nel Noddings (small group processes), and Patrick W. Thompson (constructivist curricula) in Silver, ed., *Teaching and Learning Mathematical Problem Solving*. See also the highly useful review in Mark Driscoll, *Research Within Reach: Secondary School Mathematics* (St. Louis: CEMREL, 1982); and Thomas L. Good, Douglas R. Grouws, and Howard Ebmeier, *Active Mathematics Teaching* (New York: Longman, 1983).

34. Lakatos, *Proofs and Refutations*, p. 152.

CHAPTER VIII

Practical Modes of Knowing

ROBERT J. STERNBERG AND DAVID R. CARUSO

By her fourth year, Professor H. had managed to antagonize practically all her faculty colleagues. Her research was certainly acceptable, and there was nothing terribly wrong with her teaching, but it was clear that no one wished to promote her. The thought of having her as a tenured and hence a permanent colleague dismayed many members of the senior faculty of her department. It was finally decided that her departmental citizenship had been marginal, at best, and the promotion was denied. No one overtly admitted the true reason for the negative decision: Professor H. was heartily disliked by her colleagues.

The department chairman thumbed through the course evaluation ratings of his teaching staff. The pattern of ratings depressed him. As usual, Mr. A. had received highly favorable ratings from the students in his classes. The chairman had attended a number of Mr. A.'s lectures. They were extremely entertaining, but, in the chairman's opinion, devoid of substance. Mrs. N.'s lectures, on the other hand, were rather dry, but very carefully organized and full of both substance and informed comments on this substance. Mrs. N., however, had once again received only mediocre ratings for her teaching. Despite her solidity as a teacher, she simply failed to kindle the enthusiasm of the students, and it showed in her ratings.

Each of these anecdotes illustrates a pervasive but little understood

Note: Support for work reported in this chapter was provided by a Developmental Training Grant from the National Institute of Mental Health to Yale University and by a contract with Robert J. Sternberg from the Office of Naval Research and Army Research Institute.

aspect of our daily lives: practical knowledge. Both in schooling and in research on schooling, there is tremendous interest in and concern for the nature and origins of academic knowledge. Students are repeatedly tested on their academic knowledge; they are graded on it; their admissions to further educational programs depend on it; and ultimately, their salability in the marketplace for jobs will be largely determined by it, at least for many higher-level jobs. Despite the overwhelming emphasis we place on academic knowledge, at some level we all know the inestimable importance of practical knowledge in our daily lives, and even in academic settings. Indeed, almost all of us know instances of people whose professional or personal lives have been drastically affected, for better or for worse, by their practical knowledge. In the anecdotes above, an unfavorable tenure decision and ratings of teaching provide examples of how practical knowledge can influence life courses. These are, of course, only a tiny sampling of the kinds of instances in which practical knowledge can make an important difference to people's lives. In this chapter, we seek to (a) define what practical knowledge is, (b) discuss how practical knowledge is represented mentally, (c) discuss its interrelations with other forms of knowledge and with other psychological constructs, (d) show how practical knowledge is acquired, (e) discuss the ways in which practical knowledge can be applied, and (f) summarize the main points we have to share regarding practical knowledge.

What is Practical Knowledge?

DEFINITION OF PRACTICAL KNOWLEDGE

We define *practical knowledge* as procedural information that is useful in one's everyday life. In proposing this definition, we are clearly imposing two critical restrictions on the domain of knowledge that we are willing to call practical, namely, that the knowledge be procedural rather than declarative and that the knowledge be relevant to one's everyday life.

We require practical knowledge to be procedural because of our view that practical knowledge is knowledge of and for use. We view practical knowledge as stored in the form of productions, or condition-action sequences that implement actions when certain preconditions are met.

Consider some examples of what would and would not constitute practical knowledge under our restriction that practical knowledge be procedural information stored as condition-action sequences.

1. "I know that my wife will become upset and enraged if I drop a dead mouse in her chicken soup." Under our definition, this information would constitute practical knowledge, although for formal congruence with the definition, the statement would best be rephrased as a condition-action sequence: "If I drop a dead mouse in my wife's chicken soup, she will become upset and enraged." The statement describes the procedure that will bring about a certain emotional state in my wife. Moreover, the procedure is one that has potential for real-world application.

2. "My mother is upset with me today." Under our definition, this statement does not constitute practical knowledge. It may be potentially useful to know that my mother is upset with me today, but the actual usefulness of the information would depend upon my being able to react in some way that takes this knowledge into account. Thus, if I know that "my mother is upset with me today, and therefore I had best stay away from her," the condition-action sequence turns the statement into actual rather than potential practical knowledge. Note that practical knowledge, like any other kind of knowledge, can be incorrect. If, for example, staying away from my mother will just make her more upset, and my goal is to relieve her upset, then the practical knowledge I have is simply wrong.

3. "If I submit my article on the nature of love to *Cognitive Psychology*, it will probably be rejected." This statement constitutes practical knowledge and illustrates that practical knowledge can be probabilistic in nature.

Now consider how the restriction of relevance to one's everyday life affects what does or does not constitute practical knowledge.

1. "If Dr. Fitzbottom wins the Nobel Prize, he will be able to take the trip to Tahiti that he has long been waiting for." This example illustrates how what constitutes practical knowledge depends upon the knower and the context in which the knower lives. If the knower is Fitzbottom or someone whose life meshes with his, then this knowledge will, at least potentially, have empirical consequences for that person's life. For that person, the knowledge will be practical. If the person's life has no intersection at all with Fitzbottom's, then the

information will have no everyday relevance and hence will not constitute practical knowledge. Knowledge becomes practical only by virtue of its relation to the knower and the knower's environment.

2. "Because helium is an inert gas, I should not expect a chemical reaction when I mix it with laughing gas." This example illustrates how a piece of "academic" information can become practical knowledge in certain contexts. For most individuals, this information will always remain strictly academic, in that it will have no relevance to their everyday lives. To a chemist doing an experiment on gas mixtures, the information could be quite relevant to his or her work and thus become eminently practical knowledge.

3. "The world will come to an end on April 1, 1987." This knowledge clearly satisfies the criterion of practical relevance, but does not satisfy the criterion that the knowledge be expressible in the form of a condition-action sequence. Unless one knows something to do with this or similar pieces of knowledge, the knowledge does not, by our definition, constitute "practical" knowledge.

REPRESENTATION OF PRACTICAL KNOWLEDGE

Having defined practical knowledge, it is important to say something regarding how practical knowledge is represented mentally. We have noted that practical knowledge is stored in the form of productions, or condition-action sequences. If a certain condition is met, then a certain action is performed. Sequences of productions are called production systems.

How does one decide what practical knowledge, or productions, to use at a given point in a mental or behavioral sequence? Such a decision requires an "executive" decision. The executive for a production system is hypothesized to make its way down an ordered list of productions until one of the conditions is met. The action corresponding to that condition is executed, and control is returned again to the top of the list of productions. The executive then makes its way down the list again, as needed, trying to satisfy a condition. When it does so, an action is executed, control returns to the top, and so forth.[1] Hunt and Poltrock have suggested that the productions in a production system may be probabilistically ordered, so that the exact order in which the list is scanned may differ across scannings of the list.[2]

An example of a simple production system for crossing the street is the following:

traffic-light red—stop;
traffic-light green—move;
move and left-foot-on-pavement—step-with-right-foot;
move and right-foot-on-pavement—step-with-left-foot.[3]

In this production system, one first tests to see whether the light is red. If it is red, one stops, and again tests to see whether the light is red. This sequence will be repeated until the light turns green, at which point one will start moving. If one is moving and one's left foot is on the pavement, one will step with the right foot; or if one is moving and one's right foot is on the pavement, one will step with the left foot. This particular production system is obviously an oversimplification, but gives a sense of how a simple production system operates.

A form of mental representation that is sometimes viewed as competing with the production system is the script, or standard event sequence.[4] Consider a commonly used example of a script, the "restaurant script." Almost all of us have stored in long-term memory a standard sequence of events that transpires when we go out to eat. We decide on a restaurant, go there, walk in, seek a table, wait or ask for menus, decide what we want to eat, order, wait to be served, eat the meal, ask for a check, tip the waiter or waitress, pay the bill, and leave. Clearly, scripts would seem to provide an attractive possibility as a form of mental representation for practical knowledge, in that so many of our action sequences are scripted. Thus, most of us have a restaurant script, a script for a visit to a doctor's office, a script for what we should say in a job interview, a script for how we can go to the office, and so on. In short, the script representation favored by the "Yale" school of cognitive science would seem to be an attractive alternative to the production-system representation favored by the "Carnegie-Mellon" school of cognitive science. We would argue, however, that these two forms of representation are not mutually exclusive, but rather complementary.

Were scripts all there were to mental representations of practical knowledge, we would be in trouble, if not desperate straits, every time there was a small alteration of a scripted sequence. Indeed, a script seems to be too general a form of representation to capture everything that can happen when one engages in a standard sequence of events. For example, although the waiter or waitress usually comes to serve us, we all know that there are certain actions we must take if, after a certain amount of time, the waiter or waitress does not appear. We may go looking for someone to serve us, or alternatively, seek the maître-d'. Similarly, when we see that the menu is in a language we do not understand (French, Chinese, or whatever), we do not usually fall to pieces, but either seek a translation from the waiter or waitress or else attempt a translation ourselves. Clearly, we would not want to posit a separate script for every possible variant on a standard scenario; nor would we want merely to say that the variants represent departures from a given script, because it is doubtful that there is ever a case where a given script goes exactly in some stereotyped or standard sequence. Rather, we have a repertoire of behaviors to handle all the variants on a script that can take place. It seems plausible to believe that the various possible subsequences of events are stored as productions. We have a list of possibilities for action in the case of each variation in the standard sequence. What we are proposing, therefore, is that the script is only a very general form of representation, which must be supplemented by a finer form of representation, and thus level of organization for practical knowledge. This finer-grain form of representation, we believe, is the production system. In effect, many production systems are embedded within the framework of a very general scriptal organization of practical knowledge.

To conclude, then, we believe that practical knowledge is probably stored, for the most part, in the form of rather specific production systems embedded within quite general scripts. Scripts, themselves, would constitute far too inflexible a form of representation for all of our practical knowledge. The production systems embedded within scripts enable the scripts to function for us in an adaptive and practically useful way.

Not all forms of knowledge are stored in this way. Nonprocedural (declarative) forms of knowledge are stored in the form of networks interrelating concepts,[5] and even other procedural forms of knowledge that are not practical may utilize production systems outside the context of scripts. Scripts seem to have their most useful application for knowledge that is of everyday use, rather than knowledge, even if procedural, that is drawn upon only on rare occasions, perhaps for nonpractical kinds of matters. What are these other kinds of knowledge whose representations may differ from that of practical knowledge? This question is considered in the next section.

COMPARISON TO OTHER KINDS OF KNOWLEDGE

The nature of practical knowledge can be further illustrated by comparing it with some other kinds of knowledge. Consider some other kinds of knowledge and how they relate to what we have called practical knowledge.

The most obvious comparison, perhaps, is with *academic knowledge.* Academic knowledge, in our view, can be either procedural or declarative, but if it is procedural, it is procedural knowledge not relevant to one's everyday life. One can thus imagine a 2 x 2 grid, as depicted in figure 1, that crosses procedural and declarative knowledge, on the one hand, with everyday relevant and irrelevant information, on the other. In this framework, all information can be classified as either academic or practical, with academic information taking up three cells of the 2 x 2 grid and practical knowledge taking up the fourth. What differentiates practical from academic knowledge is the necessity for practical knowledge having *both* real-world relevance and procedural (action) consequences. Information that does not satisfy these two constraints is viewed here as academic.

		TYPE OF KNOWLEDGE	
		PROCEDURAL	DECLARATIVE
EVERYDAY RELEVANCE	RELEVANT	PRACTICAL	ACADEMIC
	IRRELEVANT	ACADEMIC	ACADEMIC

Fig. 1. Practical knowledge is knowledge that is both procedural and relevant to a person's everyday life. Knowledge that is declarative or irrelevant to everyday life is academic knowledge.

Other kinds of knowledge can be either academic or practical, depending upon the content of the knowledge and the contexts in which it is used. In other words, other classifications of knowledge are orthogonal to the practical-academic distinction and hence can be "crossed," conceptually, with this distinction.

Consider, for example, *scientific knowledge.* For the most part, scientific knowledge will be academic in that much of it is declarative, and even that scientific knowledge that is not declarative (and hence is procedural) does not tend to be useful in the everyday lives of most people. But one can certainly envision scientific knowledge that is practical in nature. For example, the knowledge that "if my child whines, I should not reinforce his behavior by paying attention to it" is scientific in nature (following from reinforcement theory), but at the same time meets our criteria for practical knowledge. Knowledge is scientific by virtue of its mode of verification, which is independent of the use to which that knowledge will be put.

As a second example, consider *intuitive knowledge.* Intuitive knowledge can be classified as intuitive either by virtue of its mode of acquisition or by virtue of its mode of verification. Thus, I can experience an intuition and then refer to this intuition as intuitive knowledge without benefit of any kind of verification at all. Or someone can tell me something directly, and I can respond intuitively that something sounds correct to me. In this case, my mode of knowledge acquisition was not intuitive, but my mode of verification was. There are thus at least two senses of what constitutes intuitive knowledge. Intuitive knowledge can become scientific if knowledge that is at one time verified solely by intuition is subjected to and confirmed by empirical tests that meet scientific standards. Intuitive knowledge, like scientific knowledge, can be either academic or practical, depending upon its content and context. My intuitive knowledge about how to handle my children when they cry, for example, is practical knowledge, whereas my intuitive knowledge about what constitutes true poetry is not, at least not for me at this time. Intuitive knowledge having a certain content could change from academic to practical if the context changes. For example, should I decide to start writing poetry, my intuitive knowledge concerning the nature of poetry might switch from being academic to being practical.

In this section, we have sought to define how we will use the term *practical knowledge* and have provided some examples of statements that do or do not constitute practical knowledge, according to our definition. We now turn to a discussion of various modes of transmission for practical knowledge.

Transmission and Acquisition of Practical Knowledge

Although any kind of knowledge can be transmitted in a number of ways, it would seem, at least intuitively, that certain kinds of knowledge are more likely to be transmitted in certain ways, and other kinds of knowledge to be transmitted in other ways. For example, whereas a great deal of academic knowledge is transmitted through direct classroom instruction, it would seem that relatively little practical knowledge is transmitted in this way. We will first discuss three processes of knowledge acquisition and then discuss three major modes of transmission and acquisition of practical knowledge: direct learning, mediated learning, and tacit learning.

THREE PROCESSES OF KNOWLEDGE ACQUISITION

According to Sternberg,[6] knowledge acquisition, regardless of the mode of transmission, occurs through three basic processes: selective encoding, selective combination, and selective comparison. *Selective encoding* involves separating, in an array of inputs, information that is relevant for one's purposes in learning from information that is irrelevant for these purposes. *Selective combination* involves putting this information together so as to form an integrated cognitive structure. *Selective comparison* involves properly relating the new information and cognitive structure formed to old information and cognitive structures so as fully to integrate the new knowledge with knowledge already acquired. Consider an example of the application of these processes in the practical domain.

Tom, a teacher, finds that whenever he tells his class stories about his earlier experiences as a marine based in Guam their ears perk up. In particular, students begin to look directly at him, to avoid distractions around the room, and to stop conversations with each other. Soon, he begins to use experiences from his days in Guam as a reward, promising to tell a story if the class gets a certain amount of work done. In this instance, Tom has selectively encoded verbal or nonverbal cues to class interest; has selectively combined these cues to realize that together they indicate interest; and has realized through selective comparison that the stories about Guam have elicited the same reaction in each case. Again, learning has occurred through selective encoding, combination, and comparison.

Remember that this is not necessarily an example of the acquisition of practical knowledge. Simply knowing that the class becomes more attentive when they listen to war stories is not relevant to Tom's everyday life. This type of knowledge is declarative. If, however, Tom stores this newly acquired knowledge in the form of a production such as, "When I want the class to get a lot of work done I will promise them that I will tell them a war story," then Tom has acquired practical knowledge.

Consider now three modes of transmission and acquisition through which selective encoding, combination, and comparison may be instigated.

DIRECT LEARNING

Direct learning occurs when knowledge is acquired directly from its immediate source of transmission. The most common examples of direct learning are the learning that occurs from parental and school instruction. We believe that relatively little practical knowledge is either transmitted or learned in this way and that, moreover, direct instruction tends not to be effective unless it is supplemented by other forms of instruction. There are several reasons for this, at least in our own culture.

First, our culture tends, in many instances, to frown upon this mode of transmission of practical knowledge or to believe that it is more appropriate for slower than for faster learners. In secondary schools, for example, courses such as shop, driver education, sewing, and cooking are usually viewed as vocational. For college-bound students, grades in such courses are often not counted in the academic average, or if they are, they receive less weight than grades in academic courses. Students in academic tracks are often led to believe that grades in such courses are not particularly important to their futures and that low grades will be of little consequence so long as minimally satisfactory performance is rendered. Students who take large numbers of such courses are typically in "vocational tracks" and are often encouraged either to seek employment immediately after high school, without the benefit of college, or else to go to junior or noncompetitive colleges that will prepare them for those jobs that carry with them the least status in our society. When one walks into these classes, the norms of classroom performance often seem to be different from the norms in academically oriented classes. For academically oriented students, such courses often seem to be diversionary and inconsequential. For vocational students, grades often do not make much difference anyway, since the grades will not be needed for entrance into higher education or will be needed only for admittance to programs for which admission is not very competitive.

Second, practical knowledge, because of its procedural nature, often does not lend itself to transmission and learning through direct instruction. Students who have taken computer courses, for example, often comment that they did not really learn how to program until they actually used the programming in their own work. The procedural nature of practical knowledge means, almost a priori, that it is knowledge acquired by doing, not just by listening or reading. Statistics courses seem to provide the same kind of limited experience as computer courses. Research supervisors are often aghast at the statistical ignorance of students who have taken statistics courses. There seems to be an enormous gap between what students can do on course examinations and what they can do when they actually have to use the statistics in their research. As teachers of statistics ourselves, we have noted that students can have a perfect understanding of the theory of statistics without having the foggiest idea of how to implement this knowledge and understanding in their work.

Third, much practical knowledge is either unavailable or inaccessible to conscious introspection and thus is simply unteachable through direct instruction: teachers would not know what to teach! Consider typing as an example of the inaccessibility of important practical knowledge. One of the coauthors of this chapter is a rapid touch typist, typically typing seventy to eighty words per minute. Yet he finds it extremely difficult to tell someone which keys are where and could fill in the contents of an empty typewriter keyboard only with the greatest difficulty.

MEDIATED LEARNING

The concept of mediated learning is an old one, but its importance has perhaps been fully appreciated only recently. Much of this appreciation is due to Feuerstein, who has centered his theory of intellectual development around this concept. Feuerstein defines mediated learning experience as

> the way in which stimuli emitted by the environment are transformed by a "mediating" agent, usually a parent, sibling, or other caregiver. This mediating agent, guided by his intentions, culture, and emotional investment, selects and organizes the world of stimuli for the child. The mediator selects stimuli that are most appropriate and then frames, filters, and schedules them; he determines the appearance or disappearance of certain stimuli and ignores others. Through this process of mediation, the cognitive structure of the child is affected. The child acquires behavior patterns and learning sets, which in turn become important ingredients of his capacity to become modified through direct exposure to stimuli.[7]

According to Feuerstein, mediated learning experience is universal and crucial in the child's cognitive development. Consider first some examples of mediated learning experience in the development of the child and then why such experience is so important.

By the age of three, and often before, children become prolific askers of questions. They ask for meanings of words, interpretations of events, descriptions of unfamiliar objects, discussions of what is right and wrong in behavior, and so on. Voluminous bodies of research now indicate that the ways in which parents respond to such requests have a substantial impact upon the child's learning and formation of attitudes about learning.[8] The powerful influence of socioeconomic status on IQ is probably attributable in large part, although certainly not exclusively, to differences in the ways parents respond to requests for information from their children. Middle-class parents tend to give elaborate descriptions that describe reasons for certain events and behaviors; lower-class parents tend to give imperatives, often without providing as well the reasons for these imperatives.[9] There is a reciprocality in these two patterns of parent-child interaction with respect to questioning of children as well. In middle-class environments, parents frequently ask children questions and expect the children to develop the capacity for explanation. In lower-class environments, such questioning is much more rare. Describing one lower-class environment, "Trackton," Heath notes:

> Children do not expect adults to ask them questions, for, in Trackton, children are not seen as information-givers or question-answerers. This is especially

true of questions for which adults already have an answer. Since adults do not consider children appropriate conversational partners to the exclusion of other people who are around, they do not construct questions especially for children, nor do they use questions to give the young an opportunity to show off their knowledge about the world.[10]

This pattern of interaction is in marked contrast to that of a lower middle-class environment, such as the community of "Roadville," where young mothers begin to use questions and interpretive statements within the first month of a newborn's life. In this environment, questions are frequently asked where the questioner knows the answer, but the goal is to develop understanding and communication skills in the child.

The implications of the difference in patterns of mediated learning experience between members of different socioeconomic classes and subcultures can scarcely be overstated. Such experience not only imparts specific academic and practical knowledge, but also creates a pattern for future learning of such knowledge.

McDermott has suggested that school failure in members of minority subcultures is most appropriately viewed as an "achieved" status.[11] In other words, failure is not so much failing to do the right things as actively doing the wrong things, at least from the standpoint of the school. Whereas typical middle-class children learn how to understand, interpret, and follow the mediation supplied by the typical middle-class teacher, lower-class children may never learn these practical comprehension skills. It is not from any lack of innate intelligence. They are quite able to understand the limited and probably highly directive mediation supplied by their parents and to understand the informal mediation supplied by peers. But they never quite tune in to the right code for optimally understanding the teacher.

Thus, mediated learning experience supplies practical knowledge of two kinds and levels of organization. The first kind is the direct knowledge supplied by a particular instance of mediation. The second kind is the more general knowledge about how learning from certain kinds of mediation takes place. For the middle-class child, the learning he or she receives from parents will, in general, smoothly transfer to the school setting. For the lower-class child, there will be, if anything, negative transfer because of the mismatch between parental and school teaching styles. Laosa has attributed the pattern of failure and dropping out in Mexican Americans to precisely this mismatch.[12] Mexican-American children come into typical schools ill-prepared for the kinds of teaching and discipline that characterize the typical classroom in the United States.

In sum, we concur with Feuerstein in his strong emphasis upon the importance of mediated learning experience in cognitive development. We would extend its importance, however, to the acquisition of practical knowledge, as well as the acquisition of modes of acquiring practical knowledge. As both McDermott and Heath point out, the child of the lower classes has no lack of practical knowledge.[13] Rather, his problem is the incongruence between his knowledge and modes of acquiring that knowledge, on the one hand, and the knowledge and modes of acquisition that are expected in our society, on the other.

TACIT LEARNING

So far, we have discussed two modalities by which practical knowledge may be transmitted: direct instruction and mediated instruction. We have argued that whereas direct instruction is not very important for the transmission of practical knowledge, mediated instruction is quite important. We believe that there is a third modality for the transmission of practical knowledge that is also of great importance in the development of the child, as well as of the adult. This modality is that of tacit instruction, and its product, tacit knowledge.

Although tacit knowledge can be defined in multiple ways and may even be quite a different construct depending upon how it is defined,[14] a useful definition of tacit knowledge for our purposes is "knowledge that usually is not openly expressed or stated."[15] "Such knowledge is typically not directly taught or spoken about, in contrast to knowledge directly taught in classrooms."[16] Thus, whereas direct knowledge is acquired through direct instruction, and mediated knowledge is acquired through indirect instruction on the part of another, tacit knowledge is acquired through indirect instruction on the part of the self. It is knowledge that, metaphorically, is acquired through osmosis.

Whereas mediated learning is probably more important to the knowledge acquisition of the child than it is to the knowledge acquisition of the adult, tacit learning is probably more important to the knowledge acquisition of the adult than of the child. Indeed, we would argue that most of the practical knowledge adults acquire is tacit. Consider, for example, learning on the job. When one commences a new job, there may be a brief period of direct instruction, perhaps from a supervisor or perhaps from the individual who is being replaced in that job. Periods of direct instruction are likely to end quickly, however, with the result that one is thrown upon one's own resources. At this point, one learns on the job in a catch-as-catch-can fashion. There is usually no further formal procedure at all for learning about the job, despite the fact that almost all the learning has yet to take place. Indeed, in interviews with people in two occupations—business and academia—what we call tacit knowledge was singled out as the most important kind of knowledge for success.[17] Knowledge acquired directly in undergraduate and graduate training was seen as being of much more marginal relevance for successful on-the-job performance.[18]

Consider, for example, the situation faced by a typical first-year high school teacher in an inner-city school. No matter how good his or her training has been, probably nothing has fully prepared the teacher for some of the real basics of succeeding on the job: maintaining an atmosphere of learning while at the same time maintaining adequate discipline of the students; filling in countless reporting forms that often seem to have no clear purpose or utility; getting along with the principal and other teachers; succeeding in lunchroom duty when the students sometimes seem to have it in mind that their idea of a lunchroom is very different from one's own; finding time to prepare lessons when one comes home, after teaching seven periods and perhaps leading an extracurricular activity, utterly robbed of any strength or initiative; and so on.

The academic information one has learned about one's field of endeavor will be useless for dealing with these practical problems, and typically, even so-called "teacher preparation courses" will be far removed from the practicalities of the everyday classroom situation. At the same time, it should be recognized that the teaching profession has been very sensitive to the problem of teachers' acquisition of tacit knowledge. This recognition is shown in the programs of practice teaching and internship that are usually required for teaching certification and in the inclusion of practical courses in typical teaching curricula. Much of the current debate over the use of scores from the

National Teacher Examination focuses on whether the academic knowledge measured by this test is sufficiently relevant to practical concerns to make use of the scores valid for evaluating teaching performance. Internships are required, of course, in other fields as well (medicine, clinical psychology), and some schools are even integrating internships into their regular academic programs in a variety of subjects. Northeastern University, for example, has students in a variety of fields working in real-world settings as a regular part of their program of instruction.

One's ability to acquire tacit knowledge on the job will be a key factor in one's success or failure as a teacher. We suspect that failure to acquire sufficient tacit knowledge will result in rapid frustration and possibly early burnout.

Many kinds of learning that do not lend themselves to direct instruction do lend themselves to tacit forms of instruction. We noted earlier for instance, the great difficulty of learning the art of computer programming from courses specifically designed to teach such programming. Learning to program is largely a matter of acquiring tacit knowledge. One learns from actually doing the programming one needs and particularly from the mistakes one makes while attempting to write programs. An example of the importance of tacit learning in such endeavors is occurring at the very instant this chapter is being written, as one of the coauthors attempts for the first time to write a paper using a never-before-used word-processing program on a never-before-used microcomputer. Despite the coauthor's having read the manual for the word-processing program twice, and despite the receipt of a tutorial from his secretary, who is skilled in the use of the program, the actual writing of the paper seems to proceed from one mishap to another (which, we hope, will be reflected only in the process, and not in the product, of the writing!). To the extent that learning of the word-processing program is taking or has taken place, it has been almost exclusively from use of the program, rather than through either direct instruction from the manual or even the mediation that a busy secretary is able to provide.

Why is it that practical knowledge lends itself better to tacit or possibly mediated learning than to direct learning? Why, for example, do computer manuals and courses not work well in the absence of direct experience with computers? We believe that there are at least three reasons.

First, knowledge that is taught through direct instruction is likely to be represented in declarative form, through semantic or other networks, and is thus not likely to be accessible for practical use. In essence, the "academic" representation of the knowledge is poorly fit to practical purposes. As a result, the knowledge must often be re-represented in the form of production systems embedded in scripts, and such re-representation is likely to be more clumsy than initial learning that is represented in this form.

Second, practical knowledge is closely linked to the context of its use, and direct instruction does not serve well to link knowledge to context. Tulving and Thomson have proposed an encoding specificity principle whereby knowledge will be retrieved only if the retrieval cues available at the time of access match the cues that were encoded with an item of knowledge.[19] The circumstances of learning and of use may be so different in direct instruction of practical knowledge that the information is inaccessible because of the mismatch between cues learned at the time of storage with respect to those needed at the time of retrieval.

Third, learner motivation may flag when practical knowledge is taught through direct instruction. Knowledge that "comes alive" in the actual setting of its use may seem quite dull in classroom or other academic settings and may seem so abstracted from the context of its use that it loses its appeal to those who will eventually have to use it.

These caveats regarding the use of direct instruction for practical knowledge may have several implications for situations in which, for one reason or another, direct instruction must be used for transmitting practical knowledge. Consider three such implications. First, the instruction should be as concrete as possible and should emphasize use of the knowledge. Second, the instruction should emphasize condition-action relations and integrate them with each other and with other kinds of relations, such as those in semantic networks. In this way, the student will have a chance to form links between items of procedural knowledge and to link such knowledge to declarative knowledge. Finally, the instruction should take into account how knowledge is organized in the mind of the learner, not just in the mind of the teacher.

The instructor may have formed all of the necessary links and thus fail to recognize that the cognitive structure of the learner will not permit the level of abstraction and decontextualization that is possible for an expert, but not a novice, to comprehend.

Although we have emphasized the importance of tacit knowledge in adult activities, it is clearly important in the activities of children and adolescents as well. We previously noted the importance of mediated learning experience in adapting to a classroom. But classrooms differ from home life, and they differ from each other as well. Each teacher has his or her own set of expectations and ways of doing things. Many of the procedures the teacher sets up—whether for overt classroom activities or for covert patterns of verbal and nonverbal instruction in the classroom—are never explicitly communicated. In essence, the child is left to his or her own devices to figure out the regimen the teacher has in mind. Very often, the teacher himself or herself is only vaguely aware or even unaware of what the full regimen is. A child who is able to get the sense of the classroom quickly and accurately will be at an enormous advantage in meeting the expectations of the teacher. As noted by McDermott,[20] as well as by others, early bad impressions can be quite difficult to correct, and early favorable impressions often serve one long after they cease to be justified.

To summarize, tacit knowledge is an essential form of knowledge for success, both among children and among adults. It differs from direct knowledge and mediated knowledge primarily in the locus of the instructor, which is the individual doing the learning rather than an other who serves, directly or indirectly, as teacher. Much of one's successful performance in everyday functioning can be traced to the acquisition and effective activation of tacit knowledge.

Applications of Practical Knowledge

In the course of discussing three ways by which practical knowledge is acquired, we discussed as well some of the ways in which practical knowledge is used. In this section of the chapter, we shall formalize some of our earlier discussion, in particular, by providing a framework for understanding three ways in which practical knowledge is applied in people's lives. This framework proposes that practical knowledge is used in three main forms of interaction with the everyday world—adaptation, shaping, and selection—and that practical knowledge is applied in its use to three main objects—the self, others, and tasks.

ADAPTATION

By adaptation, we refer to the process of accommodating oneself to the demands of the environment, however these demands may be imposed. One is thus adjusting oneself to the press of situations as they arise, attempting to gain as good a fit as possible between the self and these situations. Note that we use the term *adaptation* in the narrow sense of accommodating oneself to the environment, rather than in the broad sense of any action that "fits" in the environment.

Demands for adaptation may be generated by oneself, by others, or by tasks. Consider, for example, the situation faced by a person who has just entered college, a bewildering situation indeed for the typical freshman. Many kinds of adaptation will have to take place. For one thing, one will set certain demands of oneself: one may have decided to try to maintain a certain grade-point average, to participate in certain extracurricular activities, to establish a few close friendships as quickly as possible, or whatever. In each of these instances, the press for adaptation is self-generated. One uses one's practical knowledge in order to meet these various kinds of self-generated demands. Adaptive demands will also be generated by others, for example, to conform to social or academic demands. And finally, adaptive demands will be generated by the tasks one confronts—writing papers, taking exams, starting one's own checking account (probably for the first time), and so on. In each case, one draws upon practical knowledge in order to meet the demands of the environment, many of which will be new to one's life.

In new situations, such as one's first days at college, there will be intense demands not only upon existing scripts for action, but also upon one's cognitive resources for creating new scripts. For example, most first-year students will have no script for setting up a checking account, or even for living with a freshman roommate. Script creation will proceed through self-modifying production systems.[21] One will take whatever productions one might have from old scripts, and use productions whose function it is to create other productions to invent new productions, and to recombine existing ones into new production systems. One's ability to create new scripts through the formation of new productions and production systems is, in large part, the essence of one's "adaptive intelligence."

The above logic suggests that whereas practical knowledge can be quite situation-specific, the ability to acquire and apply practical knowledge is probably more general than is the knowledge itself. Recent research has tended to emphasize the situation- and domain-specificity of practical knowledge. Thus, expertise in chess is attributed to level and organization of chess knowledge;[22] and expertise in solving physics problems is attributed to level and organization of physics knowledge.[23] But for all the specificity of such knowledge, the representations and mental mechanisms proposed in this chapter would seem applicable in a variety of domains and hence more general than the knowledge they create. If one looks only at developed expertise in various domains of everyday life, domain-specific knowledge will indeed appear to be extremely important. But if one looks as well at how one must acquire such knowledge, some fairly general skills of production creation and modification would seem to come into play.

SHAPING

In some instances, adaptation proves to be inadequate to the demands of oneself, others, or the tasks one confronts. For example, one may be dissatisfied with one's roommate or may find one's course burden excessive. In such cases, adaptation may eventually prove to be counterproductive. One would scarcely want to mold oneself to suit every disagreeable roommate who came along. In certain instances, one may try to shape the environment so as to make it more suitable to one's needs or wants. Thus, for example, one may be able to shape one's roommate's behavior. In the case of an excessive course load, one may do better to reduce the course load than to attempt to meet demands that have simply become excessive.

It is interesting to consider those people who are unusually successful in their field of endeavor, whatever it may be. Such people seem to be precisely those who are unusually able to shape their environments so that the environment accommodates to them, rather than their adapting to the environment. The talents involved in such shaping may be extremely variable. One successful business executive may exert his influence through a magnetic personality; another may achieve success through extraordinarily shrewd investment decisions; yet another may have a knack for knowing how to maximize his company's productivity. In each case, the executive shapes the environment, rather than merely allowing himself to be shaped by it. It is important to note that in these and in other similar cases, merely looking at classical patterns of abilities (verbal, spatial, numerical, and so on) or looking only at extent of knowledge acquired (about productivity gains, investments, or whatever) would fail to capture the bases for the extraordinary successes of these executives. They direct their practical knowledge toward shaping situations, rather than toward letting those situations shape them. In effect, they have higher-order practical (and procedural) knowledge that enables them most effectively to employ the lower-order practical knowledge that others may have but do not as successfully exploit.

Shaping, like adaptation, can be instigated by demands that emanate from the self, others, or tasks. Thus, one might decide to change oneself in any of various ways that will make one more effective—through exercise, speed-reading courses, or whatever. In many such cases, the demand to become more effective will be self-initiated, often because of one's dissatisfaction with the way one's life is progressing. Alternatively, demands for change may come from others, or from the tasks one faces. In each case, such demands may evoke a response that shapes oneself, others, or tasks in a way that may be more effective than mere adaptation to existing circumstances. Of course, shaping is not always more effective than adaptation and sometimes can be disastrous. Some of the worst foreign-policy decisions in the history of the United States, for example, have emanated from ill-conceived and ill-fated attempts to shape the history of other nations as well as our own. To this day, some of this country's attempts at shaping the world constitute what some, at least, might perceive as the blackest marks in the country's history.

To summarize, environmental shaping constitutes a second avenue of utilization for practical knowledge. Shaping is most often employed when adaptation fails. However, it may be initiated in its own right without prior attempts at adaptation. In almost any endeavor, adaptation and shaping will best function in a kind of equilibrational balance, much as assimilation and accommodation function in such a balance in Piaget's theory of cognitive processing.[24] The new principal who enters a school and decides at once to change all existing procedures is likely to be unsuccessful and at the same time to arouse the enmity of those in the system. But the principal who merely adjusts to extant circumstances without trying to implement any changes at all is likely to be viewed as passive and uncreative. Achieving the right balance between adaptation and shaping can be one of the most important assets of an individual's practical intelligence.

SELECTION

Both adaptation and shaping presuppose the attempt to work things through within an existing environmental framework. Thus, the student may choose to adapt to his or her roommate or, alternatively, to shape the roommate's behavior, but in each case, one stays with the roommate. Similarly, the student who feels overwhelmed by his or her academic load may try either to adjust to his load or to reduce it, but these two solutions presuppose staying in the college environment that produced the load in the first place. In most instances, adaptation or shaping will be suitable for dealing with a practical problem. However, there exist instances in which a third process of interaction with the environment, selection, is used in preference to adaptation or shaping. The mental effort in selecting a new environment is not necessarily greater than that in adapting or shaping. In many instances, the amount of effort will be less. We mention selection last because, in practice, it is usually used as a last resort after adaptation and shaping have failed.

Consider, for example, the situation in which one has discovered that one is grossly overplaced in the college one has chosen to attend, and cannot seem to meet even the minimal standards that the college imposes. In such cases, the appropriate course of action may be selection of a wholly different environment. Such a solution is often a last resort, but a necessary one. As a professor, one of the coauthors has encountered any number of graduate students who were apparently misguided, whether by themselves or others, in their choice of psychology for a graduate career. Although they do not perform well in psychology, they usually show signs of having great potential that is simply being wasted in their chosen field. Often, their best course of action would be to find some other field in which they could live up to their unexploited potential.

The decision to select another environment, like the decisions to adapt or shape an existing environment, can emanate from oneself, others, or tasks. One may decide one "has had it"; someone else may tell one that "one has had it," as when a student fails in school; or one may find oneself unable to perform successfully the tasks the environment presents. In any of these cases, environmental reselection may be the suitable course of action to take.

In sum, there are situations in which there is no course of action within an existing environment that will render an optimal or, possibly, even satisfactory fit between oneself and the environment. In such instances, one may decide to opt out of that environment and select another one instead. Such a decision may, in these cases, be the best use to which one's practical knowledge can be placed.

In our discussion of the applications of practical knowledge we have avoided a hierarchical ordering of adaptation, selection, and shaping. We feel that the "better" solution or response to a given problem is a function of the individual's resources and goals, as well as the nature of the situation. The more practical knowledge a person has, either in terms of the number of relevant productions or in terms of script acquisition and modification abilities, the more flexibility and ability there are to meet the demands of the environment and to achieve desired goals.

Conclusions

In this chapter, we have defined and elaborated the concept of practical knowledge. First, we considered just what practical knowledge is and how it relates to other kinds of knowledge, such as academic knowledge. Next, we considered how practical knowledge is mentally represented. Then, we discussed three means by which practical knowledge is acquired: direct learning, mediated learning, and tacit learning. Finally, we considered three ways in which practical knowledge can be applied, through adaptation, shaping, and selection. Despite its signal importance in our everyday lives, perhaps no form of knowledge has been less highly regarded, and more noticeably disregarded, than practical knowledge. It is of low status in most schools and, for the most part, is only indirectly transmitted outside the schools. There are at least three reasons, we believe, why practical knowledge has received so little attention and esteem. First, schools are perceived first and foremost as academic institutions, and if there is any kind of knowledge that is viewed by society as distinctive from practical knowledge, it is academic knowledge. Hence, the philosophy behind much schooling almost precludes serious consideration and transmission of practical knowledge, especially to the most able students, for whom the schools are seen as a training ground for future leadership roles in society. Second, there is a feeling on the part of many, at least today, that practical knowledge does not train one to think or prepare one for the leadership roles that are so important to society, at least in the early stages of career preparation. Thus, future leaders are often encouraged—rightly, we believe—to pursue broad liberal-arts training in college, and to eschew until graduate or professional school the kinds of practical know-how that will be needed in specific occupations. In the teaching profession, for example, graduates of nuts-and-bolts teachers colleges are today often viewed as less desirable candidates for teaching positions than are graduates of liberal-arts colleges. Third, practical knowledge is procedural and often tacit. It is thus harder to teach and even to identify than are many other kinds of knowledge. For the most part, we are not even aware of the practical knowledge we have.

Perhaps because of our own identification and introjection of contemporary norms, we believe that the stress today laid upon academic knowledge is essentially correct. At the same time, we believe that at least certain kinds of practical knowledge have received insufficient attention, both in schools and outside them. For example, although we, too, would stress academic preparation for teachers, especially in a time of decreasing academic skills among teachers, we believe that transmission of practical knowledge should not be underplayed. To the extent that a teacher experiences early burnout, feelings of incompetence in the classroom, inability to cope with the demands of the teaching profession, and so on, we suspect that these feelings will emanate more from lack of practical preparation than from lack of academic preparation. Similarly, a strong liberal-arts training needs to be supplemented by practical training to achieve adequate preparation for business or the professions. In his first year as a college professor, one of the coauthors remembers frequently bemoaning his lack of preparation in skills and knowledge relevant to activities such as writing grant proposals, preparing for multiple new courses, and reviewing journal articles. Practical knowledge, then, should not be a negligible portion of school achievement, even for bright students for whom its acquisition seems at times to be, if anything, discouraged.

Practical knowledge is also increasingly being recognized as an important aspect of intelligence. With a few exceptions,[25] traditional factorial theories of intelligence have emphasized academic rather than practical knowledge and skills, as have traditional tests (although individually administered tests, such as the Wechsler and the Stanford-Binet, have provided more representation of practical knowledge in their test items than have group-administered tests). More recent information-processing theories of intelligence have, if anything, given even less stress to the practical in information processing.[26] But in the last few years, increasing re-recognition of the importance of real-world adaptation to intelligence, stressed by early writers such as Binet and Simon[27] and Wechsler,[28] has led theorists to place more emphasis on the role of the practical in intelligence.[29] We thus view theories of intelligence as returning to their roots and again stressing the importance of a balance between the academic and the practical in intelligence, rather than excluding one and focusing only upon the other.

In sum, then, we believe that the concept of practical knowledge is an important one, both for educational and psychological theory and practice, and we hope that this chapter, and other writings like it, help in the reemergence of a balance between the academic and the practical.

Footnotes

1. Allen Newell and Herbert A. Simon, *Human Problem Solving* (Englewood Cliffs, N.J.: Prentice Hall, 1972).

2. Earl B. Hunt and S. E. Poltrock, "The Mechanics of Thought," in *Human Information Processing: Tutorials in Performance and Cognition*, ed. Barry H. Kantowitz (Hillsdale, N.J.: Lawrence Erlbaum Associates, 1974).

3. Newell and Simon, *Human Problem Solving.*

4. Roger C. Schank and Robert P. Abelson, *Scripts, Plans, Goals and Understanding: An Inquiry into Human Knowledge Structures* (Hillsdale, N.J.: Lawrence Erlbaum Associates, 1977).

5. John R. Anderson, *Language, Memory, and Thought* (Hillsdale, N.J.: Lawrence Erlbaum Associates, 1976).

6. Robert J. Sternberg, *Beyond IQ: A Triarchic Theory of Human Intelligence* (New York: Cambridge University Press, 1984).

7. Reuven Feuerstein, *Instrumental Enrichment: An Intervention Program for Cognitive Modifiability* (Baltimore, Md.: University Park Press, 1980), pp. 16-17.

8. See, for example, Eleanor E. Maccoby and John A. Martin, "Socialization in the Context of the Family: Parent-Child Interaction," in *Handbook of Child Psychology*, ed. Paul H. Mussen, 4th ed. (New York: Wiley, 1983), vol. 4, pp. 1-101.

9. Shirley B. Heath, *Ways with Words: Language, Life, and Work in Communities and Classrooms* (Cambridge, Mass.: Cambridge University Press, 1983).

10. Ibid., p. 103.

11. R. P. McDermott, "Achieving School Failure: An Anthropological Approach to Illiteracy and Social Stratification," in *Education and Cultural Process*, ed. George Spindler (New York: Holt, Rinehart and Winston, 1974).

12. Luis Laosa, "School, Occupation, Culture, and Family: The Impact of Parental Schooling on the Parent-Child Relationship," *Journal of Educational Psychology* 74 (December 1982): 791-827.

13. McDermott, "Achieving School Failure"; Heath, *Ways with Words.*

14. See, for example, Michael Polanyi, "Tacit Knowing," in *Theories in Contemporary Psychology*, ed. Melvin Marx and Felix Goodson (New York: Macmillan, 1976).

15. *Oxford English Dictionary* (Oxford: Clarendon Press, 1933).

16. R. K. Wagner and Robert J. Sternberg, "Practical Intelligence in Real-World Pursuits: The Role of Tacit Knowledge," *Journal of Personality and Social Psychology*, in press.

17. Ibid.

18. See also, Sylvia Scribner, "Mind in Action: A Functional Approach to Thinking" (Paper presented at the meeting of the Society for Research in Child Development, Detroit, Mich., 1983).

19. Endel Tulving and Donald M. Thomson, "Encoding Specificity and Retrieval Processes in Episodic Memory," *Psychological Review* 80 (September 1973): 352-73.

20. McDermott, "Achieving School Failure."

21. David Klahr, "Transition Processes in Quantitative Development," in *Mechanisms of Cognitive Development*, ed. Robert J. Sternberg (New York: Freeman, 1984).

22. William G. Chase and Herbert A. Simon, "Perception in Chess," *Cognitive Psychology* 4 (January 1973): 55-81.

23. Michelene T.H. Chi, Robert Glaser, and Ernest Rees, "Expertise in Problem Solving," in *Advances in the Psychology of Human Intelligence*, vol. 1, ed. Robert J. Sternberg (Hillsdale, N.J.: Lawrence Erlbaum Associates, 1982).

24. Jean Piaget, "Intellectual Evolution from Adolescence to Adulthood," *Human Development*, 15, no. 1 (1972): pp. 1-12.

25. For example, Joy P. Guilford, *The Nature of Human Intelligence* (New York: McGraw-Hill, 1967).

26. See, for example, John B. Carroll, "Ability and Task Difficulty in Cognitive Psychology," *Educational Researcher* 10 (January 1981): 11-21; Earl B. Hunt, "Intelligence as an Information-Processing Concept," *British Journal of Psychology* 71 (November 1980): 449-74; Robert J. Sternberg, "Sketch of a Componential Subtheory of Human Intelligence," *Behavioral and Brain Sciences* 3 (December 1980): 573-84.

27. Alfred Binet and Theophile Simon, *The Development of Intelligence in Children* (New York: Arno Press, 1973).

28. David Wechsler, *The Measurement and Appraisal of Adult Intelligence*, 4th ed. (Baltimore, Md.: Williams and Wilkins, 1958).

29. J. Baron, *Rationality and Intelligence* (New York: Cambridge University Press, forthcoming); Howard Gardner, *Frames of Mind: The Theory of Multiple Intelligences* (New York: Basic Books, 1983); Sternberg, *Beyond IQ.*

CHAPTER IX

Spirituality and Knowing

DWAYNE E. HUEBNER

A chapter entitled "Spirituality and Knowing" in a National Society for the Study of Education Yearbook suggests a new direction in the continuing dialogue between traditions of education and traditions of religion in the United States. For several decades educators in the United States have made efforts to distance their work from its origins in Christian, primarily Protestant, traditions. For instance, the McGuffey and New England readers were replaced by reading textbooks informed by the newly developing psychology of learning. Thus began the merger of the traditions of education and those of the scientific and technical enterprises, culminating in the symbiotic relationship of the testing industry and the traditions of schooling.

The merger of the scientific and educational traditions did not dampen questions of values and ends. It merely altered the rhetoric. In the early decades of this century, these questions were questions of what is best for the person. The emerging developmental literature within psychology became the idiom for framing the questions. In the 1930s and 1940s, questions of value were questions of the good society and were often framed in the language of sociology and anthropology. After the Second World War the value question turned to problems of prejudice and intergroup relations, using social-psychological language. But the language of value increasingly was dominated by formal and technical concerns, particularly for the teaching educator. Questions of value became questions of objectives, and behavioral language became the most desirable idiom. The historical questions about the meaning and significance of life gave way to technical questions of control and behavior. The distancing of education from the religious traditions was complete. In spite of the fact that questions of life's meaning and significance loom large within the religious traditions, the dependency of education upon those traditions appeared to yield to dependency upon the traditions of science, often narrowly defined as scientistic by the educator. However, questions of value could not be suppressed.

During the past two decades questions of value have resurfaced, frequently cloaked in scientific and developmental language. The cognitive emphasis of the post-Sputnik era influenced this in two ways. By emphasizing individual intellectual achievement, the social and historical fabric of human life became an easily forgotten and often neglected background. A corrective for blatant individualism was a renewal of interest in personal responsibility for maintaining social standards and hence a concern for values and ethics. Attention to a disembodied mind led quickly to an awareness of a feeling body and an interest in moral and spiritual values to discipline the body and its passions. The social fabric could be held together by the threads of personal morality and spirituality. Kohlberg assumed a pivotal place in the rhetoric of moral values. Using the currency of developmental theory, he neatly used the educator's attachment to scientific traditions to raise age-old concerns for the moral dimensions of education. Simon's concern for value clarification used the educator's commitment to the technology of method to do the same for the teaching educator.

These concerns for moral and spiritual values managed to maintain the separation of the religious and educational traditions. They did so by subsuming value questions under the scientific inquiry that undergirded education, and by identifying them as necessary components of a democratic culture. The links of education with science and with the political-economic-social structures obviously are extremely necessary and vital. But the long-standing dialogue between the traditions of education and religion is not thereby overcome or replaced. The dialogue is merely displaced to new and different questions and concerns. On the one hand, there has been increased interest in parochial schooling since the civil rights debates and struggles, particularly within Protestant traditions. On the other hand, individuals who recognized the importance of the separation of religious and educational traditions also recognized how diverse religious traditions informed cultures, societies, and persons; hence education. Examples of this are the increased interest in Eastern religions in the West since World War II and the renewed interest in American Indian religions since the new ecological awakening. As a result, comparative religions and the objective study of religion have found places in some school curricula. These interests in diverse religions help make and maintain a distinction between religion as a significant historical phenomenon influencing every culture and religion as personal meaning with the very real problem of internalization and ownership of the tradition. At issue, of course, is the possibility of objectivity, particularly of teachers and materials, in dealing with religious traditions and the obverse possibility of indoctrination or conversion.

As of this writing, the relationship between schooling and specific religious traditions is being publicly debated as Congress considers the place of silent and spoken prayer in schools. The hard-earned separation of religious practices from public schools, the gradual shifting of attention to appropriate and more difficult issues (for example, values), the place of the home and religious community in the education of persons, and the significance of religious traditions in the history of particular cultures are being eroded by a simplistic political solution to a profound historical problem.

By phrasing the relationship between religion and education in new and different ways, the editors of this yearbook contribute to the more difficult dialogue. Suggesting relationships between knowing and spirituality does not raise new questions historically, but brings into the educational community possibilities for new dialogue with those within religious traditions. Concern for the spiritual provides other perspectives for considering issues of values, the comparative objective study of religion, and even the place of prayer and meditation in education.

How Shall the Words "Spirit" and "Spiritual" Be Used?

Are the words "spirit" and "spiritual" restricted to the domains of religious language? Does their use in education imply an intrusion of religious traditions into the educational enterprise? Certainly the words have had a dominant place in religious discourse, and their usage has been primarily within religious contexts. This is less so of the word "spirit" than of "spiritual." "Spirit" is not owned by religious traditions, nor is its use limited to religious contexts. A person or team may be described as having "spirit," suggesting drive, optimism, hope, enthusiasm, acceptance of one's condition. Animals, also, are often described as "spirited." A person who lives with and overcomes handicaps with courage and acceptance is spoken of as a person who has "spirit." Political and social movements are sometimes spoken of as being a manifestation of the "spirit" of the times or age. One can be considered to be "out of spirits," depressed for various reasons, internally or externally. A creative person is often spoken of as being "inspired." The word sometimes refers to intentions, such as the "spirit" rather than the "letter" of the law. The word also refers to alcohol, and its consumption often results in "high spirits" as well as the "low spirits" of the afterglow. The word is also associated with the strange and the ethereal—fairies, sprites, and other beings of strange and different worlds, whether romantic or demonic. This usage leads easily into the occult and the dimensions of spiritism and spiritualism, to disembodied "souls," evil "spirits," and the ability to be in contact with "forces" and "spirits" outside the human world known by most persons.

However, the words "spirit" and "spiritualism" are associated primarily with diverse religious traditions. The religions of East and West—of Buddhism, Hinduism, Islam, Judaism, Christianity, of the American Indians and the peoples of Africa—all acknowledge the spiritual as an integral aspect of human life. For all of these religious traditions, human beings participate in a spiritual dimension of existence, something more than the material, the sensory, and the quantitative. To speak of the "spirit" and the "spiritual" is not to speak of something "other" than humankind, merely "more" than humankind as it is lived and known.

One who uses these words, then, need not fall unintentionally into a religious domain, and hence into the metaphysics and ontologies that are part and parcel of great religious traditions. However, the use of these words does require careful attention, lest the conversation bring forth connotations of superstition or uncritical and unwarranted religious positions. The untangling of these diverse uses would be a major study in itself, clearly a needed work. Required would be a major study of the contexts and uses of the words over the centuries and among different cultures. Such a study would map the uses of these words in various contexts and determine their boundness to and freedom from various traditions. Such studies are not readily available, nor is that the function of this chapter.

Available today, however, are movements that question today's prevalent culture and point to other dimensions of reality not usually associated with the empirical and materialistic structures of the West. The interests of the 1950s and 1960s in higher, or deeper, consciousness, such as Zen Buddhism or transcendental meditation, point to popular concerns, perhaps even needs, to acknowledge the suprasensory. A variety of scholarly and popular works supported those concerns or needs. For instance, Suzuki compared the meditative and mystical traditions of East and West.[1] In *Beyond the Post-Modern Mind*, Huston Smith called attention to the increasing body of scientific and philosophic literature that questions today's prevailing mind-set.[2] He critiqued the dependency upon the quantitative that hides qualitative dimensions, and acknowledged a sacred consciousness or spirit, a less difficult task after the unmasking of modern consciousness by Marx, Freud, and Jung.

Are there ways of talking about spirit and spiritual that do not reflect particular religious traditions—ways that point to or suggest how these aspects of human life have been experienced and acknowledged by others within and without religious traditions? One beginning is the dictionary. The Oxford English dictionary indicates that "spirit" is derived from the Latin word for breath and breathing. "Spirit" refers to "the animating or vital principle in Man (and animals); that which gives life to the physical organism, in contrast to the purely material elements." Spirit refers to that which gives vitality, that which gives life, not merely to the forms of life. It indicates that life is more, or can be more, than the forms in which it is currently lived. The expression "that a person has spirit" suggests that one has gone beyond the forms and norms of everyday life that might pull one down. To be "inspired" by someone else is to be encouraged to go beyond the usual. To "have spirit" is to be in touch with forces or aspects of life that make possible something new and give hope and expectations. Spirit refers to the possible and the unimagined—to the possibility of new ways, new knowledge, new relationships, new awareness. Spirit refers to that which makes it possible to acknowledge that present forms of life—the institutions, relationships, symbols, language, habits—cannot contain the human being. That quality of life, that participation in the deeper, hidden dimensions of life made possible these forms. They provide the vehicle wherein the everydayness of life can be lived with reasonable comfort and reasonable freedom from anxiety and unpredictability. These forms do not contain life, although they can box it in for one who lacks "spirit." Rather, life contains these forms. They are a part of life, life is not a part of them. They are a manifestation of life, not vice versa. This going beyond, this "moreness" of life, this transcendent dimension, is the usual meaning of "spirit" and "spiritual."

Talk of the "spirit" and the "spiritual" in education need not, then, be God talk, even though the traditions wherein "spiritual" is used most frequently are religious traditions. Rather, the talk is about lived reality, about experience and the possibility of experiencing. Another sphere of being is not being referred to. The "spiritual" is of this world, not of another world; of this life, not of another life. But the spiritual is not necessarily contained, nor even acknowledged, in the way that we presently know and live in this world.

Nevertheless, within the various religious traditions are veins of language about the spiritual. They should be mined for the educator. They contain centuries of experience and experiencing of the suprasensory, the qualitative, the transcendent—experiences that are stored in histories, stories, myths, and poems. Interpreting them requires more hermeneutical skill than reading textbooks, newspapers, scientific reports, behavioral science descriptions, or histories based upon more tangible traces. With sufficient care, usages and meanings can be located to inform and enlighten the understanding of knowing in its diverse modes, and hence inform and enlighten the understanding of education. No single religious tradition should be consulted or ignored. If a particular religious tradition shows forth too strongly, the appropriate response is not a cry of prejudice but argument and discussion that would further inform and enlighten.

What are these histories, stories, myths, and poems? They are symbols of moreness, of otherness, of the transcendent—symbols that life as lived can be different. The otherness, moreness, the transcendent is demonstrated in creativity. It shows forth in insight and new understanding, and is anticipated in hope for the future. The symbols may be stories of relationships—of struggle, conflict, forgiveness, love—during which something new is produced: new life, new relationships, new understandings, new forms of power and political control. There are symbols of wholeness and unity: of the body and mind, of self and others, of the human and natural world, of past, present, and future. There are symbols of at-one-ness when the inchoate and disturbing cohere in new meanings. There are symbols of liberation, of exodus from various forms of enslavement and domination: personal, interpersonal, or social. They are symbols of more than the present, more than current forms for life. These are the symbols of the spirit and the spiritual and how life as lived is, and can be, informed, reformed, and transformed.

The symbols of the religious traditions point to dimensions of human experience. They are descriptions of how particular people have encountered or acknowledged the spiritual. The presence of these symbols points to the fact that encountering, experiencing, and acknowledging the spiritual are possible. Everyone experiences, and continues to have the possibility of experiencing the transcending of present forms of life, of finding that life is more than is presently known or lived. This is what education is about. Education is only possible because the human being is a being that can transcend itself.

The condition for experiencing the spiritual is openness and receptivity. This experience requires acknowledging one's fundamental vulnerability and accepting that one can be overpowered and transformed. This openness and receptivity is a fissure, a "fault" in our knowledge and current forms of life. Doubt is one such fissure. It is an awareness that what we are and what we know can never completely contain what we might be or what we might know. It is epitomized by science, a human activity that at its best keeps looking for negative proofs, for novelty, newness and data that upset and overthrow current theories and paradigms. Siu, who brings together in one person the traditions of Eastern spirituality and the traditions of scientific research, speaks of this dwelling in as "no-knowledge."[3] This is a state of vulnerability and openness, not a condition of ignorance. Ignorance is associated with embarrassment, fear and trepidation, impotency from the inability to control or predict. The vulnerability and openness of the spiritual are accompanied by hope, by patience and forbearance, by sensitivity to the otherness of the world, and by love. With these qualities existing forms of knowledge can be used without idolatry, brought under question, and new forms invented or created.

Are There Spiritual Modes of Knowing?

The questions guiding this undertaking now can be posed and answered. Are there spiritual forms of knowing? Is it possible to know spiritually? Are there particular forms of understanding that can be identified as spiritual? Is there any particular kind of understanding that is secured within a dimension of life called the spiritual? Can spirit, which gives vitality, force, and transcending capability to human life, be known? These questions have only one answer: No.

That "no," however, is a consequence of the way the questions are asked. Of primary interest to the educator is the relationship between knowing and the spiritual. Questions should explore that relationship. It does not have to be expressed as "knowing the spiritual" or "spiritual modes of knowing." These two do not exhaust the possible relationships among these two words.

Three dimensions can be explored. The first is the relationship between knowing and the experience of the spiritual. When one has an experience that appears to be associated with the spiritual, does that necessarily imply that the person "knows" the spiritual or that the experience leads to knowledge of the "spiritual"? The second dimension concerns the publicly stored or symbolized records, traces, or memories of others who "experience the spiritual." Should these stored traces—histories, stories, myths, poetry, or other symbolic forms—be considered knowledge of the spiritual? The third dimension is the relationships of the spiritual to all modes of knowing. How are various forms of knowing or knowledge related to the spiritual? These questions raise necessary and crucial epistemological issues. They can be considered here only very superficially.

The claim has been made that people experience moments when present forms of behavior are somehow transcended. These moments might be explained or depicted as growth, education, insight, intuition, power. They could be a result of struggle and work, of suffering and pain, of ecstasy and joy. They could be a consequence of something or someone new breaking into their present form of life, of being loved and cared for by someone. A spiritual reality is not claimed, only the possibility of transcending oneself. The vitality or power of life that makes this possible has been commonly labeled "spiritual." The experience itself is important; not the source, the reason that explains, nor the label that names. People need not reach behind or beyond the experience to know something hidden or elusive. As these experiences continue throughout life, individuals begin to recognize patterns within their own lives. They can identify commonalities in these moments. They can offer a variety of explanations for these experiences. Patterns of availability, openness, and vulnerability can be detected, often linked to relationships with others. From these experiences an awareness of being vulnerable, open, and available for others and the new is developed. What is known from personal experience is not the spiritual, but the story of one's life, its many transforming and transcending moments, and the qualities or attributes needed or associated with such moments. Knowledge of one's self accompanies and follows from these experiences, not knowledge of the spiritual. To anchor this awareness in consciousness, a social fabric, a speaking and symbolic community, is required.

The need for this social fabric, this language or symbol world, points to the second dimension: histories, stories, myths, poetry, or other symbols. These are the records of those who have been transformed, or have experienced transcending moments, individually or communally. They are traditions that conserve and make available the language and the social fabric to anchor personal experience into a broader historical matrix.

The claim here is that throughout human history other individuals, and groups of individuals, have also experienced transforming and transcending moments and that these moments have been stored within the various traditions of these people. The fact that these stored traces assume the status of what Tracy calls "religious classics"[4] speaks to the importance of these records, these texts. They provide a language, a symbolic world within which one can project and understand one's own possibilities. If that textual language enters into the thinking and speaking language of the person, then the tradition becomes part of the person and the person becomes part of the tradition.[5] Consequently, this experience is brought into a usable consciousness, capable of being made public and integrated, or at odds, with the community's story. These stored memories—histories, stories, myths, poetry, and other symbolic forms—are usually maintained and honored within specific religious traditions, often being labeled "sacred." They are one part of the religious tradition connecting personal experience of individuals to the experiences of the historic community.

Can it be said that these provide knowledge of the "spiritual"? That claim might be made within the religious community. A more limited claim, appropriate within this context, is that the texts make possible knowledge of other people. They are not modes of knowing the spiritual, but ways to know others, and consequently also ways to know one's self. The knowledge that comes from these histories, stories, myths, and poems can claim only as much truth as similar symbolic materials. Their sacredness does not reside in the knowing that comes from encountering them or even in what they reveal. The sacredness resides in the community's allegiance to them and the place that they have in the life and history of the community. As narrative, historical, poetic, and mythical structures, they provide ways to think and talk about one's self, with others, from birth to death. They provide possibilities, to be chosen or rejected. The choice is not only a function of the text and the personal experience of the reader, but of the community that is the context of both.

The religious traditions store these transforming and transcending moments in their religious classics, and they also store them in various disciplines. Within these traditions they are sometimes known as spiritual disciplines. These are the disciplines of worship, prayer and meditation, text study, and disciplines of action in, and sometimes withdrawal from, the world. These are disciplines by which persons keep themselves open, available, and vulnerable so that they can be transformed and participate in experiences of transcendence. These are not knowledge-producing disciplines. In fact, one fourteenth-century writer referred to them as disciplines that enabled one to be in the "cloud of unknowing."[6] They are disciplines for staying open and hopeful. Again, these are not necessarily privileged modes of access to openness. For instance, Parker Palmer refers to the disciplines necessary for the spiritual formation of the teacher.[7] He refers to the traditional disciplines of his own religious community. But he also calls attention to disciplines within academia that also keep one at risk, open, and available. These are studying outside one's own discipline, teaching in a new field, becoming someone else's student, and the discipline of trying to get inside someone else's skin.

The claim has been made that there are no modes of knowing the spiritual. There are modes of knowing self, others, and their traditions. Through personal experience the self can be known as vulnerable, open to the world, and capable of being transformed or capable of transcending one's current forms of life. The openness, vulnerability, and experiences of transformation of others can be known through their histories, stories, myths, poetry, and other symbols. These others have also handed down disciplines that enabled them to stay open and to hope for or expect moments of being transcended. These disciplines can be known, in the sense of being able to use them and to make them part of one's habits. "Knowing the spiritual," then, refers to knowing one's self and others and their traditions.

The claim also has been made that there are no spiritual modes of knowing. To claim spiritual modes of knowing is to assume privileged access to realms of experience, knowing that would be free from the rules and warrants governing forms of knowing. The work of centuries to free various forms of knowing from the dogmas of particular religious traditions would be compromised if this claim were to be accepted. However, an active dialectic between religious traditions and the many and diverse modes of knowing must be maintained. Religious traditions should not dominate any particular mode of knowing, nor should the various modes of knowing dominate religious traditions. Religious traditions not open to developments in the various fields of knowledge become closed, sometimes idolatrous, and their proponents unnecessarily defensive. The study of sacred texts has been significantly altered and facilitated by developments in historical-critical methods, and more recently by the developments in literary criticism. Theology always finds new expression in developing philosophical idioms. The understanding of religious traditions is usually enriched by new developments in the various fields of knowledge. The reverse is also true. To the extent that various modes of knowing are separated from religious traditions they become closed in upon themselves and lose their vitality, their "spirit," their creativity, and the possibility of being transcended. Phenix states that "study and teaching in each discipline, in depth, thus constitutes de facto acts of religious devotion, even though conventional religious symbols and concepts may not be employed."[8]

The point of this essay, however, is not to explore this dialectic, but to indicate how various modes of knowing are suffused with the spiritual. That this suffusion is not commonly recognized is a consequence of enlightenment tendencies, now increasingly brought under question by philosophers of science and other epistemologists.[9] These enlightenment values have been more or less assumed by educators, hiding from view how the qualities associated with the spiritual are foundational in every mode of knowing. Space does not permit attending to each mode of knowing, as Phenix does in *Education and the Worship of God*, but a general framework for beginning that hard work of analysis can be suggested.

Every mode of knowing is a mode of being open, vulnerable, and available to the internal and external world. The form of a human being is complete and fixed only at death. Aspects of the self and most of the external world always remain beyond the structures and schemas of knowing. Present forms of knowing are always incomplete, always fallible. Behind every confidence and certainty is residual doubt. As scientists have pointed out, the only thing known for certain is what is not true, what has been disproved. There is always a better way of being in the world, more complete prediction, more perfect expression of experience and feeling, more just meetings with others, better techniques and instrumentalities. Heidegger speaks of truth as openness to being.[10] Truth acknowledges the incompleteness and expects to uncover something else. This is the fissure in human knowing, the openness that is part of the spiritual. If it is blocked from consciousness, truth is weakened, the person falls into a state of hubris, into patterns of oppressive authority, into increasing alienation from the sensory and interpersonal world, and perhaps into psychotic states. In children and scientists, openness takes the form of curiosity and inquiry. In the arts, openness is indicated by the search for new and different experiences. In the practical, openness takes the form of problems—unresolved and "problematic" situations. Identification with those who are broken, marginal, or clearly different from self is a manifestation of being open in interpersonal modes of knowing.

Every mode of knowing is also a mode of being in relationship. It is a relationship of mutual care and love, often distorted into mere attentiveness and sometimes distorted into control and oppression. When vulnerable one must either recognize and accept the other and the necessity of care or love, or one must seek control of the other, who is both threat and possibility. As those who live close to and in harmony with the land know, and as the modern ecology movement suggests, the land, also a threat, will care for those who care for it. The knowledge between two people—parent and child, or two in love—points to this dialectic between knowing and loving. The dialectic is also suggested by the Biblical Hebrew word for "to know," which also means sexual union. Often the scientist comes to care for that which becomes known and in the caring process comes to know even more. By letting one's self be in the care of a part of the world one is informed by it. The distortion of this relationship occurs only when caring is for the self and knowing becomes an act of control, often an act of violence. The significance of the relationship of caring and knowing is reflected in the increasing interest in communication transactions and dialogue within the social sciences. The primary influence in this awareness of the dialogic structures is, of course, the seminal work of Martin Buber,[11] although today the importance of Habermas[12] and diverse other scholars must also be acknowledged.[13]

Every mode of knowing is also a mode of waiting—of hoping and expectancy. Knowledge is not produced by a process of accretion of additional parts, as things are produced on production lines. All who have tried their hand at creative writing, or the arts, or even speaking something other than the tired talk of gossip are aware of the importance, and the risk, of waiting. The pause is important in speech, the incubation period in creative work. A body full of jumbled and partial ideas, formless intuitions, and vague inarticulate feelings often requires changed focus, perhaps even sleep, before form emerges or takes over. Hard work and preparation are insufficient. Bringing previous structures and forms under question, stumbling around in the muck and mire of problems, filling the head with sensations and data are necessary. These discomforting and unsettling actions are possible because of hope and expectation. If hope gives way to despair or is prohibited by time pressures, the formless is filled with premature form, accompanied by nagging doubt and dissatisfaction. The various modes of knowing are grounded in the possibility of a different future. To wait actively and expectantly for that different future is a manifestation that modes of knowing are grounded in more than merely present forms of knowing. They are grounded in and depend upon hope.

Every mode of knowing is participation in the continual creation of the universe—of one's self, of others, of the dwelling places of the world. It is co-creation. If knowing is in language forms, then the events between self and the other create new language forms.[14] If knowing is in visual and plastic forms, then co-creation is change in the qualitative and sensory aspects of the world. If knowing is practical and technical, it modifies the forms of the ever present but changing relationship between the human and the other than human. If it is knowing of the other, it is the creation of new relationships—of exclusion or inclusion, of love or enmity, of dialogue or control.

Every mode of knowing witnesses to the transcending possibilities of which human life is a part. All knowing requires openness and vulnerability. This means that present forms of knowledge, which relate the person to the vast otherness in the world and which hold together past, present, and future, must be acknowledged as limited, fallible, insufficient. To have new forms emerge, old forms must give way to relationship: love takes priority over knowledge. Love and care, however, provide not certainty but hope. Hope makes possible patience and peaceful waiting in the midst of turmoil and unsettledness. With openness, love, and hope, new creation is possible. Old forms can be transcended. New containers for the overpowering vitality of life emerge for the time being, and the cycle begins again. The cycle is not new. Openness, love, hope—this is the story of human life as celebrated in religious traditions—the traditions that keep the spiritual acknowledged in collective and individual consciousness.

The problem, of course, is that schools and other institutions of education are not places of knowing, but places of knowledge. Knowledge is the fallout from the knowing process. Knowledge is form separated from life. It stands by itself, removed from the vitality and dynamics of life, from the spirit. It becomes part of life only when it is brought once again into the knowing process of an individual. Until then it is dead. To bring knowledge to life, to enliven it, it must be brought into the living form of the human being, into the form that is a form of the transcendent. If the student is brought into the deadness of inert knowledge, the student is also deadened, alienated from the vitality that co-creates the worlds of self and others. By enlivening knowledge, the student is also empowered. To enliven knowledge is to accept it with doubt and to place it back into the eternal cycle of openness, love, and hope. Knowledge that falls out from the modes of knowing, that becomes alienated from openness, love, and hope, risks becoming idolatrous.

But Tennyson said it better:

> Flower in the crannied wall,
> I pluck you out of the crannies—
> Hold you here, root and all, in my hand,
> Little flower—but *if* I could understand
> What you are, root and all, and all in all,
> I should know what God and man is.

Footnotes

1. Daisetz T. Suzuki, *Mysticism: Christian and Buddhist* (New York: Harper and Brothers, 1957).

2. Huston Smith, *Beyond the Post-Modern Mind* (New York: Crossroad Publishing Co., 1982).

3. Ralph G. Siu, *Tao of Science: An Essay on Western Knowledge and Eastern Wisdom* (Cambridge, Mass.: M.I.T. Press, 1958).

4. David Tracy, *The Analogical Imagination* (New York: Crossroad Publishing Co., 1981).

5. Paul Ricouer, *Interpretation Theory* (Fort Worth, Texas: Texas Christian University Press, 1976).

6. Ira Progoff, trans., *The Cloud of Unknowing* (New York: Julien Press, 1957).

7. Parker J. Palmer, *To Know as We Are Known: A Spirituality of Education* (San Francisco: Harper and Row, 1983).

8. Philip H. Phenix, *Education and the Worship of God* (Philadelphia: Westminster Press, 1966).

9. Michael Polanyi, *Personal Knowledge: Toward a Post-Critical Philosophy* (Chicago: University of Chicago Press, 1962); David Bohm, *Wholeness and the Implicate Order* (London: Routledge and Kegan Paul, 1980).

10. Martin Heidegger, *Being and Time*, trans. John Macquarrie and Edward Robinson (London: SCM Press, 1962).

11. Martin Buber, *Between Man and Man* (London: Collins, 1961).

12. Jürgen Habermas, *Communication and the Evolution of Society*, trans. Thomas McCarthy (Boston: Beacon Press, 1979).

13. Richard J. Bernstein, *Beyond Objectivism and Relativism: Science, Hermeneutics, and Practice* (Philadelphia: University of Pennsylvania Press, 1983).

14. Paul Ricouer, "Structure, Word, Event," in *The Philosophy of Paul Ricouer*, ed. Charles Reagan and David Stewart (Boston: Beacon Press, 1978), chap. 8.

Part Three
IMPLICATIONS FOR EDUCATIONAL PRACTICE

CHAPTER X

Personal Practical Knowledge and the Modes of Knowing: Relevance for Teaching and Learning

F. MICHAEL CONNELLY AND D. JEAN CLANDININ

Those of us whose job it is to tease out the implications of the modes of knowing for educational practice have either a remarkably easy assignment or an impossible one, depending upon one's construction of the relationship between the two. If we assume a logistic relationship,[1] in which practice is directed by applied theory, the easier task unfolds. To draw out an implication is to say the unsaid but logically contained. There are several such implications in the account of the modes of knowing presented in this volume, and we shall recount some of them. But if the modes of knowing and the events to which they refer are taken to be in a different domain from the practice of teaching and learning, then there are no implications per se. There are, instead, "possibilities" depending on one's notion of knowing in teaching and learning and on the connecting assumptions made between the modes of knowing and the practice of teaching and learning. The burden of our effort in this chapter is to construct a basis for a consideration of these possibilities.

Our method of introducing the connection between modes of knowing and teaching and learning is to begin the paper with the aesthetics of our assigned task. This permits us to set forth our own point of view amidst the context of modes of knowing given in this volume. The distinction between theory and practice permeates our discussion and is used to make three further distinctions: (a) between conceptual modes of knowing as theory (for example, aesthetics) and teaching and learning (for example, an art class) as practice; (b) between conceptual modes of knowing as theory (for example, aesthetics) and the events (for example, art) to which they refer as practice; and (c) between experiential classroom modes of knowing as theory (for example, image of the classroom as home) and teaching and learning (for example, the gingerbread boys episode) as practice.

We introduce the necessary terms and distinctions in the section on "The Aesthetics of the Task." In the sections entitled "Implications of the Modes of Knowing" and "Learning the Modes of Knowing," we trace some of the implications of the conceptual modes of knowing for teaching and learning. We link the idea of conceptual modes of knowing with the notion of experiential classroom modes of knowing in the section "Modes of Knowing within Narratives of Experience." In effect, we link the second and third sets of theory-practice terms. The remainder of the paper gives an account of experiential classroom modes of knowing illustrated with a set of research notes on what we call "the gingerbread boys episode." We develop experiential terms for thinking about modes of knowing within classrooms, specifically, the notions of narrative unity, image, and rhythm. The chapter concludes with a summary and a consideration of practical classroom matters.

The Aesthetics of the Task

Our construction of the relation of the modes of knowing to school practice depends upon whose perspective we adopt: the theoretician of modes of knowing or the practitioner of teaching and learning. There is a tension in educational inquiry between these two perspectives, and there are heroic efforts, of which this volume is an example, to enhance practice through theory and vice versa. Still, the tension remains and is experienced by most of us in our own work. Our own experience is illustrative.

We have been philosophically trained in the modes of knowing, have inquired into schooling, and have written "our own construction of other people's constructions of what they and their compatriots are up to."[2] This leaves us with the unsettling sense of living with two conflicting perspectives. When we study philosophy, and reflect on the philosophers' inquiry into the experience of knowing, the theoretical structure "modes of knowing" makes sense and feels right. Furthermore, the contrariness of account also makes sense as writers such as Kuhn[3] and Phillips (see chapter VIII of this volume) help explain diversity via historical argument. Our adoption, then, of the philosophers' perspective yields a meaningful understanding of the modes of knowing, and we feel persuaded of their potential-practical utility. We are inclined to "take for granted," without reason or argument, the presence of practical implications for teaching and learning.

But when we work in school this taken-for-grantedness dissipates. To begin with, few people in schools talk the language of modes of knowing. If we do so talk, the kindest response is likely to be "that's interesting." When we identify an act as fitting a mode, the identification slips away in the wash of all the other modes at work. For instance, a child drawing in an art class turns out, among other things, to be acting "interpersonally" (pleasing the teacher), "intuitively" (grasping the whole), and "formally" (arranging line, space, and color). We can, of course, classify a child's art drawing as aesthetic, his mathematic problem solving as formal, and his science experiment as scientific. But this has little aesthetic appeal for us since it is the knowing in the child's act that is our interest and this knowing is much more, and perhaps of a different order of knowing, than that implied in the name. Indeed, what we call aesthetic in this case may partly be a proper blend of all of the aforementioned. To say that the mode of knowing in the art class is aesthetic is to call it by someone else's name. Social anthropologists talk the language of the culture under study, and we, it seems, should talk school.

When we shift our attention from the child learning to the teacher teaching, the sense of inappropriateness is heightened. A teacher teaching mathematics, even if in a deliberate attempt to teach a formal mode of knowing, cannot be well understood in "formal" terms. The teacher plans, explains, demonstrates, remonstrates, praises, evaluates, and reflects with voice and with body. She does not know her teaching "formally." Nor can we, with a great deal of meaning, characterize our knowing of her mathematics teaching act as "formal." There are, of course, formal elements to both. But for neither, nor for the students' learning of mathematics, is the term "formal mode of knowing" a satisfactorily telling characterization. What does feel right in the circumstance is the overall rhythm of teaching and learning and the more detailed shifting kaleidoscope of knowing that is occurring. The thought of applying the notion of modes of knowing disrupts this sense of appropriateness.

But just as the "modes of knowing" feel disharmonious when we are in school, our school thoughts feel disharmonious when we are in the philosophers' pages. The language of image, narrative unity, ritual, cycle, routine, and rhythm which help to characterize ways of knowing in school seem, in the pages of theory, ill-defined and ultimately undefinable with precision and exclusivity. The school events in which we participate feel, from the security of the philosophers' pages, unendingly variable and thoughtless.

We are, accordingly, on both sides of the fence. Both sides are informative and pleasing in their own terms. And when we carry one side into the other, especially when we entertain implications of theory for practice, the effect is disharmonious. Why should this matter of perspective make the difference it does to our aesthetic sense of what is appropriate? There are two partial answers to this question, both of which take their place within the difference between inquiry which leads to school talk and that which leads to modes of knowing talk.

KNOWING THE EXPERIENCE OF TEACHING AND LEARNING VERSUS KNOWING THE MODES OF KNOWING

The first reason stems from Geertz's definition of anthropological inquiry earlier noted. Within the practitioner's perspective, our constructions are of their constructions of knowing while, in the pages of philosophy, the constructions are of knowing more directly. The intervening subject "their constructions" is missing. In school inquiry we say, "These are the forms by which I describe the ways teachers and students know teaching and learning," while in philosophic inquiry we say, "This is how I describe the forms of disciplined thought." In both cases, of course, the forms constitute a meta language and are not necessarily part of the situation described. But, for each, the correspondence is sufficiently close to the experience described for a degree of practitioner acceptance to obtain. Practicing artists tend to feel comfortable with the language of aesthetics; similarly practicing scientists feel comfortable with the philosophy of science. Likewise, teachers tend to feel comfortable with the discussion of images, rhythms, cycles, and routines. For each class of practitioner, the disciplinarian and the school person, the subject and purpose of inquiry contained in the respective perspectives are sufficiently close to the practitioner's experience to create a sense of appropriateness. When we shift perspective, neither subject nor purpose coincides with the respective practitioner's experience.

A second reason why perspective makes the aesthetic difference it does is given by a consideration of the role of experience in inquiry. In contrast to the philosophical construction of modes of knowing, our constructions of schooling are given in terms of narratives of experience. They are given historically and biographically. Our notion of teaching and learning is one in which teacher and student actors are subjects of interest. Because of this attitude to teaching and learning, actions are not merely performances; they are minded, knowing actions. Accordingly, for us knowing is an experience. Action and knowledge are united in the actor, and our account of knowing is, therefore, of the actor with her personal narratives, intentions, and passions. This practical knowing of teachers and students is complex because it embodies in a history, in the moment and in an act, all modes of knowing aimed at the particular event that called forth the teaching and learning act.

In contrast, the theory of modes of knowing is essentially conceptual and cognitive. Philosophical accounts of the modes of knowing offer, on the whole, a conceptual account of disciplined inquiry. For example, Noddings writes about mathematics, Arnheim about any disciplined inquiry, and Phillips about philosophy of science. In this writing, the reader is offered a formal expression of the knowledge of inquirers' experience. Moreover this knowledge, for the most part, is of the formalized and adjudicated products of disciplined inquiry and its arguments. It tends not to be of the act of inquiry but of the formal outcome of inquiry. This sets a strikingly different context for "knowing" than does the study of the narrative experience of teaching and learning.

These observations bear on the problem of the aesthetics of perspective since the narratives of practitioners in each are, respectively, guided by experiential and formal intentions. Teachers are concerned with the child, and the best teachers are sensitive to the child as a person and not only as a carrier for the subject matter taught. Their concern is with how the child copes with his learning, and they take as evidence of their teaching achievements the child's happiness, career goals, ambitions, and sociality. Accordingly, inquiry into schooling that takes narrative as its subject comes within the experiential, intentional character of teacher practitioners at work.

Practicing disciplinarians, however, tend to be governed by formal, experientially free, intentions. The objectification of concepts and concept structures and the adherence to methodological rule for the removal of inquirer bias are the imagined end. Mathematicians, biologists, and artists alike aim at a stable, formal product with conceptual status. Accordingly, philosophic inquiry into formal modes of thinking comes within the conceptual, intentional character of disciplinary practitioners' work.

Thus, while a teacher imagines a child living when she teaches, and a child lives with what he is taught, the disciplinarian imagines a conceptual form. Likewise, the narrative study of schooling recounts knowing as experiential while philosophic inquiry of formal thought recounts knowing as conceptual. In brief, the imagined outcomes by practitioners within each perspective correspond in kind to the outcomes of inquiry into their practices. In part, this compatibility accounts for the sense of appropriateness we feel for the modes of knowing when in the pages of philosophic inquiry and for the vagaries of practice while in school. And because the imagined ends of each are different—experiential versus conceptual—there is a sense of inappropriateness when the two perspectives are interchanged in a quest for implications of one for the other.

We shall now briefly adopt the philosopher's perspective and say their implications of the modes of knowing for teaching and learning. Following these considerations we will examine the interface of the two perspectives and then turn our attention to knowing from the perspective of the schools.

Implications of the Modes of Knowing

This volume expresses a rich conceptual structure of modes of knowing. By implication curriculum needs to be alive to a diversity of modes. No more would the schools monolithically adopt a view of knowing based mostly on one mode as, for example, the operationalism, logical positivism, and the various misinformed versions of Dewey's *How We Think.*[4] We see manifest in this volume the richness of the best in human thought with the implication that the schools nurture all of the modes. And to the extent that we value richness in personal lives, the implication is that the nurturing occur for each person and not merely for the curriculum as a whole where some might become formal thinkers, others aesthetic thinkers, and so forth. Each child would be encouraged to develop sensitivity to, and skill in, the uses of diverse modes of knowing.

A second implication is drawn from the flavor of disputation and argument within writings on the modes of knowing and from the sense that the modes of knowing, as known, are the outcome of a kind of historical process such as that described for science by Phillips and argued for mathematics by Noddings in preceding chapters of this volume. Indeed, for some fields, such as science, there is more diversity in the formal and theoretical discourse about them than there is diversity within the fields themselves. Serious scientific disputes at any time may be limited to two or three in number whereas, apart from fashion that creates a false sense of agreement, legitimately different theories of scientific knowing abound. The implication of this diversity is that teaching and learning need to be self-consciously open to alternative constructions of scientific knowing, of aesthetic knowing, and so on. Just as it is good current pedagogical theory to teach the grounds and argument of competing theoretical views within the school subjects, so too it is good pedagogical theory to cast teaching and learning acts in the context of alternative epistemologies.

These, then, are two of the implications that may be said from the perspective of theories of modes of knowing.

Learning the Modes of Knowing

The theoretical and conceptual status of the modes of knowing permits a consideration of their teaching and learning consistent with an understanding of concept learning more generally. The "modes" are no more complicated as curriculum content than topics such as Greek mythology, human nature in Shakespearean drama, and elementary calculus. Accordingly, the modes of knowing may become part of the stock of knowledge taught and learned. They may be learned by students (a) as philosophers (for instance, as students of Arnheim, Eisner, and Phillips), (b) as teachers of teachers, (c) as teachers, and (d) as school students. We might imagine gradations in principle according to these four categories of students: philosophy students learning the principles by which the modes of knowing structures are generated, as well as the modes themselves; the teacher of teachers learning something of the diversity of modes across fields and something of the analytic ability to reconstruct a mode of knowing embodied in, for example, a set of curriculum materials; the teacher learning contemporary modes at work in her field as well, perhaps, as some of the field's history of inquiry; and school students learning something of the sense in which claims are validated in particular subjects. We might, furthermore, imagine five possible accomplishments for the study of concepts of modes of knowing: (a) transmission of part of our intellectual heritage, (b) enhancement of students' capacity for critical judgment, (c) training the mind to think in terms of certain "modes," (d) fostering intellectual tolerance and a respect for the different "modes" of thought of others, and (e) enriching students' reflective armory. We may also imagine an array of methods by which the modes of knowing may be taught: by didactic transmission as a form of knowledge, as for example in lecture and textbook; by narrative either of the intellectual history of a "mode" or by biography of key figures; by inquiry either through the hermeneutics of close reading of exemplary thought, through constructed classroom settings, as for instance in the use of laboratory, or through apprenticeship as in the training of doctoral candidates; and by reflection as in the uses of a student's personal narrative unities as the subject matter for consideration of a "mode of knowing."[5]

Many will argue that for some students the modes of knowing should not function as curriculum content but only as a principle for the organization of curriculum materials and instructional methods. We concur. It is clear that any set of curriculum materials, teaching act, or learning situation embodies, consciously or otherwise, modes of knowing. A science curriculum aggressively built around experimental laboratories will tend to foster understandings about one kind of science while another, which supplies reports of inquiry and focuses on reading and reflection upon them, fosters another kind of science, while still another kind of science would be obtained from a science curriculum read out of a textbook. It is implied, according to this notion of the modes of knowing as a curriculum-planning principle, that anyone involved in the curriculum-planning process needs to understand a diversity of modes of knowing and needs to manipulate this form of knowledge in the context of curriculum and instruction situations.

This sketch of teaching and learning implications of the philosopher's perspective on the modes of knowing will suffice to illustrate their major uses as concepts. We now undertake a transition to this same problem from the perspective of the schools.

Modes of Knowing within Narratives of Experience

Theoretical concepts, such as the modes of knowing, may, as Polanyi shows, be thought of as tools.[6] They may be felt as extensions of our body, subsumed in our awareness for use in the pursuit of our intentions. Just as a pencil may be used for writing, a mode of knowing may be used for understanding. In skilled use, the user "dwells in" the tool and is only subsidiarily aware of it as his attention is focused on its use. We attend to what is written, not to the pencil, and we attend to what is thought and not to the mode of knowing by which we do our thinking.

This account brings us to a point of contact between the perspective of the modes of knowing theoretician and that of the teaching and learning practitioner. The theoretician's aim is to celebrate the mode of knowing: to twist and turn it and recount the shades of meaning reflecting from its multiple faces. But the user's goal is to put the modes of knowing out of "sight." The more effective the tool, the less the user attends to it. A butcher's knife comes mostly to the butcher's attention when dull; likewise, the pencil for the writer and a mode of knowing for the thinker. Furthermore, depending on their generality, tools are many things according to their many uses. A pencil, for example, may be a device for writing, drawing, poking holes, enhancing eye-hand coordination, or jabbing a friend. It would, in fact, be difficult to imagine all the things a pencil is and may be; and what is said for pencils is multiplied for modes of thought. Hence, while the philosopher may imagine a sophisticated account of the ideal expression of thought, the teaching and learning user, if he thinks about it at all, will imagine any number of uses, none of which is likely to include formal inquiry uses.

The submersion of physical and cognitive tools in our awareness and their multiple uses depending on the intentionality of particular situations highlight still another point of interest at the interface of our two perspectives, one named by Bridgman as "doing one's damndest with one's mind."[7] Bridgman, downplaying the role of inquiry principles, argued that a problem-solving scientist does everything possible, no holds barred, when confronted with a problem. In terms of tools this suggests that any and all tools are, as Schutz would say, "on hand" in inquiry.[8] Moreover, in submersion, cognitive tools become something else; something conditioned both by the user's narratives of experience and by the demands of his problem situation, which is, of course, the focus of his current narrative unity.

We develop this notion of narrative unity more fully below. For now, however, suffice it to say that in our studies of schools, the modes of knowing called forth by practitioners in teaching and learning situations are more properly understood, characterized, and named in terms of narrative than in terms of the "modes of knowing." Bluntly put (and, in some respects, too strongly), school practitioners do not know their teaching and learning situations in terms of the modes of knowing. We are *not* saying that the modes of knowing have no place. They do, precisely as concepts to be embodied and submerged as tools thereby becoming part of an ongoing narrative unity or initiating a new one. Just as sugar sweetens the tea but is lost from sight and recall, the modes of knowing "sweeten" one's personal knowledge while disappearing from sight. And they are *not* "on call." A user does not call up a mode of knowing in the sense that he tries out different cars or recalls items for a test. In the pages of philosophy, and in the textbooks and methods of instruction, the modes of knowing have this quality of identifiability. But this quality is lost in a user's submersion of it in his mind and body. Something else, which we call "personal practical knowledge," is "on call." And because personal practical knowledge is experiential, embodied, and reconstructed out of the narratives of a user's life, it does not have an identifiable conceptual status. Instead, as we know from our daily doings, we "do our damndest" as needed in our situations. We react this way now, another way later, drawing on experiential images, habits and bits of experience, including those of conceptual origin. This entire armory is "on call," and the calling forth is not a matter of shopping for the named elements of use in the situation but is, instead, a re-collection, a process of crystallization, out of the narrative unities of life experience.

Personal Narrative Unities and the Knowing of Teaching and Learning

In this account of the interface between the two perspectives, we have considered the "best case" from the point of view of schooling. It is the case where the modes of knowing become submerged as tools and take their place in the learner's narrative. When this happens the modes are lost from sight and are not identifiable in action. It might be said that they have passed beyond the stage of easy recall and expression, as, for example, in their expression in testing situations. If concepts are learned as concepts they are not necessarily submerged but remain visible and identifiable, and may be recalled, for example, for achievement tests. From this perspective high recall scores indicate high understanding of the modes. But from the perspective of the user, precise recall may be a sign of incomplete learning. It is a sign that the concepts have been learned as concepts, not as narrative, and that they are, therefore, not "on call" except in the lesser sense of recall upon demand. Using a Crites distinction, we say that concepts are recalled, narratives are re-collected and on call.[9]

From the perspective of schooling our purpose is to understand how teachers and learners know their situations. From this vantage point our inquiry is not a study of modes of knowing but is, rather, a study of knowing-in-practice. It is a study of knowing as expressed in teaching and learning acts.

One consequence of this direction to our inquiry is that in the study of school practice we observe a unified intellectual and material event, for example, a teaching act. In this act there is no separation of theory and practice. The act is not an application of theory although, with due regard to the reduction involved, it might be called theory-in-action. More accurately, it is narrative-in-action. It is the expression of biography and history (in which theoretical learning has a place) in a particular situation. Theory and practice are unified in the actor through her narrative unities of experience; likewise, for the unification of various modes of knowing. Knowing and doing are reflections of one another. Knowing a teaching and learning situation is a matter of the recollections from one's narratives that are called forth by the situation. These recollections are personal, in that they are derived from *a* person's narrative, and they are practical, in that they are aimed at meeting the demands of a particular situation. These recollections are, of course, also theoretical, both in the sense of containing conceptual content such as the modes of knowing and in the sense of typifying the particulars of a situation; and they are cultural, in the sense that individual narratives are embedded in cultural and historical narratives.

A NARRATIVE FRAGMENT: THE GINGERBREAD BOYS EPISODE

For several years we have been conducting an anthropological style study of how teachers know their teaching situations. Part of the methodology consists of the writing of field notes and the preparation of interpretive accounts of the notes and other aspects of the field research experience. The interpretive accounts are the first formal step in the interpretive process and are used as letters to our participants for purposes of initiating discussion on the substance and direction of our constructions.

In the following paragraphs we present an excerpt from an interpretive account directed to Stephanie, a grade one teacher.[10] The account refers to a teaching episode which we shall use paradigmatically to illustrate our current understanding of teachers' modes of knowing. We shall show how an interpretation of the teaching episode in terms of Stephanie's narrative history yields a set of experiential terms by which we understand Stephanie's knowing. The example also illustrates how narrative unity contributes to a unity of knowing in any teaching and learning act.[11] The teaching episode takes place as Christmas nears. The account is written to Stephanie.

At Christmas time, you asked me to make gingerbread boys with the students. I was becoming quite accustomed to baking with the students so I said I would try. We had initially discussed the gingerbread early in December. I had assumed we would make it on the last day of school so the children could eat it as a party treat. The following field note segments record some of our discussions around the gingerbread.

> At lunchtime on Friday, Stephanie and I had a discussion about the gingerbread. Stephanie wanted to start the gingerbread on Monday. I was surprised as I thought she would want to put it off for several days in

> order to have the fresh gingerbread for a party treat. The party was almost two weeks away! (Notes to file, December 9, 1981)

The day we made the gingerbread you told me you wanted to poke holes in the unbaked dough so they could be used as tree ornaments.

> She sat down and started to poke holes in their heads so that the children could hang them on their trees if they wanted. Earlier, I had remembered to do that with two of the batches. The children said they had no intention of hanging them on trees. They all meant to eat them. (Notes to file, December 16, 1981)

I was not in school on December 17, 1981 and when I arrived on the morning of December 18, 1981, the gingerbread boys had been turned into a beautiful display.

> The gingerbread men were all decorated. Each was on a separate paper plate and they were arranged on the back table. Stephanie had arranged the plates on a strip of red velvet material. She pointed several of them out to me, and said they were all very nicely decorated. She told me that Mrs. Jones had been there to help the children decorate them. By this time, the children had started to arrive. The children came in and Stephanie greeted them. A number of children came back to look at the gingerbread men and to show me which ones were theirs. I was standing at the table with the children and they were pointing out their gingerbread men. (Notes to file, December 18, 1981)

Later that morning you made it clear that the gingerbread boys were first for display and then for eating.

> She asked two students if they had taken the gingerbread boy to Tereena. Tereena had been absent from school. They said they had and said she had eaten it right away. Stephanie said we were going to be good, and "not eat ours yet." (Notes to file, December 18, 1981)

Unities in the Narrative

In this account of Stephanie's practice, we see Stephanie planning her program, organizing a learning activity, arranging a learning environment, evaluating student actions, interacting with students, and encouraging student interaction. It is a teaching act with many of the practical everyday matters we commonly think of as characterizing teaching practice.

The episode, of course, is only a narrative fragment, but even in the short space of nine days, a shifting interplay of these practical matters is visible. A unity of practices, often theoretically thought of and treated as discrete matters, is in evidence. When she first talked of making gingerbread in early December, Stephanie "knew" how and when she would teach and evaluate her planning. Stephanie's plan to make gingerbread boys leads to her teaching, already imagined in the planning, *and* her teaching leads to evaluation, already imagined in the planning and teaching. There was, in this sense, a unity in the kinds of activities we commonly name as comprising teacher practice. We say that Stephanie knows the various practices as a unity given by the temporal movement, the history, defining the narrative fragment.

Of even more interest to the subject of this chapter is the evident unity of modes of knowing of which the aesthetic is perhaps most in evidence. All the children participated in the making of the cookies, and the making was done artfully with artistic ends. Stephanie intended that students display the cookies as Christmas tree decorations both in the classroom and in the homes of those who celebrated Christmas. She further heightened the aesthetic dimension by her "art show" display of the cookies on the red velvet table cover. Given this descripton we might well, from the perspective of the modes of knowing, name the gingerbread boys episode as one of instruction in aesthetics. We could describe Stephanie as a teacher of aesthetics to first-grade students.

But closer inspection of the narrative fragment reveals the inadequacy of such a characterization. For if we see her practice of making gingerbread boys as instruction in aesthetics, how do we account for the moral overtones surrounding their use and design? The researcher's "knowing" of this classroom practice differed from Stephanie's and was "corrected" by Stephanie as she turned the cookies into ornaments by punching holes in the unbaked dough and in her later comment to the children that they be "good" and not eat the cookies until they had been hung on the tree. This moral dimension is a sign that there is something more comprehensive at work in this practice. At the very least we need to describe the aesthetics of the narrative fragment partially in moral terms.

But when this narrative fragment is seen in its larger narrative context, these moral overtones take on extended meaning. The knowing expressed in the gingerbread boys episode is an expression of Stephanie's personal practical knowledge of classrooms, in particular of her image[12] of the "classroom as home" and of her rhythm of teaching. The aesthetic and moral dimensions of the episode are rooted in these narratively grounded ways by which Stephanie knows her classroom. The plausability of these constructions, the image of home and the rhythm of teaching, depends upon a detailed recording and interpretation of Stephanie's narratives of experience which cannot be reproduced in a few pages. Detail is found elsewhere.[13] We must rely on the good humor of our readers and take refuge in Geertz's remark that "if, as I have, you construct accounts of how somebody or other . . . glosses experience . . . you feel at each stage fairly well away from the standard styles of demonstration."[14]

The image of the classroom as home. In brief, Stephanie's image of the classroom as home emerges from the narrative unity of her experience in her own schooling, in her home, in her professional training, and in her teaching. The image is of a place where people can interact and cooperate but where each person has her "own space" and is "free to march to her own drummer." It is an image of a space full of treasured things, an area in which to "live," and an environment in which she and her students can feel comfortable and cared for. Moral and emotional dimensions to the image are evident. The classroom should have certain dimensions. For example, it should be a place where she and the students can live and treat people as individuals and humans, and it should be an environment full of treasured things such as plants, art work, and personal things. The image has an emotional coloring drawn from the home and school experiences in which it is rooted. Stephanie's own early learning and teaching experiences were ones in which she did not experience the closeness and the relational aspects of interacting and cooperating. The emotion inherent in her experiences colors the image of classroom as home in which these experiences coalesced.

The image of classroom as home as expressed in Stephanie's practice of making gingerbread boys highlights the emotional and moral character of the image. (The practice of making gingerbread boys is, of course, but one expression of many possible expressions of the image.) Stephanie felt strongly that the gingerbread boys contribute to enhancing the homelike environment of the classroom both in the process of making the cookies and in the display created with them.

It is Stephanie's ongoing private and professional life experience that creates the narrative unity out of which her image is crystallized and formed when called upon by practical situations. Accordingly, the aesthetic, moral and emotional dimensions of the narrative fragment, when interpreted in context, are rendered meaningful in terms of Stephanie's narrative. What appeared as an aesthetic experience with moral overtones turns out to be an aesthetic of proper home life with all that entails morally and emotionally.

The rhythm of teaching. For Stephanie, her image of the classroom as home is given cultural meaning by her particular rhythms of teaching. Just as there are rhythms in our North American, Christian home life tied to cultural givens such as the work week and cultural holidays such as Christmas, Thanksgiving and Easter, there are similar rhythms in Stephanie's classroom life.

Rhythms serve to modulate an individual teacher's imagery and the narrative unities of which the imagery is a part. In our paper on rhythm we saw the power of cultural rhythms to moderate and therefore smooth out and make harmonious personal and social action.[15] Stephanie is Jewish, and she is a teacher in Bay Street School with an essentially Christian school cycle. The rhythm she knows is not strictly one nor the other. It is one in which she expresses the rhythms of her culture at the same time as accommodating the cultural holidays of others. The result is a harmonious living out of the school year in such a way that her own personal and cultural rhythms and those of her students find expression in her classroom.

We use the term rhythm in the commonplace sense of something occurring repetitively, perhaps cyclically, and which has an aesthetic quality as performed. Baseball players, musicians, writers and teachers can name the times and places when they are "in the groove." For Stephanie, being in the groove is, partially, a matter of conducting her curriculum according to the cycle of cultural holidays. Thus, September begins a sequence of activities leading up to a Thanksgiving party, and the sequence repeats from then to Christmas. Arithmetic is done by counting out the days to the next celebration; shape and color may be studied with "Thanksgiving" leaves; and language arts activities are always "in season." Physically, the classroom wilts, is transformed and blooms as, for example, with gingerbread boys as Christmas decorations and, of course, with many other things and activities. The sequence of activities climaxes with a classroom party.

The rhythm is the personal practical knowledge, the mindedness, behind Stephanie's habit of acknowledging and celebrating the main school holidays and the variety of celebrations for the children of diverse cultural origins in her classroom. Her practice of making gingerbread boys is an expression of her rhythm of the school year, part of the Christmas celebration. Because of the cultural context for knowing the classroom, the gingerbread boy fragment has spiritual significance for Christian children in Stephanie's class. Even for non-Christian children, participation in the rhythm conveys a sense of the spiritual, particularly since Stephanie conducts "minor" celebrations for children of other cultures. Accordingly, this rhythmic knowing of the school year is an important narrative context for the gingerbread boy narrative fragment. The aesthetic, moral, and emotional dimensions of the fragment are given cultural meaning by the rhythms.

Personal practical knowledge and narrative unity. Thus, the gingerbread boys episode is aesthetic in itself, in the sense of expressing proper home life and in the sense of celebrating a cultural holiday. And it is more. The episode is an expression of Stephanie's personal practical knowledge, an embodiment of the way she knows her teaching and learning situation. Her practice is a continuation of her ongoing narrative. The gingerbread boys are not merely made as a Christmas party treat as was our original interpretation. Witness Clandinin's surprise at their early preparation (Field notes, December 9, 1981). Nor are they merely part of a lesson in aesthetics, although they certainly are this as is easily seen in the beautiful display on the red velvet and in their use as decorations for school and home Christmas trees. There are, as well, moral and emotional dimensions at work, and these, along with interpersonal and spiritual dimensions, are given meaning in the context of Stephanie's image of home and as part of her rhythm of the school year. Her practice is one of living out and knowing the classroom rhythmically and as a home. Because she knows the classroom in these ways, the making of gingerbread boys is a way for Stephanie to make the children feel "at home" and to permit them to participate in her culturally influenced rhythms of the classroom. We understand the gingerbread boys episode, then, as taking its place within Stephanie's narrative unity of experience.

To review, we see in her practice of making the gingerbread boys a unity in the act and in Stephanie, the actor. And in this act and in the actor, there is no separation of the modes of knowing. We do not see the act as a reflection of any one mode of knowing. Rather, any teaching act and anything learned are, at once, a reflection of all of the modes of knowing discussed in earlier chapters: the aesthetic, scientific, formal, interpersonal, intellectual, intuitive, and spiritual modes of knowing. Thus, in the gingerbread boys narrative fragment, we do not see Stephanie knowing aesthetically and then knowing interpersonally and then knowing formally. Instead we see a teacher knowing her practice and this knowing of practice, this acting knowingly, as having aesthetic, interpersonal, moral, emotional, and spiritual dimensions. Home and culture are combined in the narrative fragment.

Education as the Creation and Revision of Narrative Unities

Our focus has been on a conception of knowing teaching and learning situations from the perspective of teacher practitioners. We now shift our attention to an account of the educational possibilities of this conception. So far we have used the gingerbread boys episode to illustrate how Stephanie's practice is part of her narrative unity and is an expression of her personal practical knowledge. We can see, through the interpretation of Stephanie's practice, the sense in which teachers are constantly constructing and reporting various of their own narrative unities in their classroom practices.[16] Stephanie's practice of making gingerbread boys is part of her narrative unity, reported and revised through its expression in the classroom with the researcher and with her students.

Let us pursue this observation further and think of it not only as an interpretation of the teacher's experience but also as a way of thinking about the education of students. If in our lives we are constantly constructing, reporting, and revising various narrative unities, then education should somehow draw on, develop, remake, and introduce such narratives. Education cannot, from this perspective, occur unless it calls up and makes use of some aspect of each student's dominant narrative unities. What makes sense to an individual, therefore, will depend in large part on which narrative structures are blended together in his or her life and just how the blending occurs. We can see this in the sense of learning through the ongoing experience of schooling and in the sense of learning formally through reflective discussion of the experience in terms of the modes of knowing. Let us return to the gingerbread boys episode to understand how we see the practice of teaching and learning in these terms.

It will be recalled that the aesthetic quality of the gingerbread boys episode was not only descriptive of how it was experienced by Stephanie but also of how she felt it should be experienced by her students. The children were required to act as "little artists" by making their own cookies and then were told to be "good" and not eat them but instead to use them for display and decoration. Even the researcher was educated in this respect as Stephanie showed her what to do with the children and then drew her attention to several of the more pleasing cookies.

This heightening of the aesthetic dimension of experience is done in a more formal way in creative art courses when children's attention is specifically drawn to the aesthetic dimension of knowing. It is similar to the way in which some professors teach aesthetics to teachers and philosophy students. We are reminded in this of Maxine Greene and Elliot Eisner, who teach aesthetics to teachers by having them reflect on the aesthetics of their everyday experience, and of Mark Johnson, who teaches aesthetics to philosophy students in a similar way.[17] In such practices, instructors are not, as Stephanie was not, asking their students to know aesthetics conceptually but, instead, to know it experientially. By reflecting on the aesthetics of their personal experience, the experience of knowing aesthetically is heightened.

For us, this going back over an experience and heightening a dimension is a "giving back" of the experience, aimed at the seeing of an experience in new lights. It is, in our terms, a revising and remaking of each learner's narrative unities. Accordingly, we can understand the gingerbread boys episode as one of revision and re-creation of the narrative unities of Stephanie's students. By "giving it back" experientially rather than by teaching it conceptually, the aesthetic experience is encountered morally, emotionally, interpersonally, and spiritually. Indeed, to call the episode a lesson in aesthetic knowing runs the risk of diminishing this more complete sense of how this teacher and her students know the teaching and learning situation. It is, for them, a unity of knowing.

Giving it back, of course, means different things for different children depending on their narratives. Some children will come from homes where gingerbread boys are made at Christmas; others from homes where the cookies are made but not for any special occasion; others from homes where the cookies are not made at all but where baking is part of a tradition of celebration; and others, perhaps, from homes where neither baking nor celebration is featured in home life. In the latter case we might better think of the episode as one of the instructional initiation of new narratives separate from the ongoing narrative unity of the children. But even here a close and detailed study of the children's narratives would reveal related student experiences in friends' homes, in the shops, through the media, on the playground, and in past school activities. To some degree, then, all students have some narrative context for the making of gingerbread boys.

A sense of giving back the children's experience for reflection is, then, inevitable for almost all Stephanie's children and in ways that make the gingerbread boys touchstones to home experience and to cultural cycles. She is calling forth the students' experience and giving it back in the new setting of the classroom with its multicultural make-up. A Christian child, for example, now sees her personal narrative, and the celebration of Christmas, through the eyes of teacher and classmates. Both Stephanie and the other children have their own experiences, and these, in turn, are, depending on the child's culture, embedded in different cultural and historical narrative unities. This "seeing through the other's eyes" occurs because other children's narrative unities have been celebrated in the class. The experience of Christmas for the Christian child is, therefore, enriched in the classroom because the child's experience is broadened to acknowledge, respect, and understand the cultures of others. The classroom experience of making gingerbread boys may resemble a home experience of making gingerbread boys. But its educational value goes beyond mere replay. For the child who shares in the cultural and historical narrative unity of which the Christmas baking of gingerbread boys is a part, this seeing of the experience as it is seen by others with different narrative unities is a revision and re-creation of an ongoing narrative unity. Life is seen to be more than a cycle of Christian holidays. In a similar way, a new narrative, and with it insight into the personal and cultural narratives of others, is begun for those students whose narratives are embedded in different cultural and historical narrative unities. For them, life is now seen as more than their own cultural narrative unities.

We do not wish to make more of the gingerbread boys narrative fragment than is warranted by life in the classroom. It may seem that by seeing the making of cookies as embodying aesthetic, moral, emotional, interpersonal, and spiritual modes of knowing and by seeing this experience as a touchstone to home and culture, and as a way of enhancing children's personal and cultural narratives, we are making much ado about a little. And it is true that we would be so doing if the episode was an isolated act. But because the episode occurs as an expression of Stephanie's modes of knowing the classroom as home, rhythmically lived out in terms of cultural holidays and home life, the gingerbread boys are part of the ongoing educative experience of giving back for reflection the children's narratives of experience. There is a narrative unity about the fragment which is given, and seen, in terms of Stephanie's personal practical knowledge of her classroom.

Thus, for us, two points emerge from our interpretation of Stephanie's practice. The first is that in the ongoing business of teaching and learning in Stephanie's classroom, we see Stephanie "giving back" each child's experience in her Christmas practice of making gingerbread boys. In this "giving back," we see her calling up and making use of some aspect of each student's dominant narrative unities. For some students, the experience of making gingerbread boys in class is a revision of an ongoing narrative unity. For others, it is the creation of a new but connected narrative unity.

Second, from the perspective of knowing teaching and learning situations, the giving back of student experiences is a desirable classroom practice. In reporting, revising and creating narrative unities, the richness of each person's experience is brought forward. Teaching and learning situtions should, we believe, continually "give back" a learner's narrative unity so that it may be revised and, perhaps, a new connected narrative unity begun.

Educational Entailments in Experiential Modes of Knowing

The following briefly summarizes our understanding of what is entailed in a consideration of knowing from the perspective of school participants. The primary entailment of the school perspective on knowing is a focus on the experiential rather than upon the conceptual. It is a focus on the making, and remaking, of meaning in teaching and learning situations. This experience of knowing school situations is one in which personal practical knowledge composed of such experiential matters as images, rituals, habits, cycles, routines, and rhythms is brought to bear. This mode of knowing the teaching and learning situation (or, if one prefers, "these modes of knowing") is re-collected from the narrative unities which make up the person's life experience and which contain experiential elements that are "on call" for this purpose. Modes of knowing in the first sense, that is, in the sense described in earlier chapters of this volume, when formally learned are submerged and take their place in the narrative unities of the teaching and learning knower. Depending on the demands of the situation at hand, modes of knowing (sense one) may be recalled as concepts as, for instance, in a testing situation or re-collected as experiential dimensions of the modes of knowing teaching and learning situations (sense two) as, for example, in Stephanie's classroom Christmas practices.

A second entailment of the school perspective on knowing, essentially a corollary of the first, is that teaching and learning acts are no mere sequences of behavior, nor are they only expressions of a conceptual, cognitive structure such as modes of knowing (sense one). They are unities of mind and body, to which we refer as "minded practice." To see a teaching and learning act is to see an experiential mode of knowing (sense two) at work. Likewise, to refer to an experiential mode of knowing, such as rhythmic knowing, is to imagine certain bodily movements. The two are inextricably intertwined. Accordingly, when it is said that Stephanie knows her teaching rhythmically, we imagine such bodily acts as the making of gingerbread boys at Christmas and the in-class celebration of each child's cultural holidays.

This understanding of Stephanie's experiential mode of knowing teaching and learning situations entails two further points of interest. The unity of Stephanie's modes of knowing her teaching and learning situations implies a unity, derived from her narrative experience, of the kind of activities it is said that teachers do, that is, such matters as planning, teaching, and evaluating; and also a unity in the personal practical knowledge brought to bear on the situation. Thus, knowing the classroom rhythmically entails a unity of considerations of planning, teaching, and evaluating. This is not to say that at any one time one of these activities would not predominate. The making of gingerbread boys in Stephanie's classroom is an example, timed according to its place in the rhythm of teaching. But in the transition, in the movement entailed in the rhythm, a planning act leads to teaching that is imagined in the planning; and the teaching leads to evaluation, and contains it reflectively both in the ongoing act of teaching and, sometimes, summatively at its end. All of these matters are in the teacher's knowing at all times. A teaching act reflects the other two named and likewise for each of the others. Similarly, a student knows his learning situation as one of evaluation as well as one of learning. His narratives of classroom experience have taught him that learning and evaluation, in formal school situations, are always simultaneously at work.

The personal practical knowledge brought to bear on a situation also exhibits unity. This is seen in the gingerbread boys episode where the aesthetic is highlighted in the decoration and display of the cookies. Because we understand that Stephanie's experiential mode of knowing her classroom is in terms of an image of home, and because she knows the year rhythmically, we understand that the aesthetic emphasis is played out as a recollection of her personal narrative unities. As such, the aesthetic experience is merely our name for what is, for her, a unity in her narrative. We reexamine the gingerbread boys episode and find moral, emotional, interpersonal, cultural, and spiritual dimensions clearly in evidence. But it is, after all, none of these dimensions at which Stephanie aims. She does, of course, want students to appreciate the gingerbread men and, thereby, to heighten their aesthetic sense. But she does so because she wants the students to feel "at home" and to partake of the cultural rhythms by which her classroom functions. They are, after all, her modes of knowing the classroom. In short, the unity of mind and body in teaching acts further entails a unity in the activities attributed to teaching and to the modes of knowing (sense one) at work.

One of the implications of this perspective, and all that it entails, is that teachers, teacher educators, and others concerned with curriculum planning, should not treat the modes of knowing (sense one) as garments to be put on according to particular situations, for example, the aesthetic for an art class, the scientific for a science class. While it is a positive move to recognize a diversity of modes of knowing (sense one), rather than treating teaching and learning as if they were mere expressions of one or two modes, there is the seductive risk of treating the modes of knowing as concepts to be applied in various teaching and learning situations according to their character. In our view, there is little to choose between diversity and singularity with such a notion.

Instead, educators need to focus on experience, in particular, teacher and student narrative unities. In drawing upon, developing, remaking, and introducing narratives, the richness of past experience may be brought forward and credited as teachers' and students' personal knowledge of their teaching and learning situations. Teaching and learning situations need continually to "give back" a learner's narrative experience so that it may be reflected upon, valued, and enriched. We want knowing to come alive in classrooms as the multifaceted, embodied, biographical, and historical experience that it is.

Footnotes

1. Richard McKeon, "Philosophy and Action," *Ethics* 62, no. 2 (1952): 79-100.

2. Clifford Geertz, *The Interpretation of Cultures* (New York: Basic Books, 1973), p. 9.

3. Thomas S. Kuhn, "The Characteristics of Scientific Revolutions" (Paper presented at the University of Toronto, November, 1982).

4. John Dewey, *How We Think* (Boston: D. C. Heath and Co., 1933).

5. Joseph J. Schwab, "Learning Community," in *The Great Ideas Today* (Chicago: Encyclopedia Britannica, 1976).

6. Michael Polanyi, *Personal Knowledge* (Chicago: University of Chicago Press, 1958), p. 59.

7. Percy W. Bridgman, "Prospect for Intelligence," *Yale Review* 34 (March 1945): 32-35.

8. Alfred Schutz and Thomas Luckmann, *The Structures of the Life-world* (Evanston, Ill.: Northwestern University Press, 1973).

9. Stephen Crites, "The Narrative Quality of Experience," *Journal of the American Academy of Religion* 39, no. 3 (1971): 292-311.

10. Stephanie is a grade 1 teacher at Bay Street School, a kindergarten to grade 8 core inner-city school in a large metropolitan area. She has been a participant in an ongoing study of personal practical knowledge since 1981. Accounts of Stephanie and of our concepts of personal practical knowledge are presented in D. Jean Clandinin, "A Conceptualization of Image as a Component of Teacher Personal Practical Knowledge in Primary School Teachers' Reading and Language Programs" (Doctoral dissertation, University of Toronto, 1983); D. Jean Clandinin and F. Michael Connelly, "Personal Practical Knowledge: Image and Narrative Unity" (Paper presented at the ISATT Conference, Tilberg University, The Netherlands, October, 1983); idem, "Teachers' Personal Practical Knowledge: Calendars, Cycles, Habits, and Rhythms" (Paper

presented at the Curriculum Planning Conference, Haifa University, April, 1984); idem, "Personal Practical Knowledge at Bay Street School: Ritual, Personal Philosophy, and Image," in *Teacher Thinking: A New Perspective on Persisting Problems in Education*, ed. A. Rob J. Halkes and John K. Olson (Caisse, Netherlands: Swets and Zeitlinger Publishing Co., 1984), pp. 134-48; F. Michael Connelly and D. Jean Clandinin, "Personal Practical Knowledge: Image and Narrative Unity," Working paper (Toronto: Ontario Institute for the Study of Education, 1983).

11. Narrative unity is a continuum within a person's experience which renders life experiences meaningful through the unity they achieve for the person. What we mean by unity is the union in a particular person in a particular time and place of all that he has been and undergone in the past and in the past of the tradition which helped to shape him. We are informed on this notion by Alasdair C. McIntyre, *After Virtue: A Study in Moral Theory* (London: Gerald Duckworth and Co., 1981).

12. Image is here conceptualized as a kind of knowledge embodied in a person and connected with the individual's past, present, and future. Image draws both the past and the future into a personally meaningful nexus of experience focused on the immediate situation that called it forth. It reaches into the past, gathering up experiential threads meaningfully connected to the present. And it reaches intentionally into the future and creates new meaningfully connected threads as situations are experienced and new situations anticipated from the perspective of the image. Image emerges from the imaginative processes by which meaningful and useful patterns are generated in minded practice. Minded practice involves the emergence of images out of experience so images are then available as guides for the person to make sense of future situations. Many images have a metaphoric quality and as such are close to Lakoff and Johnson's "experiential metaphors." See George Lakoff and Mark Johnson, *Metaphors We Live By* (Chicago: University of Chicago Press, 1980).

13. Clandinin, "A Conceptualization of Image as a Component of Teacher Personal Practical Knowledge"; Clandinin and Connelly, "Teachers' Personal Practical Knowledge."

14. Clifford Geertz, *Local Knowledge: Further Essays in Interpretative Anthropology* (New York: Basic Books, 1983), p. 6.

15. Clandinin and Connelly, "Teachers' Personal Practical Knowledge."

16. We are indebted to Mark Johnson for his insightful suggestions to us that practitioners are, through their practice, both reading their experience as a text and continuing to tell their own story.

17. Personal communication.

CHAPTER XI

Ways of Knowing and Curricular Conceptions: Implications for Program Planning

ELIZABETH VALLANCE

Introduction: Useful and Ornamental Knowledge

A musician and a mathematics teacher, late one night after a rehearsal for a community theater production in which both are involved, have the following conversation. The musician speaks first.

> "Oho, I know what you are. You are an advocate of Useful Knowledge."
>
> "Certainly."
>
> "You say that a man's first job is to earn a living, and that the first task of education is to equip him for that job?"
>
> "Of course."
>
> "Well, allow me to introduce myself to you as an advocate of Ornamental Knowledge. You like the mind to be a neat machine, equipped to work efficiently, if narrowly, and with no extra bits or useless parts. I like the mind to be a dustbin of scraps of brilliant fabric, odd gems, worthless but fascinating curiosities, tinsel, quaint bits of carving, and a reasonable amount of healthy dirt. Shake the machine and it goes out of order; shake the dustbin and it adjusts beautifully to its new position" [1]

A distinction between Useful and Ornamental Knowledge is in many ways familiar to us. It parallels other dichotomies with which school people and the public struggle in setting priorities from the national to the individual school level. It echoes, for example, distinctions between required courses and electives, the basics and "frills," the core curriculum and its complements. These and other formulations attempt to make the necessary distinctions between what needs to be taught in school and what does not. But like most dichotomies imposed on complex subjects, a distinction between

Useful and Ornamental Knowledge is deceptively simple, and the dangers of using it as a basis of choice are many.

It will be helpful to bear in mind, in the course of this discussion, the situation of the two participants in the conversation reported above. The musician is a flamboyant character, church organist and choral director, a private teacher dedicated to music and active in community activities, including now the local production of *The Tempest.* The schoolteacher is passionately dedicated to mathematics and excels at teaching it. His encounter with the musician is, we gather, something of a first for him: his dedication to the useful knowledge of mathematics has been absolute. His role with the theater is that of an accountant.

But is mathematics *only* useful knowledge? And does it function best as an orderly machine? At first glance it would seem so; many in the educational community and among the public would agree. This chapter will turn on the curricular implications of several traditional distinctions available to curriculum planners and on the changes suggested by considering them in light of the foregoing chapters. We shall see that the distinction between the useful and the ornamental is not a clear one, and that there are other choices than those between machines and dustbins. The rich variety of the ways of knowing would help both the musician and the mathematician to see their positions more clearly; certainly the lessons suggested by the multiple ways of knowing can help educators to refine the various distinctions by which they guide the choices they are able to make in planning educational programs.

The Uses of Conceptual Maps in Program Planning

It is customary to attack a curriculum-planning problem by first identifying the choices available within the prevailing conception of "curriculum" guiding the discussion. The conception of curriculum underlying a planning effort may simply be a given. This might be the case, for example, in developing the vocational skills program of a technical school where job placement in trades or industry is the accepted goal: the questions of which skills to teach and at what levels would presume consensus on the more basic questions of the dominant conception of curriculum held by the staff and community. Likewise, most basic questions may have been resolved long ago in a college-preparatory private school where the chief goal is to assure that its graduates are accepted into exclusive liberal arts colleges: the basic questions of the purposes of the school are not regularly open to debate.

Precisely because so much of the deliberation about the curriculum at practical levels can take certain decisions for granted, educators are not accustomed to clarifying the conceptual/philosophical lines along which their curriculum choices should be made. Few educators, after all, have the luxury of building a complete curriculum anew; that educators infrequently question the very bases of their enterprise is thus scarcely surprising. But the infrequency of the activity merely underscores the importance of being able to approach problems freshly when the opportunity does arise. It is in this activity of questioning the prevailing conceptions of curriculum that educators can come closest to making genuine changes in the educational system. For these reasons it is imperative that program planners have a firm and clear grasp both on a full array of choices and on the implications of each.

The choices available to educators are constrained by tradition, and the ways in which we define educational problems to begin with are constrained in the same way. Assumptions—or even conclusions reached after long debate—about what knowledge is of most worth have guided our curricular choices in one way or another for centuries, with school programs developed and reshaped continually along lines of subject matter and academic disciplines. Discussion of curriculum choices may well be colored by other principles (for example, by purposes of the economic betterment of immigrants or by conceptions of the mind as a machine to be refined), but by and large our program planning choices are shaped by an allegiance to the disciplines that was clarified during the Renaissance and has not been seriously challenged in the intervening centuries. The distinctions between college-preparatory and vocational curricula may be described in terms of which areas of knowledge are to be mastered. College "majors" follow strict departmental lines dividing the disciplines; even the exceptions to the strict rule tacitly accept it, offering "inter-disciplinary" majors or "general majors" acknowledged to cover a number of disciplines equally. Graduate and postgraduate studies continue the specialization on the disciplines as content—to be mastered, developed, applied, but always respected as knowledge *of* something. Our conceptions of knowledge, of the educated person, of expertise tend overwhelmingly to be phrased in terms of *what* is known.

Program planning choices phrased chiefly as choices among subject areas are necessary choices; selection from among the whole array of disciplines available within the western cultural tradition must indeed be defended on some grounds consistent with the school's overall purpose. The tradition of building curricula around the disciplines is one with which both educators and the general public are comfortable. Indeed most curriculum reforms refer to modifications of subject matter: adding sex education courses or modifying the subject matter to include creationist views of history are recent examples.

What may not be evident to educational planners is the extent to which an emphasis on content limits our conception of what education can be. Put a slightly different way, it is not always apparent to participants in program planning discussions just how small a subset of educational possibilities the traditional approach to curriculum structure is. Lacking any impetus to ask fundamental questions of purpose and direction, and therefore any immediate need for a conceptual system that might illustrate the broader context of our present choices, it is all too easy for educators to suppose that they are in fact addressing all the alternatives they need to consider. They may suppose that they have a map of an entire city, when in fact their map shows only a single street.

To the array of curricular choices now available, the expanded conception of the varieties of ways of knowing adds an invaluable and enriching new dimension. The extent to which the additional choices provided by this new perspective on knowledge will enhance educators' abilities to develop powerful and creative new programs is not yet known; much will depend on how broadly this conception of knowledge is accepted within the educational community. Much, too, will depend on the research it stimulates and the nature of the refinements of the general concepts offered here. If we can assume that the conceptions of knowledge outlined in this volume will survive the scrutiny of epistemologists, learning researchers, and practitioners and if experience with these ways of knowing demonstrates their power both as research tools in education and as guides to practice, then their implications for program planning could be substantial. The task of this chapter is to demonstrate the probable scope of possibilities admitted by a perspective on human knowing not previously accepted by educational practitioners.

Let us turn, first, to four systems of curriculum thought—four conceptual maps—currently available for program planning purposes and consider how the addition of a fifth one derived from this study of the ways of knowing changes the nature of the choices that can be made. The following discussion does not assume that the four systems of curriculum thought referred to here describe the full array of resources available to us. The systems outlined briefly here are selected chiefly because they approach the problems of practical choices in program planning from four quite different perspectives. As such, they illustrate quite clearly the innovative qualities of the system suggested by the varieties of ways of knowing addressed here.

Some Existing Systems of Curriculum Thought

Four systems of curriculum thought come to mind as models that have shaped the discussions about curriculum for the last decade or so. All four have not been equally useful to the curriculum profession, and it cannot be assumed that any one curriculum planner has systematically attempted to coalesce all four into a single meta-system such as will be suggested here. The point remains, however, that four systems at least are available and, in principle, could be applied in practical settings. The differences among these four systems, and the stunning practical implications of introducing a fifth system, will be the subject of the next few pages.

The chronologically first and surely the most directly influential of these four conceptual maps is Tyler's formulation of the procedures for specifying curriculum content.[2] The "Tyler rationale," enthusiastically embraced by a generation of reformists seeking to codify and streamline the program planning processes, identifies a series of sequenced steps in the curriculum development process. The steps are by now familiar to most educators: specifying of objectives, selecting learning experiences, organizing the experiences according to appropriate principles, and evaluating the extent to which objectives are met. The rationale provides a checklist in a logical progression, and its original complete formulation includes a thoughtful discussion of the issues to be addressed in making decisions at each step along the way.

The Tyler rationale may be treated simplistically and may be used to rationalize some quite superficial curriculum reforms; at its best, and used most responsibly, however, it offers a responsible guide to the procedures of constructing a curriculum. By specifying a cumulative sequence, the Tyler rationale attempts to ensure that each step in program planning is informed by appropriate decisions made at the preceding points.

Equally pervasive in curriculum thought, at least in the journals, is Schwab's conception of the "practical" concerns of curriculum planners and specifically his model of four "commonplaces" of the curriculum.[3] Not in themselves a guide to procedure, the commonplaces identify instead the points around which decisions can be made. Thus, curriculum decisions can be made concerning the subject matter of the curriculum, the teachers, the students, or the milieu in which all coexist; a decision about any one of these commonplaces will affect the other three. The commonplaces describe in general terms the features of any educational terrain, each more or less subject to manipulation by direct intervention; changes in any will color the quality of the others. Thus, for example, any change in subject matter must account for the educational preparation, capabilities, and interests of the students to whom it is addressed—and for teachers' capability of teaching it. Schwab specifies no order in which the commonplaces should be addressed; the model identifies points of change. Where Tyler's model attempts to describe *how* to construct a curriculum, Schwab's commonplaces identify *where* change can take place.

A third model of curriculum thought, commissioned over a decade ago by the National Society for the Study of Education and meeting with rather startling success, is the "conflicting conceptions of curriculum" proposed by Eisner and Vallance.[4] The model addresses neither the procedures of curriculum change nor the points at which it can happen. Rather, it identifies five sets of general *concerns* that may drive a curriculum development effort and shape the decisions it must make. The "conflicting conceptions" are the differing and sometimes mutually exclusive themes underlying much discourse about the chief problems of curriculum work. Four of the conceptions refer to broad purposes of schooling. One body of curriculum writing sees the chief concern of the curriculum as the development of cognitive processes in children, providing cognitive skills that will enable them to attack problems and master material. Another line of thought envisions the school's chief task as that of facilitating the "self-actualization" of children, liberating children to achieve their full potential in intellectual and other realms. A third would use the school deliberately as an agency of social change, a basis for reconstructing society through a curriculum attuned to social problems and current conceptions of "relevance." The "academic rationalist" conception is concerned chiefly with passing on the established traditions of western culture, usually in the form of the established intellectual disciplines. The fifth conception, "curriculum as technology," is less concerned with the specific purposes of schooling than with their efficient management and reflects a line of thought where both the human mind and the educational system are construed in technical terms, subject to ever increasing efficiency and governed by logical application of means to ends. This fifth conception comes closest to the "machine" view that the musician decries in his mathematician colleague; the "academic rationalist" view is the only one offering consistent and specific recommendations on curriculum content. And although the five conceptions are not fully parallel (and are somewhat dated by now), they do identify alternative sets of fundamental concerns held by educators. Ultimately they map out alternative goals of education, distinguishing among sets of assumptions and lines of thought held by different participants in the educational dialogue. (It is interesting to ask where a test of the musician and the mathematician in these terms would take us. It seems evident that the mathematician, in his deification of the orderliness of mathematics, is an academic rationalist; the musician is more problematic, and may be a variant of a "self-actualization" proponent, arguing that the mind be liberated from the constraints of the technological conception.) The conflicting conceptions of curriculum offer, at base, alternative and competing purposes of education from which to select.

The fourth system of curriculum thought addressed here has had a quieter life, but has always struck me as especially helpful in assessing curricular questions. Huebner's essay on "Curricular Language and Classroom Meaning" offers five perspectives from which educational activity can be valued.[5] He calls these "rationales." They are: the *technical* (concerned with the efficient mobilization of resources to meet desired ends), the *political* (concerned with the power relationships developed within an educational system and community), the *scientific* (concerned with understanding educational phenomena), the *aesthetic* (concerned with the symbolic or aesthetic impact of educational phenomena on students), and the *ethical* (the value of the educational activity for the child, and the moral implications of the teacher's responsibility for it). American education, Huebner argues, has typically emphasized the first three to the exclusion of the latter two. For example, most educators and public participants in educational dialogues acknowledge the political content in some current school reform movements (creationism, or school prayer), are much concerned with effective schools and other distillations of the technical rationale, and orient most learning research to a scientific understanding of the educational process. The aesthetic and the ethical implications of curricular change often get lost in the shuffle. In any event, Huebner's five "rationales" provide a system of questions to ask in assessing the value of any educational enterprise; they provide filters through which to *understand* practical action.

What do these four systems of curriculum thought have in common? Each provides the program planner with a number of degrees of freedom in the program planning process. Each identifies the context within which the curriculum planner operates and by identifying a set of alternatives helps the program planner to broaden his or her thinking. Each, if responsibly used, attempts to guarantee that no curriculum choice is made simply by default, for lack of alternatives. Each constitutes a kind of map ensuring that the program planner realizes that the street he or she is walking down today is but one of many possibilities, and as such encourages him or her either to consider the other alternatives or to be prepared to defend the choice in their terms. The conceptual maps available broaden our perspective, stretch the limits of our vision, keep the alternatives alive.

By way of example, consider what some of these maps might reveal about a hypothetical college-preparatory high school curriculum that is organized according to subject-matter divisions and is heavily "academic" (English, science, mathematics), with each subject allotted roughly an hour per day in a schedule structured by bells and lessons guided by textbook chapters. The success of this curriculum will be measured by scores on standardized tests and by acceptance of its graduates by colleges. Applying only some categories from two of the four systems of curriculum thought outlined here, we might be able to say that this curriculum is structured along academic rationalist lines, is technologically efficient and therefore has a high political value in the community, but is aesthetically deadening to both students and teachers. In these terms, it may contrast sharply with another program that is also structured along academic rationalist subject-matter lines but is guided more by a "self-actualizing" concern for an aesthetically rewarding experience to children and, as an experimental program, is tolerated as politically neutral and unthreatening. Even this crude and hypothetical comparison gives an idea of the function of conceptual maps in providing a common language with which to discuss different curricula and a basis on which to compare them. Having even one such "map" or system of curriculum thought meets the need for a language of discourse; the addition of other complementary maps further expands our conception of what is possible in program planning.

These four systems of curriculum thought meet different needs for program planners. They provide different sets of concepts with which to approach a curriculum problem; not all will be appropriate or valuable in every dialogue, and there is a sense in which some are logically prior to others. The identification of which of the four commonplaces is most in need of reform (Schwab), for example, may well precede any considerations of the procedure by which new objectives should be developed (Tyler). An application of Huebner's five "rationales" could initiate a curriculum reform effort by identifying dimensions on which the present curriculum is weak, or the rationales might be brought to bear afterward, as a set of judgments to be made as part of the evaluation process. A consideration of the different "conflicting conceptions of curriculum" operating in a debate over curriculum priorities (Eisner and Vallance) may not be necessary if the participants hold a shared conception of the major concerns of the curriculum, but a taking-stock in terms of that model might be advisable midway through an application of Tyler's sequence for program development to resolve a dispute over content. Conceivably any given curriculum problem could be addressed using only one of the conceptual maps described here; a leisurely and well-staffed curriculum development project might have the luxury of considering all four in some appropriate order. In either case, the conceptual map serves the simple but important purpose of pinning down at least one set of possible choices and ensuring that the alternatives are available for consideration. A good conceptual map is liberating.

In short, conceptual maps or systems of curriculum thought, when applied by program planners in practical situations, expand the options for the curriculum by defining them in general terms. Any one system does this much by itself. The adoption of more than one enlarges the program planner's scope proportionately. The urgency of an immediate crisis, the pressures of time, or the lack of resources may dictate that the whole map cannot be explored and that the program must be developed quickly according to unexamined standard conceptions. Ideally, however, the curriculum planner can gradually acquire a repertoire of conceptual systems that can guide and shape curricular thinking in a variety of settings and contexts. The richest of these repertoires will stimulate the program planner to ask questions from as many different perspectives as possible before selecting the one that seems wisest.

Before examining the fifth conceptual map provided by a consideration of the multiple ways of knowing, let us risk a bit of metatheorizing to identify the kinds of perspectives that the four fairly standard approaches to curriculum problems offer to the task of program planning. I will address this question only briefly, but the exercise will prove to be important for identifying gaps in our present lines of thinking about curriculum matters and, as such, will indicate the special contribution of this fifth conceptual map.

It is possible, for example, to argue that the four conceptual maps collectively offer two distinct kinds of assistance. One category includes those systems of curriculum thought that identify the areas to be addressed in the process of curriculum development. Schwab tells us to pay attention to subject-matter, teachers, students, and milieu, and Tyler provides a checklist of procedures to be addressed as we make changes in the curriculum (specify the objectives, identify learning experiences appropriate to them, arrange these appropriately, and evaluate the results). These two "process" maps function exactly as maps. They remind us of where we are and of what still needs to be considered before we can reach our final destination of a complete new curriculum. The contrasting category would embrace those systems of curriculum thought that themselves identify curricular options or provide criteria for assessing the appropriateness of curriculum content.

The perspectives charted by Eisner and Vallance identify some available biases in curriculum purpose and content (social reconstructionism, for example); Huebner's five "rationales" outline languages available to be used in arguing a curriculum to some public, and thereby provide bases on which to judge particular curricula. Thus, if we were to dichtomize the four conceptual maps sketched above, we would find a contrast between systems that somewhat abstractly identify things to think about in doing curriculum development (*process-oriented* systems) and those with *normative commitments* prescribing content areas and bases for evaluation. Collectively they help us to conceive of curriculum change and what it might include. None of the four, however, addresses curricular goals in terms not reducible to content mastery; none identifies or argues for a way of knowing that differs substantially from our traditional conception of knowledge as logical, linear, and scientifically guidable.

Alternatively, we can argue that the four curriculum maps serve three general purposes: (a) Huebner serves as a kind of critic and interpreter of the persuasive tools available to curriculum discourse, (b) the conceptions outlined by Eisner and Vallance themselves constitute schools of persuasion, arguments for curriculum content based on traditional conceptions of human knowledge or on critiques of social need, and (c) Tyler and Schwab both attempt to provide systems of curricular thought that are value-neutral techniques of curriculum development. The three basic approaches to understanding curriculum change—critique, persuasion, or technique—collectively ensure that our curriculum development is thorough, sensitive, methodical, and defensible against most critics. They ensure that our eyes remain open to the many kinds of questions appropriate to practical program planning. But the questions they illuminate still pertain chiefly to knowledge that is organized comfortably into subject-matter areas and taught with the assumption that sequential mastery of cognitive information is what education must be.

It is in this context, of course, that the notion of multiple ways of knowing assumes a special importance for curriculum planners. The notion that human knowing takes many forms introduces a fifth kind of curriculum map that cannot be understood in the same terms as the other four. It does not fit the deceptively neat dichotomy attempted above. For example, it neither prescribes areas of curriculum content nor provides procedures guaranteeing that the standard content options are considered. And it falls somewhere outside the three configurations argued above: it is not a system of critique, it is not a set of arguments attempting to persuade about specific curriculum content, and it is surely not a value-neutral technical system of rules. Like the system created by Eisner and Vallance, it attempts to identify some of the options available to the practitioner, but unlike that system the curricular implications of any one of the options are not clear: while "social reconstructionism" may have clear implications for the role of social studies in the school curriculum, it is hard to see what specific curricular implications arise from the concept of formal modes of knowing, or even scientific or aesthetic modes. The modes of knowing are not tied to conventional subject-matter divisions. As such, their relevance for program planning takes a new form.

The notion of multiple ways of knowing introduces a fifth perspective on practical curriculum questions. The remainder of this chapter shows how this is so and suggests the unique kinds of questions that this perspective poses for practical program-planning work.

The Ways of Knowing as a System of Curriculum Thought

To acknowledge that there is a variety of kinds of human intelligence, and that the various ways of knowing may all be equally valuable to the development of human potential, is to accept an entirely new realm of possible curricular choices. In effect, the variety of ways of knowing constitutes a new system of curriculum thought. A diligent curriculum planner attempting to integrate all four of the systems outlined above might adopt the multifaceted conception of human intelligence as a fifth system, a fifth set of questions to ask in attacking a curriculum development problem. More important, however, is that a multifaceted conception of the modes of knowing introduces questions quite unlike any others that are traditionally asked in educational planning. Thus, the practical implications of this new conception for program planning purposes will be evident on two levels: it complements the curriculum maps already available to both theorists and practitioners, but more basically it challenges the assumptions on which all other systems of curriculum thought are based. At the very least, it demands that the questions we ask in coming to curricular decisions be enlarged; at the extreme it demands that they be reformulated.

Thus, on one level we already know that we can address at least four questions in the process of program planning: what can be changed, what are our major purposes in working toward educational change, how do we go about it, and in what terms can we best understand the implications of what we have wrought? (Schwab, Eisner and Vallance, Tyler, and Huebner, respectively). To these four questions we can now add a fifth: in which mode(s) of knowing have our children been educated up to now, and which should the curriculum foster? The notion that there are many ways of knowing and that schooling has traditionally excluded whole realms of intellectual development is immensely disturbing. It is also disturbing that our conceptions of curriculum thought have deliberately fostered this omission by being themselves based on a single limited conception of knowledge. Given that the ways of knowing outlined here are an appropriate demarcation of the vast realm of human intelligence, the relevance of these insights for program planning is clear in several areas.

Without examining the impact of this new perspective on every item within each of the four curriculum models mentioned here, some examples may suffice to illustrate how a multifaceted conception of knowledge can modify the questions each model may raise in program planning. Consider, for example, the academic rationalist perspective in the Eisner and Vallance model. Typically the academic rationalist approach to curriculum development is to weigh systematically areas of knowledge against the prevailing culture to identify "what knowledge is of most worth." The question of "worth" may be considered in its own terms; that is, a discipline may be valued and included in the curriculum because it is and always has been central to the progression of the western intellectual tradition. Therefore some form of mathematics is required in all school systems in the country. Mathematics is valued for its own sake as an established discipline; it is also valued these days as a necessary skill. In the conversation reported at the beginning of this chapter the musician and the mathematics teacher agree that it is Useful Knowledge, practical and orderly. In fact, the teacher uses it in his theater work. But if we admit that there may be many ways of knowing, we are forced to ask either of two questions about mathematics: (a) Which of the many ways of knowing are embodied in mathematics (and which of them can a mathematics teacher reasonably be expected to "teach")? or (b) Given the modes of knowing that we wish to foster in our curriculum, what will be the role of mathematics? The two questions are quite different. The first allows us to retain a subject-matter division of the curriculum and challenges us to identify new qualities within it; the premise of the second defines ways of knowing as the guiding concern, with mathematics admitted as a possible medium for teaching them. The ways-of-knowing paradigm therefore allows new rationales for traditional subjects while also admitting the possibility that traditional subjects might be modified to accommodate educational goals defined in a wholly new way.

The impact of the ways of knowing on Schwab's commonplaces also forces us to ask additional questions about each of the four commonplaces. For example, in considering changes in teachers, a program planner must be sensitive not only to the teacher's influence on the subject matter, students, and milieu but also to the teacher's capacity for accommodating a broader perspective on human cognition. What must a teacher know in order to address responsibly the development of aesthetic knowing in the course of teaching a standard literature survey course? How can Hector, the mathematics teacher, incorporate his spiritual knowledge of his subject matter in a mathematics lesson so that that knowledge is accessible to students (and should he)? What does a teacher need to know in order to address formal modes of knowing in an art class? Or, looking at the commonplace of "milieu," can an aesthetic way of knowing really be fostered in a milieu characterized by rigid hourly schedules, loud bells, a curriculum chopped into subject matters arbitrarily arranged?

An admission of multiple ways of knowing also enriches the questions that can be asked in any of Huebner's five rationales. From the point of view of the ethical value of a curriculum, for example, can we be sure of the ethical coherence of a curriculum that ignores *any* of the many ways of knowing and deprives any child of the power of intelligence? What political messages are conveyed by a curriculum that limits some children to a single cognitive mode, providing access to multiple modes only to children deemed "gifted"? How does the development of interpersonal or intuitive modes of knowing enhance the ethical values of a curriculum?

The concept of multiple modes of knowing forces us to ask of Tyler's orderly sequence of curriculum development whether the formal and practical knowledge applied in that process is appropriate for developing programs where the goal is to foster intuitive or aesthetic knowing. Is the Tyler rationale itself so fully a product of one or two specific modes of knowing that it must retire, or be greatly changed, in order to be responsive to the curricular demands of this new perspective?

The questions that a multifaceted conception of cognition raises for the curriculum maps now available to us are many more than those examples cited above, and it is not our purpose here to address them in detail. It is our intention, however, to argue that one of the most important implications of this new perspective for program planning is precisely that it changes the nature of the questions we fruitfully can ask. It does add a fifth system of curriculum thought to at least the four cited here. But more than simply adding another set of categories to consider, it changes the quality of the categories which we have traditionally used in making our curricular choices. It fundamentally alters the way curriculum problems are understood.

This change is critical. Both theorists and practitioners have traditionally been bound by the strong subject-matter bias that has colored western educational thought for centuries. More or less directly, and with more or less attention to its limitations, educators have embraced the notion that building a curriculum is chiefly a question of building a responsible structure of lessons to enable students to master content. Indeed, even those educators concerned less directly with content areas and more with the generalized skills of values clarification, discovery, or other processes have tacitly accepted the predominance of formal cognitive ways of knowing. The conceptual maps heretofore available to educators have not made alternative approaches to curriculum planning possible. It is feasible now at least to conceive of a curriculum organized not by subject-matter divisions at all, for example, but according to the various modes of knowing deemed important to the culture. Taking this notion to an absurd extreme for the sake of illustration, students might move from "Formal Reasoning" in first period to "Aesthetic Modes of Knowing" just before lunch, and so on, with each period integrating content from various disciplines; college majors eventually would be identified not by subject-matter department but by the mode of knowing in which students choose to specialize. While this quick example roundly violates the subtlety that this fifth perspective argues eloquently for, it does illustrate the jolt of change that the perspective might encourage. To acknowledge that human knowing takes many forms must also be to acknowledge that the organization of the curricula by which we hope to teach children may be subject to substantial change. That change cannot come about, however, unless curriculum planners are able to change their own approaches to the questions of what is knowable and how knowing can be taught.

It remains to venture some suggestions as to what specific questions we might ask of schooling, or of any given curriculum, under this revised perspective on the varieties of modes of knowing. Quite aside from how this perspective will influence the questions asked under each of several existing systems of curriculum thought, the issue suggests some larger questions that may be independent of any particular conception of the curriculum. Granting that the nature of the general questions is at present still conjectural, as we know little about how directly this line of thought will actually affect practitioners, it is nonetheless intriguing to wonder what sets of questions might ultimately displace the question of "What knowledge is of most worth?" Some possibilities come readily to mind:

1. Given that there are at least seven ways of knowing, which of them are appropriately to be addressed by schooling and which can be left to other realms of socialization? Should the curriculum attempt to account for all the ways of knowing available to us?

2. For those modes of knowing that can or should be addressed in the school curriculum, is there a hierarchy of importance? Are some to be considered "required" and others not? Would the verdict be the same for all students?

3. Do the different ways of knowing develop best at different times in a person's life? If so, how should the sequence of the curriculum accommodate these stages in order to maximize each student's access to the full array of modes of knowing?

4. Do some traditional subject areas provide better access to some modes of knowing than to others? If so, how can this knowledge guide

our selection of curriculum content? (Example: We assume that aesthetic modes of knowing may be taught through art, but *is* art the best channel to aesthetic knowing? And might art classes also teach formal modes of knowing quite well?)

5. Might the modes of knowing themselves be an appropriate basis on which to structure the curriculum, gradually coming to replace the traditional divisions along subject-matter lines?

6. In what terms are the goals of schooling most usefully phrased? Should mastery of a variety of ways of knowing be an explicit goal of a curriculum, or can this end remain tacit, secondary to other more measurable goals?

7. At what point in a student's career should he or she be encouraged to specialize in one or more ways of knowing, and what would be the curriculum-content implications of the decision?

8. What background do teachers, curriculum developers, and educational administrators need in order to foster a curriculum that encourages mastery of a wide variety of ways of knowing?

9. By what signs or indicators will educators know that a curriculum has been successful in teaching the various modes of knowing?

10. What curriculum materials and experiences are best suited to fostering a command of a wide variety of modes of knowing? Do textbooks by definition favor one mode over others? Do some modes of knowing demand more active involvement in creating, solving problems, or analysis than others?

Many such questions must be addressed before the full range of implications of multiple modes of knowing can be understood. Clearly the most fundamental implication is simply that the prevailing conceptions of the major issues facing program developers must shift if a variety of modes of knowing is to be accommodated. The questions that have prevailed in the curriculum area for the last three decades are predicated largely on an academic-rationalist and technological conception of the curriculum, on a sensitivity to the technical, scientific, and political implications of educational change, and on a logical, linear conception of knowledge. Curricular decisions to intervene in any of the commonplaces with any systematic approach to change have largely left those assumptions intact. The varieties of modes of knowing familiar to philosophers, historians of science, aestheticians, and others have not heretofore reached educators in a practical or meaningful way. But the possibilities for reorienting our ways of thinking about curriculum problems are vastly expanded with this exciting new perspective. It remains for further research to aid educators in understanding exactly what the responsible moves might be, and for practitioners to begin examining the alternatives in the new light that this "fifth" system of curriculum thought now allows.

Is the distinction between useful knowledge and ornamental knowledge a valid one? Perhaps, but the foregoing chapters surely suggest that the traditional tendency to divide knowledge into dichotomies is questionable, and that what has typically been considered merely ornamental may have a value much greater than that label might suggest. Conceivably what is useful to one person may be merely ornamental to another, and vice versa, and it may be that in some fundamental sense *no* human knowledge is strictly ornamental. That possibility is a humbling one, for it demands of program planners that they discover some means of abolishing many standard dichotomies and of ensuring, through all the political and ethical messages a curriculum may convey to its public, that no student by virtue of his or her program of study is becoming more "useful" than any other. If the multiple perspectives on ways of knowing teach us nothing more as educators, they should teach us that the values and priorities and biases created by the modes of knowing that have shaped the education profession itself are now open to reexamination.

As to the distinction between the machine and the dustbin, through all this it still remains a compelling metaphor. Ultimately it is not the same as the distinction between useful and ornamental knowledge, as the musician suggests, for the latter refers chiefly to kinds of knowledge rather than to its uses. We may grant that a distinction between knowledge that is useful and knowledge that is not may one day disappear. It is less likely that the distinction between the machine and the dustbin will become irrelevant, for we must assume that there will always be plodders and dreamers, those comfortable with the straight and narrow path of predictability and those adventurers tantalized by the unexpected bits of glitter and disorder. Yet if educators do not seek to shape children into predictable "neat machines," neither do they aim for the uncontrolled disorder of "worthless but fascinating curiosities." Some mixtures of the two may be necessary. What will be important to remember is that mathematics is not only a machine: Hector finds it beautiful and even spiritual. And surely art, the area most often associated with the development of creativity and more likely to foster a delight in "odd gems," can be as mechanical and devoid of aesthetic knowlege as any subject. The distinction between the neat machine and the dustbin, then, may serve as a reminder and as a hope: a reminder that knowledge is more varied and more diverse than that, and a hope that knowing the variety of ways of knowing may help the education profession to find the points along a continuum between the two.

References

1. Robertson Davies, *Tempest-Tost* (New York: Penguin Books, 1980), p. 182.

2. Ralph W. Tyler, *Basic Principles of Curriculum and Instruction* (Chicago: University of Chicago Press, 1950).

3. Joseph Schwab, "The Practical: A Language for Curriculum," *School Review* 78 (November 1969): 1-23.

4. Elliot Eisner and Elizabeth Vallance, eds., *Conflicting Conceptions of Curriculum* (Berkeley, Calif.: McCutchan Publishing Corp., 1974).

5. Dwayne Huebner, "Curricular Language and Classroom Meaning," in *Language and Meaning*, ed. James B. Macdonald and Robert S. Leeper (Washington, D.C.: Association for Supervision and Curriculum Development, 1966).

CHAPTER XII

Mind as a Cultural Achievement: Implications for IQ Testing

MICHAEL COLE

For almost as long as there have been IQ tests, there have been psychologists who believe that it is possible to construct "culture free" tests. The desire for such tests springs directly out of the purposes for which tests of general intellectual ability were constructed in the first place: to provide a valid, objective, and socially unbiased measure of individual ability. Our society, founded upon the principle that all men are created equal, has never lived easily with the recognition of enormous *de facto* social inequality. We need a rationale for such inequality and our traditions strongly bias us to seek the causes of inequality, in properties of the individual, not society. At the same time, we realize that social and economic inequality can be the causes of individual intellectual inequalities, as well as their consequences.

What would be more ideal, then, than a psychological test that could measure intellectual potential that is based equally on the experience of people from all cultures. Can't we find universals in human experience and construct a test on this basis? Some psychologists have claimed not only that such tests are possible in principle, but have been applied in practice.[1]

In this chapter I will argue that culture-free intelligence is a contradiction in terms. After working through a "thought experiment" to help clarify the issues, I will turn to some implications for teaching

This chapter is an expanded version of an article that appeared in the *Annual Report (1979-1980)* of the Research and Clinical Center for Child Development, Faculty of Education, Hokkaido University, Sapporo, Japan.

of the view that mental development is always a culturally organized process that can produce great heterogeneity in specific mental skills by the time children reach school. This heterogeneity can cause great difficulties for the classroom teacher. In the final section I will note some promising leads that teachers may use in dealing with culturally organized heterogeneity in their classrooms.

Having made these assertions, I want to provide the evidence upon which they are based. My own personal strategy for thinking about these matters is to think my way back in time into the nineteenth century, when such devices came into existence. I have found it helpful to study the conditions in science and society that allowed some scholars to believe it is possible to assess mind independent of culturally organized experience. To begin, I will review some of that history, emphasizing the logic of the enterprise. I am focusing on an *anthropological* perspective on testing, but it should become clear that anthropology and psychology have always been linked in shaping our understanding of the relation between experience and mind, even when this link is obscured by divergent methods and theories.

The several decades just preceding this century provide a useful starting point from which to trace theories of culture and cognitive development, because it was during this period that both anthropology and psychology took shape as disciplines. Before that time, say the 1860s, there was no distinctive body of methods for the study of the "humane sciences," nor had scholars with different theories been institutionally divided into separate disciplines the way they are today. Obvious differences in technological achievement between peoples living in different parts of the world were common knowledge. Theorizing about sources of these differences had produced rather general acceptance of the notion that it would be possible to study the history of humanity by a study of contemporary peoples at different "levels of progress." E. B. Tylor summarizes, in what he calls "mythic fashion," the general course of culture that most of his fellow scholars would have adhered to:

> We may fancy ourselves looking on Civilization, as in personal figure she traverses the world; we see her lingering or resting by the way, and often deviating into paths that bring her toiling back to where she had passed by long ago; but direct or devious, her path lies forward, and if now and then she tries a few backward steps, her walk soon falls into a helpless stumbling. It is

not according to her nature, her feet were not made to plant uncertain steps behind her, for both in her forward view and in her onward gait she is of truly human type.[2]

Tylor's choice of imagery for "Civilization" nicely reveals another basic assumption which he and many of his colleagues made: there is no principled distinction between mind and society. The condition of culture among the various societies of mankind, Tylor tells us, reveals basic information about the laws of human thought. He even adopted the notion of a "mental culture," which he expected to be high or low depending upon the other conditions of culture with which it was associated.

Herbert Spencer, writing at about the same time, shared Tylor's belief in the fusion of mental and cultural phenomena. He also drew a very tight analogy between cultural development on the one hand and mental development on the other.

During early stages of human progress, the circumstances under which wandering families and small aggregations of families live furnish experiences comparatively limited in their numbers and kinds; and consequently there can be no considerable exercise of faculties which take cognizance of the *general truths* displayed throughout many special truths.[3]

Spencer invites us to consider the most extreme case; suppose that only one experience were repeated over and over again, such that this single event comprised all of the person's experiences. In this case, as Spencer put it, "the power of representation is limited to reproduction of this experience" in the mind. There isn't anything else to think *about*! Next we can imagine that life consists of two experiences, thus allowing at least elementary comparison. Three experiences add to the elementary comparisons, and elementary generalizations that we make on the basis of our limited (three) experiences. We can keep adding experience to our hypothetical culture until we arrive at the rich variety of experiences that characterizes our lives. It follows from this line of reasoning that generalizations, the "general truths" attainable by people, will be more numerous and more powerful the greater one's experience. Since cultures provide experience, and some cultures (Spencer claimed) provide a greater diversity of experience than others, a neat bond between cultural progress and mental progress is cemented.

Although such evolutionary schemes seemed almost transparently obvious in the enthusiasm following publication of Darwin's *Origin of Species*, events toward the close of the nineteenth century proved that there could be a great deal of disagreement about the relation between culture and thought, despite the compelling story constructed by people like Tylor and Spencer. One set of disagreements arose when scholars started to examine more closely the data used to support conclusions about relations between cultures, especially claims for historical or evolutionary sequences. Quite a different set of arguments arose around conflicting claims about mental processes.

The seed of disagreements concerning cultural sequences can be found in Tylor's own work. The main criteria for judging the stage of a culture were the sophistication of industrial arts (including manufacturing techniques for metal tools, agricultural practices) and "the extent of scientific knowledge, the definitions of moral principles, the conditions of religious belief and ceremony, the degree of social and political organization, and so forth."[4] However, in Tylor's words, "If not only knowledge and art, but at the same time moral and political excellence, be taken into consideration" it becomes more difficult to scale societies from lower to higher stages of culture.

This latter theme in Tylor's work was taken up by Franz Boas, who submitted the cultural evolution position to a devastating critique at the close of the nineteenth century. On the basis of his own ethnographic work, Boas concluded that a great deal of the evidence apparently supportive of evolutionary schemes was so deeply flawed that no clear conclusions ranking one culture above another could be accepted.[5] Boas did more than show the flaws in evolutionists' data and arguments concerning *culture*; he also delighted in showing that examples of "primitive mind" produced as part of this argument were based on misunderstandings.

Consider the following example from Boas's classic, *The Mind of Primitive Man,* which repeats evidence used by Spencer to make some generalizations about properties of primitive mind:

> In his description of the natives of the west coast of Vancouver Island, Sproat says, "The native mind, to an educated man, seems generally to be asleep. . . .

On his attention being fully aroused, he often shows much quickness in reply and ingenuity in argument. But a short conversation wearies him, particularly if questions are asked that require efforts of thought or memory on his part. The mind of the savage then appears to rock to and fro out of mere weakness."[6]

Spencer's text goes on to cite a number of similar anecdotes corroborating this point. But Boas produces an anecdote of his own.

> I happen to know through personal contact the tribes mentioned by Sproat. The questions put by the traveller seem mostly trifling to the Indian, and he naturally soon tires of a conversation carried on in a foreign language, and one in which he finds nothing to interest him. As a matter of fact, the interest of these natives can easily be raised to a high pitch, and I have often been the one who was wearied out first. Neither does the management of their intricate system of exchange prove mental inertness in matters which concern them. Without mnemonic aids to speak of, they plan the systematic distribution of their property in such a manner as to increase their wealth and social position. These plans require great foresight and constant application.[7]

Thus, Boas tells us that the entire scheme was wrong. Cultures cannot be ranked using evolutionary age as a basis for comparison, and "mind" cannot be seen as rank in developmental age. (Boas also demonstrates the total hopelessness of deducing cultural differences from any differences, real or imagined, in genetic makeup.)

Finally, and very importantly, Boas was a leader in a subtle, but essential change in anthropological thinking about the concept of culture itself. Educated in Germany, Boas had begun his career imbued with the romantic concept of "Kultur," the expression of the highest attainments of human experience, as expressed in the arts, music, literature, and science. This is the conception of culture that allowed Tylor to talk about "the conditions of culture among various societies." Tylor, like Boas as a young man, conceived of culture as something groups and individuals had more or less of. It was a singular noun: one talked of higher or lower *culture*, not more or fewer *cultures*. By the same route that led him to deny the basis for ranking cultures in terms of a hypothetical, evolutionary sequence, Boas arrived at the idea that different societies create different "designs for living," each representing a uniquely adapted fit between their past and their present circumstances in the world. This point of view is central to anthropology, and it clearly has to be taken into account if we want to rank the intellectual achievements (levels of mental development) of people growing up with different cultural experiences. It renders simple more/less comparisons of cultures difficult and restricted, with parallel effects on our inferences about mind.

Enter Psychology

As we entered the twentieth century, anthropology was still pursuing its goal of reconstructing the history of mankind by studying cultures in different parts of the world. But that goal was now blocked by serious methodological problems (such as those raised by Boas) that needed to be settled before further theoretical progress could be made.

The birth of psychology is usually dated back to 1879, when Wilhelm Wundt officially opened an experimental laboratory in Leipzig. The exact date is not important, because several laboratories opened almost simultaneously in different industrialized countries. But the *reasons* for these laboratory openings are very important indeed.

Boas's critique of developmental theories, whether of mind or culture, produced controversy in both domains of inquiry. Boas earned the enmity of anthropologists who believed his criticisms of their general theories unjust; they sought to rescue the more general theories, criticizing Boas and his students for "historical particularism" (to use Harris's apt phrase). While new competitors for an overall approach to understanding historical links between cultures became a central activity for the new discipline of anthropology, psychologists were people who took up the other half of Boas's critique, problems of specifying mental mechanisms.

The major difficulty facing those who became psychologists was to devise methods for specifying pretty exactly what sorts of activity an individual engages in at those times we want to make claims that some sort of "thinking" is going on. No one could be very precise about what was meant when psychologists referred to a mental process. Competing claims were evaluated by constructing settings to control as exactly as possible the kinds of events a person experienced and to record the kinds of responses these experiences evoked. Since the presumed processes were not observable (they were, as we say, "psychological"), psychologists spent a great deal of time and ingenuity devising ways to pin down what these nonobservable processes might be. The rapidly growing ability to control electricity and to build precision machinery was exploited to the fullest; the early psychology laboratories were marvels of inventions. Their instruments allowed psychologists to present people carefully controlled lights and tones for carefully controlled intervals and to measure precisely the time it took to respond. In their search for ways to make mind observable, they used electrophysiological devices to record internal, organic functioning. The discipline of "psychophysics" advanced appreciably in its quest to relate psychological phenomena of an elementary order (discriminating tones, judging hues). There were even hopes of uncovering a "cognitive algebra" by carefully comparing reaction times to stimuli of various complexities arranged to reveal steps in the thought process.

The activities of the psychologist and the anthropologist soon contrasted very dramatically. The psychologist brought people into the laboratory where behavior could be constrained, stimuli controlled, and mind made visible. The anthropologist wandered the world talking to people, observing their customary behavior, and seeking clues about the factors that made one design for living different from another.

Whereas the anthropologists continued to concentrate on gathering data that would permit firm statements about historical relations between cultures, scholars who came to identify themselves as psychologists concentrated on resolving arguments about thinking such as those illustrated in the passage quoted from Boas. Just as anthropology evolved careful field techniques to disambiguate competing claims about "culture," psychologists developed the laboratory experiment as a way to test competing claims about "mind."

There occurred, in effect, a division of labor in the "humane sciences," a division that was primarily a matter of scientific strategy in the beginning: progress required some concentrated work on specialized subtopics. The overall task remained the same for everyone: how do human beings come to be the way they are?

Enter Testing

Despite an increasing gulf between scholars who called themselves psychologists and those who called themselves anthropologists, it was not long before these two areas of inquiry were brought together again. At the end of the nineteenth century, Francis Galton, in

England, set out to test hypotheses about mental differences among people, using the newly devised psychological techniques. His concern was not differences between people growing up in different cultures. Rather, he studied people growing up in different families. He sought the inherited sources of variability in mental abilities. Significantly, his tests were theoretically motived; he believed that speed of mental processing was central to intelligence so he created tests of rapid processing of elementary signals. Galton succeeded in finding differences among Englishmen on such tests as simple reaction time to a pure tone, but he did not succeed in relating these "psychological test" differences to human characteristics of greater interest to him such as scientific excellence or musical ability. Galton's tests, based on an oversimplified model of the human mind and the highly controlled procedures adopted from the laboratory appropriate to testing his theory, were not taken up by society. However, in creating an early precursor of existing IQ tests, Galton did begin the development of the statistical techniques that would be necessary to show how test differences correlate with interesting behavioral differences.

The difficulties that Galton encountered in trying to demonstrate that he was testing abilities of general significance were a direct stimulus to the development of that branch of applied mathematics known as statistics, upon which current testing technology relies so heavily. The fact that these difficulties have not been resolved, despite great progress in the technology for evaluating the theory, is a key problem that remains to be dealt with.

Galton did all of his work in England, but other Englishmen, including W. H. R. Rivers, travelled to the Torres Strait northeast of Australia, to see if psychological tests could be used to settle disputes over cultural differences in cognition. Rivers was in some senses an antique. He was both anthropologist and psychologist, which meant that he considered both the evidence of his tests and evidence provided by observation of the people he went to study when he made statements about culture and thought. His conclusions were consistent with Galton's data on individual differences; natives differed from each other on such simple tasks as their ability to detect a gap in a line, or their recognition of colors. But there were no impressive differences between the natives of the Torres Strait and Englishmen.

It would appear on the basis of this evidence that there are no cultural differences in thinking, at least no differences consistent with what we had been led to believe by Tylor, Spencer, and many others. However, it could be (and was) argued, that the *important* ways in which cultural differences cause mental differences were not even tested by Rivers and his associates. After all, Galton had found no relation between responses to his psychological tests and other presumed indicators of intelligence. Why would anyone, then, expect cultural differences? Perhaps the experiments, limited as they were to *elementary* psychological processes, simply failed to implicate *higher psychological processes* at all. What we needed were tests of higher psychological processes that could be used to compare people from different cultures or different people in the same culture.

This distinction between elementary and higher processes pinpoints a weakness in the basic foundations of experimental psychology, a weakness acknowledged by Wundt, its founder. It is impossible, Wundt believed, to study *higher* psychological functions in experiments because it is impossible to construct appropriately controlled environments of the needed complexity. Wundt believed that scientists should use *ethnological* evidence and folklore if they want to discover the properties of the mind that get constructed on the basis of the elementary processes that he studied in the laboratory.

Wundt's doubts about the experimental method have not been accepted in psychology, but they are very germane to understanding problems with cross-cultural developmental research, as we shall see. These doubts were not accepted because they put psychologists in a very difficult bind. Psychology had been founded on the principle that without carefully controlled environments, it is not legitimate to make statements about how the mind works. But a great many of the questions about how the mind works that interested psychologists and anthropologists alike clearly refer to "higher" psychological processes such as logical reasoning and inference. When Wundt gave up on the idea that such processes could be studied in the laboratory, he was, it seemed, robbing psychology of most of its interesting subject matter. For psychologists, the inability to study higher psychological processes in the laboratory meant that they could not be studied at all. Rejecting this conclusion, many psychologists were attracted to theories claiming that complex processes are compounded of simple ones. The basic task was to understand the elements, before tackling the compound. Relatively simple experimental models thrived, but complex behavior was rarely dealt with.

Binet's Strategy

The major push for research on more complex human problem solving came from a source seemingly outside the scientific community, although respected psychologists were involved. Early in this century, Alfred Binet was asked to deal with a practical, social problem. With the growth of public education in France, there was a growing problem of school failure, or at least severe school underachievement. It seemed not only that some children learned more slowly than others, but that some children, who otherwise appeared perfectly normal, did not seem to benefit much from instruction at all. Binet and his colleagues were asked to see if they could find a way to identify slow-learning children at an early stage in their education. If such identification were possible, special education could be provided them, and the remaining children could be more efficiently taught.

The subsequent history of IQ testing has been described too frequently to bear repetition here, but a sketch of the basic strategy of research is necessary as background to understand just how deeply IQ tests are embedded in cultural experience.

To begin with, early test makers had to decide what to test for. The decision seemed straightforward. They wanted to test people's ability to perform the kinds of tasks that are required by schools. They observed classrooms, looked at textbooks, talked to teachers, and used their intuitions to arrive at some idea of the many different kinds of knowledge and skills that children are eventually expected to master in school.

What Binet and his colleagues found was not easy to describe briefly, as anyone who has looked into a classroom can quickly testify (and all of us have done so, or we would not be reading these words). There was a very obvious need to understand graphic symbols, such as alphabets and number systems. So recognition of these symbols was tested. But mastery of the rudiments of these symbols was not enough. Children were also expected to manipulate these symbols to store and retrieve vast amounts of information, to rearrange this information according to the demands of the moment, and to use the information to solve a great variety of problems that had never arisen before in the experience of the individual pupil. Thus, children's abilities to remember and carry out sequences of movements, to define words, to construct plausible event sequences from jumbled picture sequences, and to recognize the missing element in graphic designs were tested (along with many other components of school-based problems).

It was also obvious that to master more and more esoteric applications of the basic knowledge contained in alpha-numeric writing systems, pupils had to learn to master their own behavior. They had not only to engage in a variety of "mental activities" directed at processing information; they also had to gain control over their own attention, applying it not according to the whim of the moment, but according to the whim of the teacher and the demands of the text.

It was clearly impossible to arrive at a single sample of all the kinds of thinking required by "the" school. Not only was there too much going on in any one classroom to make this feasible; it was equally clear that the school required different abilities from children of different ages. Binet realized that estimates of "basic aptitude" for this range of material would depend upon how much the child had learned about the specific content before he or she arrived at school, but he felt knowing a child's current abilities would be useful to teachers anyway.

In the face of these difficulties, Binet decided to construct a sample of school-like tasks appropriate for each year of education, starting with the elementary grades, and reaching into higher levels of the curriculum. He would have liked to sample so that all essential activities were included in his test and that tasks at one level of difficulty would be stepping stones to tasks at the next higher level. But because no firmly based theory of higher psychological functions existed, Binet had to rely on a combination of his own common sense and a logical analysis of tasks that different classrooms seem to require (for example, you have to be able to remember three random digits before you can remember four; you have to know the alphabet before you can read). He also hit on the handy strategy of letting the children themselves tell him when an item selected for the test was appropriate. Beginning with a large set of possible test questions, Binet hunted for items that half the children at a given age level could solve. An "average" child would then be one who solved problems appropriate to his or her age level. Keeping items that discriminated between children of different ages (as well as items that seemed to sample the activities demanded of kids in their classrooms), he arrived, with help from his colleagues, at the first important prototype of the modern IQ test.

Of course a great deal of work has gone into the construction of tests since Binet's early efforts, but the underlying logic has remained pretty much the same: sample the kinds of activities demanded by the culture (in the form of the problems it requires that its children master in school) and compare children's performance to see how many of these activities they have mastered. Children who have mastered far less than we would expect given a comparable sample of kids their own age are those who will need extra help if they are to reach the level expected by the culture.

This strategy is perfectly reasonable, so long as we stay within the framework that generated the item selection procedures in the first place. However, much to the disapproval of Binet, people found new uses for these tests of school-based knowledge that carried with them the seeds of the current disputes over IQ testing. Although Binet specifically warned against the procedure, his test and tests like it began to be used as *measures* of an overall aptitude for solving problems *in general*, rather than *samples* of problem-solving ability and knowledge *in particular*. Those engaged in such extrapolations acknowledged that in principle it is important to make certain that everyone given the test has an equal opportunity to learn the material that the test demands. But in practice there was no way to guarantee this essential prerequisite for making comparative judgments about basic abilities.

These are important issues in thinking about applications of IQ testing, and they are extensively discussed in the psychological literature. However, it is not until we back up and examine the possible significance of Binet's work in the light of anthropological scholarship that we can see just how limited an enterprise IQ testing was at the beginning, and how restricted it remains today.

A Thought Experiment in Test Construction

A good starting point for this reexamination is to think about what sort of activity Binet would have engaged in if he had been a member of a cultural group vastly different from his own. As a sort of "thought experiment" let us suppose that a "West African" Binet has taken an interest in the kinds of knowledge and skills that a child growing up in his part of the world would need to master as an adult. To make the thought experiment somewhat concrete, I will do my supposing about the tribal groups inhabiting the interior of Liberia, principally the Kpelle people, among whom I have worked and about whom a good deal of relevant information is available.[8]

Following in the footsteps of his French model, our Liberian Binet would want to make a catalogue of the kinds of activities that children are expected to master by their parents and the village elders. People in rural Liberia make their living by growing rice and other crops, which they supplement with meat and fish when these scarce commodities can be obtained. Rice farming is physically difficult work that demands considerable knowledge and planning for its success, but as practiced by the Kpelle, it is not a technologically sophisticated enterprise. It is carried out using simple tools such as a machete to cut the underbrush; fire to burn the dry brush; vines to tie together fence posts in order to keep out animals, and slingshots to harass.[9] Other aspects of Kpelle material culture are also relatively simple, although in every case the proper use of tools requires a good deal of knowledge about how the tools are supposed to be used. There is division of labor among Kpelle adults (men hunt, women do most of the fishing; men cut the bush on the farms, women plant the seed, children guard the crops), but far more than is true of contemporary America, everyone pretty well knows what there is to know about adult economic activities. There are some specialists (blacksmiths, bonesetters, weavers) whose work is an exception to this generalization, and study of their activities would certainly be important.

Of course, there is more to getting through life as a Kpelle than growing rice or weaving cloth. All descriptions of the social organization of Kpelle life stress that, as in America, knowledge of the social world is essential to adult status. Kpelle people are linked by a complex set of relations that control how much of the resources available to the society actually get to the individual.

Faced with this situation, how should our West African Binet proceed? Should he sample all the kinds of activities valued by adults? This strategy is almost certainly unrealistic. Even allowing for the possibility that aspects of technology make it reasonable to speak of the Kpelle as a "less complex" society than our own, it is very complex indeed. No anthropologist would claim to have achieved a really thorough description of even one such society. Moreover, like Tylor, he would have to admit the possibility that in some respects Kpelle society provides members with more complex tasks than we are likely to face. Since it is unreasonable in Liberia, as it is in the United States, to think that we can come up with a test that samples *all* types of Kpelle adult activities, why not follow Binet's example and sample an important *subset* of those activities? From an anthropological perspective, schools are social institutions for assuring that adult knowledge of highly valued kinds gets transmitted to a society's next generation (it must be transmitted, or there would be no later generations!). While the school is not likely to be a random sample of life's tasks, it is certainly a convenient place to sample activities that adults consider important, activities that are complex enough to make it unlikely that kids would learn what they need to know simply by "hanging around."

So, our Liberian Binet might decide to search for some institutions in his society that correspond roughly with the basic goals of schooling in ours. Not all societies readily manifest such institutions, so that anthropologists are led to speak of "socialization" as the broadest relevant category. Fortunately for discussion, in the case of Liberia, he would undoubtedly discover the existence of institutions called "bush schools" in the Creole vernacular.

There are no detailed accounts of the curriculum of the bush school. The three or four years that youngsters spend are organized by town elders who are leaders in the secret societies that control a variety of esoteric information. This material cannot, on pain of death, be communicated to outsiders.[10] However, we know enough about aspects of bush school activities to continue our hypothetical research; we know that youngsters learn to farm, construct houses, track animals, shoot birds, and carry out a variety of adult economic activities (children live apart from their home villages in something like a scouting camp during their time in bush school). They are also instructed in the important lore of the group. This lore is communicated not only in a variety of ceremonies, but in stories, myths, and riddles. So, let us suppose that our West African Binet decided to use "successful execution of bush school activities" as the abilities he wanted to sample.

Again, like Binet, our researcher would not be able to sample *all* such activities for his test, nor would he want to. He would not, for example, want to sample activities that all children knew how to accomplish *before* they got to school, nor would he want to sample activities considered so universally accessible that everyone mastered them well before the end of schooling. This information would not help him pick out those children who needed extra instruction. Instead, he would seek those activities that discriminated among children, activities that some mastered far earlier than others, and perhaps activities that some mastered only in later life. Once these Binet-like restrictions had been placed upon the activities selected for study, our hypothetical researcher could begin selecting tasks on which he could base test items.

In considering what sort of test would emerge, it is useful first to consider what activities would be excluded as well as those included. Cutting brush or sowing rice seed probably would not be the test; everyone knows how to do that before he or she gets to school. Nor would anyone spend time explicitly teaching children common vocabulary. However, there would be explicit instruction in such tasks as constructing houses and identifying leaves that are useful in different kinds of medicine. There would also be some mechanism for insuring that the history of the group and its laws and customs were taught to everyone often in the form of stories and dances. Finally, some children would be selected for specialist roles that would require special tests (bonesetter, weaver, midwife, blacksmith, hunter, and so on). These children would receive additional instruction.

Looking at those areas where instruction might be considered important, we can see many candidate activities for testing. We might want to see if children had learned all of the important leaf names for making medicine. Riddles are often important parts of stories and arguments, so we could test to see how many riddles children know and how adept they are at interpreting them. The specialties would be a rich source of test material, especially if we thought that rational testing of ability to perform like adults would improve the quality of our cloth or machetes. In short, it seems possible, in principle, to come up with test items that could perform functions in Kpelle society similar to the way that Binet wanted to use IQ tests.

Could we carry out such a program of research *in practice*? There is no simple answer to this question, but it is useful to consider the obstacles. For some activities such as naming leaves or remembering riddles, it should be relatively easy to make the relevant observations because the Kpelle have already arranged for them: several researchers have described children's games that embody precisely these activities.[11] We could also test people's skills at constructing houses, weaving designs, and forging sturdy hoes. However, from a Kpelle point of view, test of such skills would not be particularly interesting. The real stuff of using's one's wits to get along in the world has been excluded.

This point was made very explicitly by a sophisticated Kpelle acquaintance of mine who was versed in the more esoteric aspects of Kpelle secret societies and medicine (or magic, according to American stereotypes). We had been talking about what it means to be intelligent in Kpelle society (the most appropriate term is translated as "clever"). "Can you be a clever farmer?" I asked. "No," came the reply. "You can be a hardworking farmer, or you can be a lucky farmer, but we couldn't say that someone is a clever farmer. Everyone knows how to farm. We use 'clever' when we talk about the way someone gets other people to help him. Some people always win arguments. Some people know how to deal with strangers. Some people know powerful medicine. These are the things we talk about as clever."

In this bit of dialogue we see an emphasis on activities that require social interaction as the arena where intelligence is an appropriate concept. (Among the Kpelle and many other nontechnological groups, display of a good memory for use in discussions is often considered an important component of intelligence.)[12] This usage is quite consistent with Binet's analysis; *it is those activities that differentiate among people* in terms of the way they manipulate information that the Kpelle, like the French, use to mark intelligence.

However, once we reach this point, we face two important difficulties. First, the situations that we have selected for our study of Kpelle intelligence are exceedingly difficult to describe. Second, these contexts are very difficult to arrange. It is not enough to know riddles, everyone knows riddles. What is important about riddles is how they are used to get one's way with other people. Riddles are a resource to be used in a variety of social interactions where people's statuses and rights are at issue.

Consider the first difficulty. Bellman recounts an occasion when an elder member of a secret society told a long story about how he came to be a high ranking shaman.[13] He followed this (presumably autobiographical) story with a long riddle, which was also in story form. A novice such as myself would have no way of figuring out what part of the story was true, and I certainly would not have responded to the riddle as if its interpretation depended upon the autobiographical story; the two monologues appear to be about quite different topics. Bellman succeeds in demonstrating, however, that the riddle is closely linked to the autobiography. Not only are there formal, structural similarities (once one understands the basic categories of the relevant Kpelle belief systems). There is a rhetorical link as well. The autobiographical story actually represents a bit of self-aggrandizement by the person who told it. The man is claiming special knowledge and special power in a covert manner. The riddle reinforces the main point of the story (which raises the teller above his fellow shaman), giving the story "logical" as well as "historical" validity. The fact that listeners are constrained to agree with the riddle also gets them to agree, at least in part, with the message of the autobiographical story.

By almost any account, this man's autobiographical account plus riddle is a clever bit of behavior. It is exactly the kind of thing that our West African Binet ought to be sampling. But, at precisely this point, our cross-cultural thought experiment in IQ testing comes apart. As I have already pointed out, in order to construct a test Binet needed to be able to select a large number of items. But the "item" we have just described (very loosely) is not easily constructable. The participants in this scene were doing social work on each other; the shaman, in particular, was attempting to establish his preeminence using an account of his past history that would be difficult to check up on, a riddle whose structure was designed to reinforce his account, and his knowledge of his listener's state of knowledge concerning both the shaman's past and Kpelle social structure. This was one item; it was constructed by the subject, not the "tester." It is very difficult for me to imagine how to insure that a test includes one or more items "of this type." Furthermore, because the example's structure and content depend upon the special circumstances surrounding it, how could I insure that I would be able to present the test to the subject since it was the "subject" who did a lot of the presenting in the example I have described?

Here the contrast with Binet's situation is very strong. Like Binet, we have proceeded by figuring out what sorts of activities differentiate people according to some notion of what it means to behave intelligently. Unlike Binet, the activities we need to sample in West Africa to accomplish this goal lead us into domains that are *systematically absent from Binet's tests*. These domains involve interactions among people in which flexibly employed social knowledge is of paramount importance. They are not domains of hypothetical knowledge; rather, they always involve some real operations on the world, operations that require a great deal of care simply to describe. We have no good notion of how to make such activities happen in a manner analogous to the way that teachers make vocabulary tests and multiplication problems happen. Furthermore, even if we solved all these problems, we would have no real theory of the psychological processes that our subject engaged in. Such problems have not been studied by cognitive psychologists.

On both practical and theoretical grounds, then, it appears virtually impossible to come up with a way of testing Kpelle intelligence in a manner really equivalent to what we understand to be intelligence tests in our society. So long as we restrict our attention to Kpelle culture, this conclusion should not cause much consternation. After all, the idea of a West African Binet is rather absurd; Kpelle people have managed to pass on their culture for many years without IQ tests to help them select clever children and give extra assistance to the dull.

Some Implications for the Notion of a Culture-Free Test

Our characterization of what one has to do to be clever in Kpelle culture and what it would take to sample such cleverness in a test must be discomforting for anyone who imagines that one can construct a culture-free test of intelligence. Imagine, for example, that by some quirk it was our imaginary Liberian Binet who constructed the first IQ test, and that other West African tribal people had refined it. Next, imagine that American children were posed items from the West African test. Even items considered too simple for Kpelle eight-year-olds would cause our children severe problems. Learning the names of leaves, for example, has proven too difficult for more than one American Ph.D.[14] Our children know some riddles, but little use is made of such knowledge in our society except for riddling, which would put them at a severe disadvantage on more "advanced" items.

If our children were forced to take a test constructed by a West African Binet, we might object that these Kpelle-derived items were unfairly biased toward Kpelle culture. If the eventual incomes of our children depended in any way on their ability to interpret Kpelle riddles, we would be outraged. Nor would we be too happy if their incomes depended upon their use of their own riddles as rhetorical devices. At the very minimum, we would want a *culture-free test* if real life outcomes depended upon test performance. However, what kind of test is a West African Binet likely to dream up that we would consider culture-free? It would not involve a set of drawings of geometrically precise figures, because Kpelle, a preliterate group, do not engage in much graphic representation and they have no technology for drawing straight lines. It would not be recall of lists of nonsense syllables or even lists of words, because there are no corresponding activities in Kpelle adult life. We might try a memory test like recalling all of one's family, but here the Kpelle, who teach their children genealogies, would have a distinct advantage: what is the name of your grandmother's father on your father's side of the family? In fact, if we run down the list of presumably culture-free items that our experiment on Kpelle IQ testing turned up, we would almost certainly find none of the subtests that have been claimed as culture-free tests of intelligence in our society. The reason is very simple; our West African Binet, having scientifically sampled *his* culture, would have come up with items that reflect valued activities and that differentiate people in *his* culture, while Binet and all his successors have come up with items that do the same job in our culture. *They are different kinds of activities.*

The only way to obtain a culture-free test is to construct items that are equally a part of the experience of all cultures. Following the logic of Binet's undertaking, this would require us to sample the valued adult activities in all cultures (or at least two!) and identify activities equivalent in their structure and frequency of occurrence.

I probably do not have to belabor this point further. The simple fact is that we know of no tests that are culture-free, only tests for which we have no good theory of how culture affects performance. Lacking such a theory, we lack any guidelines that would permit us to specify clear connections between cultural experience and performance.

Return to First Principles

Our imagined study of cross-cultural test construction makes it clear that tests of ability are inevitably cultural devices. This conclusion must seem dreary and disappointing to people who have been working to construct valid, culture-free tests. But from the perspective of history and logic, it simply confirms the fact, stated so clearly by Franz Boas half a century ago, that "mind, independent of experience, is inconceivable."

The historical experience of anthropologists has led them to consider it axiomatic that the abilities you choose to sample have to be drawn from an analysis of indigenous, culturally organized activities. Because different cultures emphasize different kinds of activities, the valued abilities will differ. From this point of view, a test that is equally valid across cultures would be a test that sampled some domain of activity that occurs in roughly the same form and same frequency in the cultures being compared. While it is possible, in principle, to identify such activities, they may not be of much use for the purposes of ability testing in the tradition of IQ tests. Many psychologists and anthropologists have asserted that some core set of experiences is common to all cultures. Such assertions are at the heart of such major systems as those constructed by Sigmund Freud, Jean Piaget, and Abraham Kardiner, to name just a few important figures who have studied this problem. But it is simultaneously asserted that everyone, irrespective of culture, comes to master those basic activities common to our species. Piaget, whose work is most closely associated with the development of intellectual skills, explicitly assumes that there will be universal acquisition of basic understandings of the physical and social worlds because of universal constraints on behavior common to all cultures. There are no existing data to refute this assumption.

However, both our nineteenth-century anthropological forefathers and twentieth-century scholars such as Piaget readily admit cultural differences *associated with particular domains of activity*. Tylor, Spencer, and other nineteenth-century cultural evolutionists focused on differences traceable to technology. Piaget believes that special institutions and technologies of cultural transmission, such as the modern school, produce culturally determined cultural differences. So long as we restrict ourselves to specifiable domains, it is possible to rank cultures and, consequently, rank the intellectual achievements of individuals from different cultures within those domains. So, for example, we can rank cultures in the sophistication of their means of communication (from oral cultures, to literate cultures, to those possessing electronic media); we can rank cultures in terms of the complexity of dance movements that people are expected to master; we can rank cultures in terms of the degree of urbanization that characterizes the lives of their members, or the degree of rhetorical skill in institutionalized settings that they require.

Any time we engage in such domain-specific comparisons, we can expect cultural differences in the abilities that individual culture users will have developed to achieve the required level of proficiency. Americans will be expected to deal more effectively with graphic symbols than Kpelle or Balinese. But if we chose dance movements as our subject matter, the opposite ordering of culturally linked proficiencies is certain to emerge. In either case, from an anthropological perspective, we would have no illusions that our tests of ability were culture-fair. Why should we? After all, if we choose to compare people in domains where their experience differs, we expect mind to differ as well. That conclusion is certainly a basic legacy of nineteenth-century anthropology.

Sticking to this point of view provides us with a powerful way of understanding the relation between IQ testing and social demands. We can recognize the school as an institutionalized setting designed to provide children with massive practice in activities that are useful and valued in our society. IQ tests sample school activities, and therefore, indirectly, valued social activities, *in our culture.* Insofar as such tests are really used to insure that all children master the required skills, such tests would have to be considered extremely useful. However, insofar as such tests act as screening devices giving access to some people and not to others, without any commitment to insuring that all achieve the level of proficiency required for full participation in the adult life and access to the resources available to adults in our society, their initial purpose has been subverted and must be reexamined. This will be no easy task, since there is little current agreement on the intellectual skills needed for performing in most adult occupations.

Implications for Teaching

Teachers facing the enormous heterogeneity of classrooms in many parts of America may well be tempted to set aside this essay as essentially irrelevant to their classroom practices, whether they agree with my arguments for a culturally conditioned notion of intelligence or not. With respect to classroom organization and curriculum, what follows from the notion that children who may fumble or fail in typical classroom settings shine elsewhere? How can such knowledge be used to advantage?

Perhaps the first thing that needs emphasizing is that a child's skill in a non-classroom setting does *not* imply that poor performance in the classroom is not a problem, either for the child or for the society which uses schooling as a major means of imparting valued social knowledge. The past decade of research on the cognitive consequences of schooling convincingly shows that there are systems of cognitive activity closely correlated with modern schooling that are sharply differentiated from the systems of activity that govern a wide range of activities outside the confines of school.[15] When people who have not experienced schooling are tested using materials and interactional formats characteristic of schooling, they perform poorly. This is a social fact and an important social fact in the lives of the people involved.

While it is true that the activities associated with South Sea navigation,[16] Botswanian story telling,[17] and West African fish mongering[18] each represent highly articulated uses of intelligence, people who excel at these activities must still confront the fact that the domains of activity where these skills are valued are either being stamped out by the economic and political power of schooled, technological societies or they are being encapsulated within lower echelons of them. In the modern world, to be unschooled is to be denied access to the basic contexts where wealth and power are brokered. As Jerome Bruner and I noted more than a decade ago,

> cultural *deprivation* represents a special case of cultural *difference* that arises when an individual is faced with demands to perform in a manner inconsistent with his past (cultural) experience. In the present social context of the United States, the great power of the middle class has rendered differences into deficits because middle-class behavior is the yardstick of success.[19]

I might phrase matters slightly differently now, but I do not think that the significance of that middle-class standard has lessened in the intervening decade. In fact, with respect to a strategy that says that schools must pay increased respect to cultural diversity, the situation has become, if anything, more rigid.

UNIFORM TREATMENT METHODS

Faced with the enormous heterogeneity of many American schools and the generally poor performance of culturally different peoples, highly structured, bottom-up strategies like the Achievement Goals Program in use in San Diego City Schools have won wide approval. These methods are closely tied to means of measuring time on task and therefore serve as a means of control to insure that all children "get the basics." They emphasize very specific, highly uniform, "correct steps" in mastering the basics. I have grave concerns about these kinds of efforts because I have had too much experience in recent years with children at the bottom 20 percent of my local school system who do not make it through the structure; they seem to do all right in the early grades, but they fail to make the essential transition from "basic" to "higher order" skills in mathematics and reading. Rather than focus on the problems of this highly uniform method of resolving the problem of cultural variation, we have been interested in our research group in ways to take advantage of diversity.

A completely different way of achieving excellence that nonetheless seems to match the urge of the "back to basics" movement and to apply a single method for all children in the classroom at one time is exemplified in demonstrations such as those of Marva Collins and Sylvia Ashton-Warner.[20] These teachers focus uncompromisingly on the highest ideas of western civilization in their teaching. They teach to whole classrooms of diversely prepared students at one time but somehow find a way to involve each child in the excitement, despite very divergent cultural traditions separating children from curriculum. Here the teacher evokes deep involvement from every *individual* child by the exercise of a kind of empathetic skill that makes us call teaching an art, not a science.

As an art, this kind of activity is notorious for its failure to transfer. Marva Collins could not transfer it beyond a single, other teacher working with her at close range; her ideas came apart when the scale of activity was too great for her to control personally. Sylvia Ashton-Warner was *not* able to transfer methods developed in New Zealand among the Maori to Colorado among the privileged.

Master teachers can demonstrate to us what is possible. When the context of teaching is so arranged that the children are truly captivated, there resides a very important achievement. It provides educational science with a goal, however utopian, against which to judge its failures; why can't we make *every* classroom work?

APPROACHES EMPHASIZING DIVERSITY

Well, ordinary teachers, among whom I include myself, are not able to weave the kind of magic of a Marva Collins or a Sylvia Warner. But many ordinary teachers do not like to work in the restrictive atmosphere of an AGP school. The problem is to offer a workable, *scientific* alternative. That means an alternative that can approach the same heterogeneity of children's backgrounds as more "uniformitarian" strategies like AGP and succeed. It means an alternative that is transferable because it can be taught in teacher education programs and education schools. It means an alternative that does not cost more, or much more, than the money that is being expended on education now.

No such overall alternative formulation exists, but there has accumulated a set of educational demonstrations that, taken as a group, offers a different, culture-sensitive way to deal with academic diversity in the classroom. Among these culture-sensitive approaches it is possible to see several clusters.

First, there are studies like the Kamehameha Early Education Project (KEEP) and that of Erickson and Mohatt that can establish links between particular modes of pedagogy and the nonschool organization of experience.[21] These efforts are most appropriate in settings where there is a single distinctive cultural tradition shared by most, if not all, of the students.

The Kamehameha Early Education Project was working with Native Hawaiian children who did not succeed with structured, code-emphasis instruction in reading. As they moved into direct teaching of comprehension, they slowly evolved a lesson format that seemed to catch the children up in an active and effective way. An analysis of the successful teaching techniques revealed that the procedures they eventually developed mapped onto an indigenous cultural activity, "talk story."[22] The children had all been present on many occasions of talk story, but they were not old enough themselves to participate in talk story at home. So when they came to school they encountered reading as a variation on an already familiar pattern of instructional interactions.

This program has achieved some of the characteristics I attribute to a scientific alternative. Not only has the program demonstrated success in individual classrooms; it has been taught to new generations of teachers who have used it successfully in new classrooms.

However, many questions remain. Perhaps the correspondence between talk story and the successful KEEP reading procedures is an accident. Perhaps their teaching strategy is simply a good teaching strategy for *any* kids learning to read. The evidence on this question is not in yet, but preliminary results from our own research group suggest that there are elementary school populations for whom the procedure is *not* effective; further pursuit of the reasons why the KEEP program does and does not work will teach more about both reading and Hawaiian culture.

A different kind of demonstration is provided by Erickson and Mohatt from work among the Odawa in Canada. In this case, too, a successful educational strategy was connected to discourse modes prevalent in the children's community.[23] The analysis, based on ethnographic techniques, was specific enough to warrant treatment-specific claims about the effect of the discourse strategy.

The phenomenon that Erickson and Mohatt addressed was the apparent passivity and silence of Native American students in regular classrooms that had been studied by Phillips. Very different modes of classroom discourse feel comfortable to Anglo and Native American children living in the southwestern United States. In particular, it was found that for Native American students

> the notion of a single individual being structurally set apart from all others, in anything other than an observer role, and yet still a part of the group organization, is one that Indian children probably encounter for the first time in school.[24]

Native American children who find themselves with an Anglo teacher encounter a single, powerful person regulating the behavior of many others. They adopt the observer role that they know to be appropriate.

Like good observers, they are quiet. They also adhere to the rule that it is not acceptable to single out individuals for praise or censure on a public occasion, and so they also remain silent, or experience difficulty, when singled out to provide an answer to the teacher's questions. The result is what Erickson and Mohatt call the "often reported phenomenon of the 'silent Indian child' in the classroom." Their behavior is inappropriate to the standard mode of instruction in which the teacher acts as a "switchboard operator" who allocates speaking turns, calls on individual children, and expects active participation.

Erickson and Mohatt show that it is possible to construct rules of participation in the classroom that are a functional blend of Anglo school curriculum and Native American discourse styles that make the classroom run much more smoothly. These patterns seemed to be learnable; an Anglo teacher was observed to change his participant structures over the course of the school year in the direction of the Odawa. (These examples demonstrate that culture-sensitive pedagogy can make a difference where it is possible to be explicit about cultural patterns and there is not much cultural heterogeneity in the classroom. In each case, it is important to note that culture-sensitive does *not* mean a focus on the traditional arts, foods, and folklore of a group. Instead culture-sensitive means sensitivity to "relatively subtle aspects of interactional etiquettes [that] are likely to go unrecognized by non-Indian teachers.)[25]

CONTEXT-SENSITIVE APPROACHES

The KEEP and Native American examples are interesting precisely because they map on to identifiable cultural structures that, despite their divergence from the usual pattern of the school, are appropriate for instructional purposes. But many teachers face a situation where it is not a problem of the school having one cultural background and the children one other. Rather, the children are from *many* and varied cultural backgrounds, even if they are from the same general ethnic group. In my own region, for example, there are many Hispanic children from varying countries of origins and years of residence in the U.S., black students of similar heterogeneity, Southeast Asians from several countries, Native Americans, and many more.

What can teachers do in circumstances of extreme student heterogeneity if they are neither master teachers nor cultural experts? There is no single answer to this question, but one of the things that will be very helpful is to have as full a picture of the skills and interests of each individual child when they are *not* in school as possible. Another key element is to construct activity systems that are clearly structured, but where there is room for a good deal of creativity with respect to how each child interacts with the structure.

Activity-centered classrooms with a diversity of learning centers provide one excellent, structural format within which to connect child expertise and interest outside the school with the basic skills required by the school. They also allow a natural way for the classroom to connect with special educational resources in the community (science programs connected with museums such as Berkeley's Lawrence Hall of Science or Toronto's Science Museum, local experts among retired residents, unions, and industries).

Gottfried described the impact on classroom life of visits to the Lawrence Hall of Science, which has an outstanding set of activities for the public.[26] Gottfried studied the way that the visit to Lawrence Hall was taken up in classroom activity. When he spent time in their classrooms with an exhibit that required considerable interaction with various animal species and insects, he found that the materials evoked different patterns of expertise among the participants.

One boy, who was doing poorly in school and of whom the teacher had a rather dim opinion, turned out to be unafraid of crayfish. That alone won him unaccustomed social credits. But it also turned out that he knew more about crayfish than the teacher and more than was provided by the encyclopedia. It turned out he was an *expert* on crayfish. Other children displayed similar kinds of virtuosity, enriching the number of interesting things to be written and worried about. As a result, the teacher learned a lot about the children, and the children displayed prowess that they would not have been known to possess if Gottfried had not disturbed the usual social order. A great deal of basic skills training resulted from the episodes.

No single such activity will captivate everyone, but everyone has some activity that can capture them. The trick is to figure out how to organize experiences out of school and variety in the classroom that will serve as the essential starting point for successful instruction. An activity-centered classroom has the great virtue of allowing parallel activity structures that are only loosely coordinated in time and space.

This permits teachers to apply a variety of approaches to a particular area of academic concern, embedding reading (for example) in many contexts. Specific activity structures facilitate connections between the classroom and the outside world, enabling teachers to create occasions for transfer of home-based knowledge into school-based contexts for basic skills.

In our own research we have pursued the special power of computers to create educationally useful activity systems.[27] We have sought to create carefully scripted activity which embeds exercise in the basic skills in ways designed to maximize transfer. Thus, instead of content that replicates the format of pages of printed text, we seek to embed literacy and numeracy activities in activity structures which have some larger goal and are often game-like in their structure. Viewing the computer as a medium for interaction rather than a surrogate teacher leads us to arrange it so that more than one person is usually working at a single console at any one time and that the entire set of operations has a clear socially accepted goal.

In other work on reading we create activity structures that are *group* enterprises, organized around a script with teachers, college students, and children mixed together with respect to roles and expertise.[28] Even children with long histories of educational failure can be caught up in these systems enabling a keener insight into the difficulties and a better chance at remediation.

CULTURE AND CONTEXT SPECIFICITY

I know of one educational innovation that combines aspects of both types of systems described above. Like the context-specific activity centers, it arranges for education to occur in contexts that can recruit children's out-of-school accomplishments so that both the children and the teacher can succeed at a school task. Like the work in Hawaii and with the Odawa, this case uses cultural understandings that all of the children have in common outside of the classroom and that are not usually used inside the classroom.

Moll and Diaz worked with Hispanic children who had fairly good literacy skills in Spanish, but were failing to learn how to read in English in spite of organized bilingual instruction.[29] When English was being taught in the classroom, the children could not rely on their Spanish skills. The instruction was organized so that a teacher who spoke only English taught them English reading. They worked with a Spanish teacher for other parts of the day, including times when they worked on reading in Spanish at quite a high level—not only complicated comprehension work but even book reports. Yet, when they went to the English class they were faced with what looked like first-grade work. The instructional program was arranged so that until the children could do fairly well in oral English, they would be kept at a beginner level in reading. These children did quite poorly. They did not advance.

The teachers were surprised to see videotapes of the children reading in the two settings: it was hard to believe that children who were so competent at reading in one language were so incompetent at learning to read in another language. No one was happy with this situation.

Moll and Diaz created an intervention that was later picked up by a "real teacher" who had the necessary attributes: she was bilingual, biliterate, and could teach reading. Moll and Diaz had discovered a way to move the children into English reading, and at an advanced grade level. They gave the children English books to read—the very same fourth-grade books that their classmates were reading. The children read the English text, getting a bit of casual help from the teacher, if they asked for any, using either Spanish or English as the medium of communication. Because the teacher and the children could both use Spanish, sometimes the questions and answers were in Spanish. When the children had finished a first reading of the text, the group conversation turned to what it meant. Again, the conversation was in Spanish or in English, whatever seemed most helpful. The children understood the story very well; the problems they had in comprehension were on the same sorts of text and questions that their monolingual English classmates had trouble with.

The children were, very suddenly, reading English at grade level. Granted, in English they could not display their ability as easily. But reading English they were. An "extra" ability of theirs had been the ability to speak Spanish—and they used this ability from home to *read* English. The interesting punch line to this case is that the children changed in another way: once they were allowed to use Spanish to do English reading lessons, they started to use a lot more English. Their lack of ability in speaking English had kept them from reading English in the ordinary instructional program; ironically, Moll and Diaz created a way to "get around" the first problem, only to end up finding an indirect way to solve it!

Final Comments

In the decades ahead, we can be certain that the issue of student heterogeneity in our schools is going to be important, even if no one has anything particularly useful to say about it. We do not have to subscribe to the pseudo-scientific aspects of Huxley's *Brave New World* to realize that increased requirements for technical expertise are likely, even when combined with increased technical assistance for gaining expertise, to create a situation where the intellectually rich get richer. There is also no serious doubt that one could use any of several commercially available culture-fair tests and come up with a statistically significant prediction of who is most likely to become a highly educated, technologically successful, person.

One-sided notions of culture-free testing covertly create a uniform, quantifiable, notion of what intelligence *is*. Although as yet not particularly strong as a scientific and pedagogical tool, a culture-sensitive approach to testing and intelligence seems to provide guidance in the creation of mixed systems of education that will take advantage of the heterogeneity instead of suppressing it. Context-sensitive approaches appear to be especially helpful in dealing with situations of extreme diversity, because they allow the kinds of flexibility that can organize a variety of resources to assist children in benefiting from their educational experiences; they can be shown to work. However, they remain enough of an "art" so that transfer and generalization are still very problematic in many cases. Very often they remain no more than demonstrations, with no scientific framework or bureaucratic structure to engineer their uptake in the educational system.

A decade from now, when the next time rolls around for the National Society for the Study of Education to be thinking of yearbook articles on this topic, it will be interesting to see if the currently successful brands of context- and culture-specific science and pedagogy will have been able to survive, not to say prosper, in a world people are currently fond of calling the "coming information age."

Footnotes

1. For example, see Arthur Jensen, "g: Outmoded Theory or Unconquered Frontier," *Creative Science and Technology* 2, no. 3 (1979): 16-29.

2. Edward B. Tylor, *The Origins of Culture* (New York: Harper and Row, 1958), p. 69.

3. Herbert Spencer, *The Principles of Psychology*, vol. 5 (New York: D. Appleton, 1886), p. 521.

4. Tylor, *The Origins of Culture*, p. 27.

5. Franz Boas, *The Mind of Primitive Man* (New York: Macmillan, 1911).

6. Ibid., pp. 110-11.

7. Ibid., p. 128.

8. See, for example, Beryl L. Bellman, *Village of Curers and Assassins: On the Production of Fala Kpelle Cosmological Categories* (The Hague: Mouton Press, 1975); Michael Cole, John Gay, Joseph A. Glick, and Donald W. Sharp, *The Cultural Context of Learning and Thinking* (New York: Basic Books, 1971); James L. Gibbs, "The Kpelle of Liberia," in *Peoples of Africa*, ed. James L. Gibbs (New York: Holt, Rinehart and Winston, 1965).

9. See John Gay, *Red Dust on the Green Leaves* (Thompson, Conn.: Inter-Culture Associates, 1973) for a much better account on this process.

10. See Bellman, *Village of Curers and Assassins*, for the most detailed account of these practices.

11. Cole, Gay, Glick, and Sharp, *The Cultural Context of Learning and Thinking*; David F. Lancy, "Studies of Memory in Culture," *Annals of the New York Academy of Science* 307 (1977): 285-97; Alfred A. Kulah, "The Organization and Learning of Proverbs among the Kpelle of Liberia" (Doctoral dissertation, University of California, Irvine, 1973).

12. See, for example, Ernest F. Dube, "A Cross-cultural Study of the Relationship between 'Intelligence' Level and Story Recall" (Doctoral dissertation, Cornell University, 1977).

13. Beryl L. Bellman, "Ethnohermeneutics: On the Interpretation of Subjective Meaning," in *Language and the Mind*, ed. William C. McCormack and Stephen A. Wurm (The Hague: Mouton and Co., 1978).

14. E. S. Bowen, *Return to Laughter* (New York: Doubleday, 1964).

15. Donald W. Sharp, Michael Cole, and Charles Lave, *Education and Cognitive Development: The Evidence from Experimental Research*, in *Monographs of the Society for Research in Child Development* 44, nos. 1, 2 (1979), Serial No. 178; Harold W. Stevenson, Timothy Parker, Alex Wilkinson, Beatrice Bonnevaux, and Max Gonzales, *Schooling, Environment, and Cognitive Development: A Cross-cultural Study*, in *Monographs of the Society for Research in Child Development* 43, no. 3 (1978), Serial No. 175, pp. 1-92; Barbara Rogoff, "Schooling and the Development of Cognitive Skills," in *Handbook of Cross-cultural Psychology*, ed. Henry C. Triandis and Alistair Heron, vol. 4. (Boston: Allyn and Bacon, 1981).

16. Thomas Gladwin, *East is a Big Bird: Navigation and Logic on Puluwat Atoll* (Cambridge, Mass.: Harvard University Press, 1970); David H. Lewis, "Observations on Route Finding and Spatial Orientation among the Aboriginal Peoples of the Western Desert Region of Central Australia," *Oceania* 46, no. 4 (1976): 249-82.

17. Dube, "A Cross-cultural Study."

18. Naomi Quinn, "Do Mfantse Fish Sellers Estimate Probabilities in Their Heads?" *American Ethnologist* 5 (1978): 206-226.

19. Michael Cole and Jerome S. Bruner, "Cultural Differences and Inferences about Psychological Processes," in *Annual Progress in Child Psychiatry and Child Development*, ed. Stella Chess and Alexander Thomas (New York: Brunner/Mazel, 1972), pp. 47-63.

20. Marva Collins and C. Tamaricus, *Marva Collins' Way* (New York: Houghton-Mifflin, 1982); Sylvia Ashton-Warner, *Spearpoint: "Teacher" in America* (New York: Knopf, 1972).

21. Kathryn H. Au, "Using the Experience-Text-Relationship Method with Minority Children," *Reading Teacher* 32 (March 1979): 677-79; idem, "Participation Structures in a Reading Lesson with Hawaiian Children: Analysis of a Culturally Appropriate Instructional Event," *Anthropology and Education Quarterly* 11 (Summer 1980): 91-115; Ron Gallimore and Kathryn H. Au, "The Competence/Incompetence Paradox in the Education of Minority Culture Children," *Quarterly Newsletter of the Laboratory of Comparative Human Cognition* 1 (July 1979): 32-37; G. E. Speidel, Guest Editor, *Educational Perspectives* 20, No. 1 (1981); Frederick Erickson and Gerald Mohatt, "Cultural Organization of Participant Structures in Two Classrooms of Indian Students," in *Doing the Ethnography of Schooling*, ed. George D. Spindler (New York: Holt, Rinehart and Winston, 1980), pp. 132-74.

22. Steven Boggs, *Speaking, Relating, and Learning: A Study of Hawaiian Children at Home and at School*, with the assistance of Karen Watson-Gegeo and Georgia McMillen (Norwood, N.J.: Ablex, forthcoming).

23. Susan Phillips, "Participant Structures and Communicative Competence: Warm Springs Children in Community and Classroom," in *Functions of Language in the Classroom*, ed. Courtney B. Cazden, Vera P. John, and Dell Hymes (New York: Teachers College Press, 1972).

24. Ibid., p. 391.

25. Erickson and Mohatt, "Cultural Organization of Participant Structures," pp. 166-67.

26. Jeffrey Gottfried, "Activity-based Outreach Programs" (Lecture given at the Laboratory of Comparative Human Cognition, University of California, San Diego, n.d.).

27. Laboratory of Comparative Human Cognition, "Culture and Intelligence," in *Handbook of Human Intelligence*, ed. Robert J. Sternberg (New York: Cambridge University Press, 1982), pp. 642-719; James A. Levin and Randall Souviney, eds., "Computers and Literacy: A Time for Tools," special issue of the *Quarterly Newsletter of the Laboratory of Comparative Human Cognition* 5 (July 1983).

28. Peg Griffin, Michael Cole, Stephen Diaz, and Catherine King, "Model Systems for Re-mediating Reading Difficulties," in *Cognition and Instruction*, ed. Robert Glaser (Hillsdale, N.J.: Lawrence Erlbaum Associates, forthcoming).

29. Luis C. Moll and Stephen Diaz, "Bilingual Communication and Reading: The Importance of Spanish in Learning to Read in English" (unpublished manuscript, 1984).

CHAPTER XIII

Ways of Knowing: Their Meaning for Teacher Education

VINCENT ROGERS

The education of America's teachers is an enormously complex enterprise. This chapter, however, is concerned with one aspect of teacher education: the nature and quality of the intellectual life of students enrolled in preservice and in-service teacher education programs. I assume at the outset that there is a relationship between the intellectual quality of teacher education curricula and the intellectual growth of students exposed to such curricula. I also accept the fundamental conclusions of the preceding chapters, namely, that human cognition occurs in many ways and that there are varieties of intelligence. Finally, I assume that preservice and in-service teachers should have the opportunity to use their minds fully and completely, in all of the mind's dimensions, and that intellectual growth is a significant goal of teacher education programs at all levels.

I shall discuss here what those teaching in schools and colleges of education might do *within the framework of existing programs* to enhance the quality of intellectual life for students in those programs. Readers will be disappointed if they seek some master plan, some formula for improvement, some "program" that can be easily adopted. I have no intention of substituting one rigidity for another by creating a new, fragmented teacher education curriculum focusing separately on aesthetic, scientific, interpersonal, intellectual, formal, and practical modes of knowing. I propose to examine the ideas presented in preceding chapters and to sift through and sort out those ideas that seem most important, most neglected in conventional programs, and most doable in a practical sense.

As I read the preceding chapters a number of fundamental insights emerged. Each idea most often grew out of an examination of the material presented in a given chapter. On the other hand, each seems to have broader, overlapping qualities as well. Thus, for example, "creating, inventing, and improvising" are associated with all the ways of knowing discussed in Part Two, yet have their origins in my reading of Arnheim's work on intuitive intelligence.

Characteristics of Teacher Education Programs That Foster Intellectual Growth

What then are the characteristics of teacher education programs suggested by the preceding chapters? What kinds of experiences foster teachers' intellectual growth in the areas suggested in this book? How might teachers spend the limited amount of time they can devote to professional growth? What is the nature of a teacher education program designed to foster and encourage intellectual growth?

As I see it, such programs would be characterized by the following features.

1. *The opportunity to create, invent, and improvise.* If indeed many of the most complex problems we face are practical in nature and cannot be resolved by measurement, calculation, logical deduction, or straightforward inference, it is essential that teachers become involved in formal and informal experiences in which inventive, intuitive modes of thinking are called for. The opportunity for genuine improvisation and creativity on the part of teachers is relatively rare in conventional programs of teacher education. On the contrary, current practice suggests that teachers would do better if they taught more uniformly, followed curriculum guides and textbook outlines more closely, and improvised less.

2. *The opportunity to practice the art of perception.* To teach well, one must learn to see with all of one's senses. Painters, dancers, poets, musicians, comedians, and other artists have developed this skill far beyond the level of ordinary people. They see the subtleties, the nuances, the absurdities in everyday life that others often overlook. To teach, teachers must know the people who populate their world in and out of schools. Such knowing depends upon one's ability to see and understand the subtle cues and signals given by children, colleagues, and others with whom one comes in contact both in and out of school settings.

3. *The opportunity for reflection.* Teacher education, and indeed teaching itself, is often a hurried, time-dominated activity. One learns to deal with daily crises, but seldom has time to search for the meaning inherent in events. Thus there is a need to stand back, examine events from a number of perspectives, to apply theory to practice, and indeed, practice to theory.

4. *The opportunity to represent ideas and experience.* I wrote earlier of the importance of perception—the ability to see beyond the obvious meaning of events. But to perceive well is not enough. It is equally important to be able to disclose, to make public, to communicate or represent what one perceives to others. Teachers need the opportunity to represent their perceptions in a variety of ways, as do children.

5. *The opportunity to collaborate.* Teaching has been (and continues to be in most settings) a lonely profession. Teachers need the opportunity to work with each other in a variety of ways, sharing interests, enthusiasms, questions, and concerns. Such collaboration may take the form of seeking answers through research, curriculum building, and the development of teaching materials. Whatever the form, teacher education programs should offer students the chance to build collaborative habits early in their professional lives.

6. *The opportunity to engage in genuine inquiry.* Inquiry is, essentially, "finding out." It need not be goal-oriented (although it usually is), and one does not necessarily know in advance what one is seeking. Teachers need to inquire about education, to learn how it functions in certain settings, to identify and isolate problems, to seek, gather, analyze, and synthesize data, to build theory as well as test it, and to share and discuss these theories with their colleagues in training and in schools.

7. *The opportunity to experience.* If one is to create, perceive, reflect, represent, collaborate, and inquire, one must have something to create, reflect, and inquire about. Thus, teacher education ought to provide opportunities for rich experience in preservice and in-service programs both in schools and in the wider community. If teachers, like other human beings, are partly the product of their prior and continuing experience, then the nature of in-school and out-of-school experiencing provided in teacher education programs is of vital importance.

8. *The opportunity to study ideas and settings holistically so that*

relationships and connections may be explored. What goes on in the cafeteria or art studio is indeed related to what goes on elsewhere, both within and outside the school. Similarly, what goes on in first grade is related to what happens in seventh grade, and what occurs in the science curriculum is related to what occurs in language arts and social studies. The modes of knowing described in earlier chapters strongly suggest a holistic approach to the study of educational issues.

9. *Opportunities to participate in mentoring, modeling, and apprenticeship activities.* If the intellectual qualities listed above are indeed important, both preservice and in-service teachers must be exposed to teachers and educational settings in which these characteristics are practiced and valued.

10. *An emphasis on growth, on learning "in-process."* An acceptance of the nine characteristics described above also suggests an approach to teacher education characterized by openendedness. Whatever the experiences and activities engaged in, they are never "completed," never finished. Teachers need continuing opportunity to create, perceive, reflect, represent, collaborate, inquire, and experience.

Experiences for Fostering Intellectual Growth: Some Examples

If one takes these ideas seriously, what kinds of experiences might be designed to foster the intellectual growth of preservice and in-service teachers? How might time be spent by at least some of our students, at least some of the time? I shall describe here three major and a number of minor strands I have developed in my classes that may suggest directions for others to investigate. I believe that some of my work with graduate and undergraduate students is relevant to the ideas expressed in preceding chapters and illustrative of how those ideas might be developed in practice. I conceive of these activities as a series of encounters offering enormous possibilities for intellectual growth and activity. These experiences make it *possible* for preservice and in-service teachers to use the various modes of knowing. However, there are no guarantees that what I describe will indeed produce more inventive, perceptive, receptive, reflective, collaborative, inquiring, growing teachers. The best any of us can do is to create a learning environment that at least allows for and encourages the development of these qualities. If existing teacher education programs are fragmented, authoritarian, passive, regimented, routinized, competitive, and time-dominated (and many of them are), intellectual growth of the sort described in this volume will have little chance to occur.

THE TEACHER AS WRITER

My "Writing for Teachers" course or my writing workshops were not developed to teach the specific set of intellectual characteristics outlined above. On the other hand, it seems clear that writing allows and encourages teachers to perceive, create, reflect, represent, and occasionally to collaborate.

Let me illustrate by reproducing excerpts from a letter I received a few years ago from one of my students. A middle-school English teacher, Jack had found what he was looking for when he enrolled in one of my "Writing for Teachers" courses. He became a successful, well-published teacher-writer, and his letter was a sharing of ideas for potential new articles:

> Whatever it is, I've suddenly turned into a writer. For heaven's sake, I even carry around a notebook, and I'm forever writing sketches. . . . This vacation was totally work. I did research in the library, digging out odd facts about Stamford. I sat in McDonald's at around 9:30 P.M. and listened to the conversation of two old, lonely men. I turned that into a poignant essay on this town without a heart—don't know if it's marketable, but I like it. Then, I went into Caldor's and counted electric gadgets and appliances and wrote a piece about America's love affair with things electric. That was the hardest piece I've ever done; it took over eleven hours. And I'm not sure it's good. But I learned a lot from it. I also wrote an essay of sketches of three of my students; it's a beauty. And another piece of how I, a father, learned that mothering is not a respecter of gender. It's good, very good, and may be worth a lot of money, but I expect it'll take me months to market it. Finally, I came up with seventeen additional ideas, none of them on education. There's an interview I want to conduct with some Haitians; Stamford has 5,000 living here, the second most to Miami, and they live in fear and poverty. . . . I want to do a history of the Citizens' Savings Bank, of all things. I want to find out how many donuts "Mr. Donut" sells and talk to the donutmaker, an ebullient Puerto Rican. I want to find out why Stamford never buried its power lines when an editorial in 1881 called for it. "It's a mark of a primitive civilization," snarled the editor. . . . The more I write, the harder writing is. One would think I'd be perfecting my craft. But the craft part isn't the problem; the art part is the rub. It makes me even more sensitive to the gentle criticism that's required in working with kids. Gentle, gentle, encouraging, encouraging.

Through his writing, Jack had become a sensitive "seer." He learned that good stories exist almost everywhere, if one has the ability to see beneath the surface, to look with fresh eyes. Of course, it would be pretentious to claim that Jack became the perceptive, creative writer that he is solely because he took my course. On the other hand, the course opened the door for him. It gave him the opportunity to think about what he wanted to say, to look for significance in the everyday events occurring around him, to read and reflect on the writing of others, to share his work with his mentor and his classmates, and, most important, to write.

I think it is fair to say that teacher educators generally leave writing concerns of this sort to English departments at the undergraduate level and virtually ignore writing (other than the production of term papers and theses and the writing of examinations) at the graduate level. This seems a tragedy to me, since writing offers so many opportunities for intellectual growth.

A sampling of the sort of work my teacher-writers have produced through the years will illustrate the quality of intellectual life made possible by participation in the "Writing for Teachers" experience. (Each of the passages reproduced here is, of course, an excerpt from a longer book or article.)

Jim Delisle became one of the few single foster parents licensed by the State of New Hampshire. His foster child, Roger, had been a student in Jim's special education class for the preceding four months. This article describes their relationship.

> Roger's entrance explodes the silence of my small, square classroom: fists bloodied, cheeks streaked with tears, his once white shirt stained and soaked with sweat. He has had another fight.
>
> This time Roger knows there is no second chance, that he must go away once again. As before, his short fuse was ignited by the comments of other kids who do not understand that just because he lives with his teacher, Roger is not "queer." And as before, he now regrets having gone out for recess and exposing himself to these taunts.
>
> He is sobbing and breathing, sobbing and breathing, trying to mouth the words "I'm sorry" through his tense, quivering lips. All that comes out is air. As his teacher, as his father, I hold him close. His blood and sweat now stain my clothes as well.[1]

Jack McGarvey describes Richard, one of his eighth-grade students, in a piece entitled "Portraits of Three Students."

There is Richard. Dark, deep-set eyes. Quietly observant. Athletic build.

One day he stopped shyly by to ask for help with an idea for a personal essay. And along the way, we talked of suffering. I asked him if he knew of it. He told me, yes, he suffered from migraine headaches. I was surprised. True, I'd noticed he was absent a bit more than most students, and sometimes he'd be in school in the morning and gone come class time. But never once did I see distress on his handsome face. Nor did he once ask for an extension for an assignment due.

I asked him what suffering migraines was like, feeling both gentle and foolish. Helplessness and pain, he said. Helpless tests at Yale-New Haven Hospital, helpless encouragement from the best of helpless doctors. I told him that I'd never seen him use his illness as a crutch. He couldn't do that, he said, surprised. "I've had them since I was little." "You get used to them then?" "Never." "And your parents? How have they handled this?" "They've handled it well, except that sometimes my mother is frustrated. She can't do anything except come get me and see that my room is dark and quiet. She sometimes feels so helpless that she becomes impatient."

I understand, I said. I understand what she feels. My little girl, since she was two, has had chronic bladder infections, and all I can do is rush her off to the doctor for a urinalysis and then on to the pharmacy for some antibiotics that can cause anemia. I understand the impatience your mother feels at the denial of being able to cure with cool hands on forehead. The denial of being able even to comfort. "Yes," he said, and in his response was wisdom far beyond his fifteen years.[2]

Ellen Stratton writes about the last fly still living in February:

The last fly still living in February is in my classroom. That's okay. He fits right in. He's rushing at the windows, buzzing the hot chocolate, bouncing off the walls like the rest of the kids on a break. Like them, he's as much at home here as is possible for a fly who knows there are better places to be in the world.[3]

Shirley Bostrom, a special education teacher, describes her first experience working with a severely handicapped child named Jennifer.

Five years is such a short time to be alive. I will never forget Jennifer. Few people will. Ironically, I'm not sure she was aware of us. I don't know what being alive meant to her.

I met Jennifer for the first time on November 29, 1979. I had been asked to attend a Planning and Placement Team meeting at a regional center as a representative of the local school district. Jennifer was almost three years old then, and her educational program would soon be our responsibility.

It was a bright, brisk autumn morning as I arrived with little time to spare. I did not know anyone attending the meeting, and I was both apprehensive and excited. As I entered the room I saw eight unfamiliar faces. One of them was Jennifer's. I did not expect her to be there. I wanted to turn and run to the safety of my car. There I would not have to face her reality.

Jennifer was lying there. Her mouth was open, and there was a plastic tube in her nose. Her breathing was labored. Unfocused eyes were half open. Her hand appeared too large for a three-year-old. It rested at an awkward angle. I looked no further.

All my experience in special education had been with socially maladjusted or learning disabled students. Both of these groups appear normal physically. I was still uncomfortable with trainable retarded students. They look different, and their language is often impaired. I should be comfortable with them. I felt this deficit was mine, not theirs.[4]

Other students have written and published work with different emphases. For example, there is Steve Barish's piece on feeding his book habit, Chris Stevenson's description of an incredible scam carried out by his sixth-grade students, Ruth Kirkwood's interview with a brilliant young Maine architect, Sonja Nixon's poems about loneliness and rejection during a stay in Japan, Karen Vetrone's interview with a local actress, Cynthia Talbot's and Ellen Cosgrove's views on excellence, Ann McGreevy's reflections on Charles Darwin, and Karol Sylcox's sensitive description of an extraordinarily creative senior citizen poet who lives in a nearby nursing home.[5]

Still other students have added a visual dimension to their writing. Susan Baum and Robert Kirschenbaum, for example, used photography in their analysis of the special needs of talented students who were labeled "learning disabled." Penny Miller also used photography in her description of her seventh-grade children's study of the growth patterns of guinea pigs, while Karen List's award winning photographs have been used not only to buttress her own writing but also to illustrate the work of others.[6]

It seems clear to me that important things are happening here. One cannot write this sort of material without perceiving well, inventing, reflecting, and inquiring. We often collaborate as we review and critique each other's writing. And the entire process of sharing one's thoughts through writing and photography is obviously a form of representation.

THE TEACHER AS NATURALISTIC RESEARCHER

Research of any kind offers teachers the opportunity to become intellectually involved and engaged. Naturalistic or qualitative research offers unusual opportunities for teachers to practice the arts of creation, invention, improvisation, perception, reflection, representation, collaboration, and holistic inquiry. I have written extensively elsewhere of the potential value of qualitative or naturalistic approaches to the study of educational phenomena.[7] Qualitative techniques allow us to study a much broader range of educational questions—questions that do not always lend themselves to more conventional research methods.

Apart from the insights and understandings the results of such research bring to the field of education, the process of *doing* naturalistic research offers an incredibly rich opportunity for intellectual growth on the part of the researcher. In fact, I am struck by the close connection between the most basic ideas relevant to the modes of knowing discussed in earlier chapters of this volume and the characteristcs that qualitative researchers associate with their methodology. For example, qualitative researchers believe that:

1. The study of children, teachers, and classrooms is enormously complex and subtle. What occurs within classrooms is closely related to what goes on in children's homes, on the playground, in the cafeteria, and on the street. To study one dimension of a child's experience while ignoring others leads to incomplete and inadequate description.

2. An educational question, process, or event needs to be studied longitudinally, over long periods of time, if we are genuinely to understand it.

3. The most effective way to study a given phenomenon is through direct, on-site, face-to-face contact with people and events in question. What people do is often different from what they say.

4. It is vitally important to understand the *meaning* behind behavior, to understand how others view their world. High school students may indeed join informal groups or cliques in school, but such information is relatively useless unless we know why students choose

to associate with one group rather than another, what their perceptions are of the values and purposes of such groups.

5. The basic function of the qualitative or naturalistic researcher is to provide the reader with the richest, fullest, most comprehensive *description* possible so that the subtleties in human behavior may be revealed.

6. Research questions emerge as the researcher becomes involved in his or her study. While researchers have a general idea of where they are going, new and unpredictable questions are likely to develop as one "gets into" the data.

A few years ago I became convinced that my students ought to become involved in this kind of seeking or inquiring, not only in master's or doctoral theses, but also as a part of their day-to-day approach to the study of educational questions that seemed important to them. The qualitative research course I have developed at the University of Connecticut has led to student involvement in such projects as those described here.

A study of the use of out-of-school time. Various reports on American education suggest that education could be improved by lengthening the school day and year and by increasing the amount of homework. The superintendent of schools of Farmington (Connecticut) thought it might be wise to find out how his students were using their out-of-school time before rushing into a series of changes that might or might not be effective. A group of my students agreed to carry out a study of the use of out-of-school time by Farmington's children. While a number of data-gathering devices were used in the study, the fundamental source of data was a daily log kept by 179 students in the third, sixth, seventh, and ninth grades. Analyses of the logs by my students led to the raising of a number of important questions our research team thought needed discussion prior to any decision to increase the school day or year.

For example, we found a "seventh-grade slump," that is, seventh graders watch more television, dislike school more, participate less in learning-related activities, and so forth, than do all other grades studied. It seemed to us that special study should be made of the nature of seventh-grade academic programs, extracurricular activities, and out-of-school learning opportunities. In addition, we found that Farmington's children do not participate to any great extent in clubs, lessons, hobbies, community service activities, or out-of-school jobs. Perhaps most important, we found that parents spent relatively little time with their children.

A study of interethnic relations in a middle school. A team of graduate students collaborated with a group of middle school teachers and administrators in order to investigate the nature of ethnic relations in their school. A group of twenty volunteer teachers worked directly with the university team as the project evolved. During the study, teachers, administrators, and students were interviewed and observed, curriculum materials were examined, and emerging data were shared with the staff. Ultimately, the research team concluded that (a) children entering the middle school from a series of culturally isolated "feeder schools" needed help in adjusting to the cultural diversity of the middle school; (b) the bilingual English as a Second Language program and the bilingual program for gifted and talented children seemed to have a divisive, segregating effect on the children participating in such programs; (c) some teachers appeared to ignore aspects of the formal curriculum that dealt with ethnicity and ethnic relations; and (d) many extracurricular activities were not available to minority group children because of busing schedules.

Teacher and student perceptions of a high school sex education curriculum. The sex education curriculum at the Westport (Connecticut) high school was selected as an "exemplary" program by a group of national experts. The curriculum was thorough, well organized, clearly written, practical, and specific. Nevertheless, what was selected as "exemplary" was the *written* curriculum guide. Teachers and administrators responsible for the program wanted to know more about how the teachers teaching the course and the students involved viewed its content and methods. Thus we sought student and teacher perceptions of the nature and quality of the relationships among students and between students and teachers in the course; of the quality and effectiveness of the various activities of the course; of the major strengths and weaknesses of the program; of the possible value and meaning of the course and its relative importance compared to other courses; and of the ways in which the school as a whole supports or undermines the goals of the course. Some of the more significant student perceptions are summarized here.

1. Virtually all students stated that they perceived the sex educa-

tion course to be value-free, that teachers did not take positions on various issues. Yet students' elaborated responses indicated that this was not necessarily the case in practice. For example, students responded that they learned that "birth control was desirable, certainly not a sin," that it is a "sensible, reasonable practice for intelligent adults." Other students reported that they now feel "less guilty about sexual feelings," that they are "normal and natural," and that sexuality and one's body are essentially "good" rather than evil or "something to be ashamed of."

2. Students also disagreed about the perceptions of the milieu of the school itself as a whole vis-à-vis the positions emphasized in the human sexuality course. Some thought the course existed virtually apart from the school as a whole, having little or no influence on other teachers, students, or programs. Some reported that many teachers "had sexist expectations" and that they "stereotyped boys and girls." Many girls stated that there is still a double "social standard" in the school and community for boys and girls, that is, "it's okay for boys to sleep around but if a girl does it, it's wrong." Some girls felt that "boys still don't accept girls as equals," although this view was perceived as changing by some girls.

All these activities have led to the development of a new course to be offered at the University of Connecticut for the first time in September, 1984. The course was designed jointly by the Departments of Educational Administration and Curriculum and Instruction. Simply stated, it will focus on the study of the teaching-learning act in its classroom setting. Teams of university students will develop data-gathering techniques on campus and then move into the schools for an intensive clinical experience. As a result of these activities, we hope that both our students and the participating teachers and administrators will have developed a number of more effective ways of examining the complex phenomenon we call teaching. How these techniques are eventually used in any given school will of course depend upon the needs and interests of that school. The response to our proposal for this course has been overwhelmingly positive.

I have described these approaches at some length because it seems to me that engaging in this sort of inquiry inevitably involves the preservice and in-service teacher-researcher in all of the intellectual modes I outlined earlier. That is, the student must perceive, create and invent, collaborate, represent and reflect. To design and carry out these sorts of activities allow no other choice.

THE TEACHER AS STUDENT OF CHILDREN

The study of children in their natural settings can be one of the most rewarding activities of teaching. Surely all our great teachers, from Montaigne to Montessori and Piaget, *created* and *invented* ways to understand their pupils better. They *perceived* the complexities of children's thinking and *inquired* into them; they *reflected* upon those perceptions, *collaborated* with colleagues, and *represented* their ideas in writing.

Currently my students and I are engaged in a number of investigations of student perceptions of what has been taught—what Goodlad would call the "experienced curriculum."[8] Persons make their own meanings out of the experiences that would appear to be "common" to all. What we teach is the "taught" curriculum; what learners learn is the "experienced" curriculum. And despite our most valiant efforts, they are not always the same.

We are intrigued with the notion of the experienced curriculum partly because we know little about how to assess it, partly because of the massive efforts underway at all levels of education to ignore it by concentrating on assessment largely by standardized, paper and pencil testing, and partly because of the obvious opportunities it offers teachers to do what teachers ought to do, that is, get to know and understand children's minds in a more probing, Piagetian way. How then do we assess this "curriculum of the mind?"

Schools and colleges of education could do, of course, what has been done effectively for the past decade or so at the Prospect School in Bennington, Vermont. The Prospect Archives and Center for Education and Research has a unique fourteen-year collection of data on children, including samples of individual children's paintings, drawings, work with clay, writing, number work, video tapes of classroom activity, and teacher observations. These data are used by graduate and undergraduate students in education as well as by the Prospect School staff and are obviously a great help to anyone seriously interested in discovering the meaning of school experience to a given child.

My students and I took a different approach to the question.

During the last two years, we have put together a collection of techniques designed to assess the curriculum elementary children *experience*. The collection, of course, is constantly in flux. We develop ideas, try them out, discard some, retain others. Some of our more successful approaches are described here.

1. *Card sorts.* Assume, for example, that a group of eleven-year-olds has been studying a foreign nation—Ghana. Assume also that one of the goals of the unit was to help children understand that Ghanians live in a country that is both old and new, rich and poor, developed yet developing.

We show the child a collection of pictures of modern apartment buildings, slum-like shacks, an airport, television studio, modern hospital, a rickety bus on a muddy dirt road, children dressed smartly in school uniforms on the way to school, children sitting in an outdoor, rural village school, and so forth. Obviously, pictures should be chosen to match the general thrust and purpose of the social studies curriculum and of the teacher. Then we ask the child to sort pictures into three piles: first, people and places you *would* find in Ghana; second, those you would *not* find in Ghana; and third, those you are not sure of. After the sorting, we ask the child to explain the reasons for sorting the cards as he or she did.

2. *Object sorting.* Continuing with our Ghanian example, we gather a group of commonly used objects (toothbrush, nail file, scissors, watch, calculator, ballpoint pen, pocket radio, and the like) and ask the child to sort these and explain as in the card sort.

3. *Picture interpretation.* We choose three or four pictures from the social studies chapter under study at the time, perhaps a Spanish explorer in armor, a picture of a tribal chieftain in full ceremonial dress, a Japanese businessman walking down a Tokyo street. We ask the child to tell about these persons. Who are they? Where do you think they live? Tell about their houses, their families, their children. What do they do? Why do you think they do whatever they do?

We use many other techniques, of course. We have discussed samples of music, paintings, graffiti. We have tried sentence-completion exercises, word association ("Which words best describe how you feel about Ghanians?"), triad sorts ("Which two pictures or objects are alike, which one is different?"), simple listings ("List the things Ghanian children do."), miniature models of various structures, articles of clothing. And we have used simple, straightforward, one-on-one interviews. Fundamentally, we are trying to find ways to probe beneath the surface, to see what remains after the lesson has been taught, to get closer to the minds of children. These activities call for intellectual involvement on the part of preservice and in-service teachers who are themselves creating, testing, revising, and evaluating the devices and the data they yield.

In this chapter I have tried to identify some significant issues suggested by the theoreticians in the earlier chapters of this volume and to illustrate them with practical illustrations drawn from my own work at the University of Connecticut. Clearly, these ideas are intended to suggest possibilities rather than to prescribe solutions.

Footnotes

1. Jim Delisle, "Notes to Myself: Roger and Jim," *Media and Methods* 16 (April 1980): 69.

2. Jack McGarvey, "Portraits of Three Students," *English Journal* 71 (December 1982): 20.

3. Ellen Stratton, "The Fly," *English Journal* 73 (February 1984): 58.

4. Shirley Bostrom, "Jennifer," *JASH Journal* 8 (Spring 1983): 58.

5. See Steve Barish, "Addicted to Print: A Diary," *New York Times*, 20 March 1977, p. 30; Chris Stevenson, "Meet Jason, Our Classroom Spirit," *Learning* 10 (April/May 1982): 34-37; Ruth Kirkwood, "Auburn Architect," *Maine Life* (October/November 1981): 40; Sonja Nixon, "Poems on Japan" (unpublished); Karen Vetrone, "Joan Kendall Walsh, Actress," *Port Washington News*, 6 October 1983, p. 24; Vincent Rogers, Cynthia Talbot, and Ellen Cosgrove, "Excellence: Some Lessons from America's Best Run Companies," *Educational Leadership* 41 (February 1984): 39-41; Ann McGreevy, "Charles Darwin," *G/C/T* (September/October 1980): 59; Karol Sylcox, "Extraordinary Resources: Our Elders," *Neighbors* 1 (January 1984):1.

6. See Susan Baum and Robert Kirschenbaum, "Recognizing Special Talents in Learning Disabled Students," *Teaching Exceptional Children* 16 (Winter 1984): 92; Penny Miller's photographs in "Guinea Pigs," *National Geographic World* 102 (February 1984): 4.

7. Vincent Rogers, "Qualitative Research: Another Way of Knowing," in *Using What We Know about Teaching*, ed. Philip L. Hosford (Alexandria, Virginia: Association for Supervision and Curriculum Development, 1984), pp. 85-106.

8. John I. Goodlad, *Curriculum Inquiry* (New York: McGraw-Hill, 1979).

CHAPTER XIV

Educational Research and Evaluation

JILLIAN MALING AND BRUCE KEEPES

Both research and evaluation attempt to inform, to impart knowledge. Both are activities that aim to get at the truth. They are not, of themselves, forms of knowledge or ways of knowing. One assumes that both researchers and evaluators know. One reads research and evaluation reports in order to inform oneself, to know, and to understand. However, in both research and evaluation the form of knowledge has, until the last ten to fifteen years, been drawn largely from a single paradigm of knowledge. Indeed much of the work currently undertaken in educational research and evaluation in what might be termed the "mainstream" still exists within that single knowledge paradigm.

The Dominant Paradigm of Educational Research and Evaluation

Twenty years ago evaluation was seen largely as a form of measurement. As such, this form of evaluation is referred to here under the generic name of quantitative evaluation. The techniques and approaches were very largely those of a classical form of educational research, dominated by paradigms drawn from agricultural botany. The method is essentially a hypothetico-deductive one derived from mental testing and psychological testing movements, with many of the statistical and experimental techniques used being developed first in agricultural work.

> Students, rather like plant crops, are given pretests (the seedlings are weighed or measured) and then submitted to different experiences (treatment conditions). Subsequently, after a period of time, their attainment (growth or yield) is measured to indicate the relative efficiency of the methods (fertilizers) used.

> Studies of this kind are designed to yield data of one particular type, that is, "objective" numerical data that permit statistical analyses. Isolated variables like IQ, social class, test scores, personality profiles and attitude ratings are codified and processed to indicate the efficiency of new curricula, media, or methods.[1]

Basically, the approach aims at developing a science of educational practice by discovering the laws underlying human behavior. The general epistemological model is that of the scientific. The central problem becomes one of controlling experimental conditions and developing precise measurements for subsequent statistical analysis.

The various forms of quantitative evaluation have in common the need to predict, or as Stake has termed it, to establish preordinate variables.[2] Much quantitative inquiry is also designed to construct universal propositions and theories that can be used to explain, predict, and control behavior. The theories and generalizations are developed through processes of observing that behavior, forming generalizations and hypotheses based on the observations, and subjecting these hypotheses to empirical verification. Quantitative inquiry has a distinctive approach to the manner in which generalizations are made, as it builds inferential bridges across populations.[3] A quantitative evaluator will examine a randomly chosen sample of a larger population and will focus attention on the sample only insofar as it is representative of that general population.

Those adopting the quantitative approach view reality as separable into distinct components. The role of the researcher is to explore the situation with a list of a priori independent and dependent variables, and categories of behavior that are central to the study being undertaken. Attempts are made to control all the other variables seen as confounding; those *seen* as extraneous are ignored. The separate independent and dependent variables are then analyzed statistically in order to determine significant relationships. It follows that quantitative inquiry is most concerned with obtaining a high degree of interrater and interobserver consistency.[4] This in turn necessitates focusing on very discrete aspects of overt behavior that have been operationally defined.

Various measures are used to assess intended outcomes including tests, attitude surveys, interest surveys, anecdotal records, student artifacts, and interviews with students. In each case, data are gathered and analyzed in terms of the preordained categories. Data are abstracted and combined into numerical indices, which are then analyzed using statistical procedures. Student achievement tests relating to intended outcomes may be norm-referenced (which enables comparison of individual and group performance), or they may be criterion-referenced (which permits assessing the ability of students to perform observable behaviors against certain predefined criteria such as curriculum objectives.)[5]

An extension of the above is to compare the performance of students exposed to different curricula in terms of some prespecified domain of learning. This particular method of curriculum evaluation has been very popular, although Walker and Schaffarzick,[6] after reviewing more than fifteen years of work of this kind, reached the conclusion that different curricula are associated with different patterns of achievement and that the differing patterns of achievement are in turn associated with different patterns of emphases found in the curricula. More directly, students learn what they are exposed to rather than what curriculum developers necessarily intended that they should learn.

In the quantitative paradigm, evaluation studies in education (unlike, for example, the health professions) have basic difficulty in finding suitable control of comparison groups and in being able to assign students randomly to control and treatment groups. Difficulties in this area led to the debate in 1960 between Cronbach and Scriven about the value of comparison groups in evaluations and, more recently, to the suggestion that quasi-experimental time series investigations should be particularly useful quantitative tools.[7] Here the major focus of the research report also lies in the numerical index, which can be used to assess the extent to which intended outcomes have been achieved. In most cases, the index will indicate both the strength of the observed relationship between intended outcomes and student achievement and the likelihood of obtaining such a result from chance rather than from a specific intervention, for example, a curriculum innovation. Again, the epistemological model is that of the scientific.

Some Criticisms of the Dominant Paradigm

The criticisms that follow are not intended to apply to all quantitative evaluations or any specific evaluation. Rather, they are presented to highlight some of the limitations of the dominant paradigm and to summarize the major criticisms that have appeared in the literature.

First, the approach emphasizes statistical significance rather than educational significance. If most four-year-olds who watch "Sesame Street" regularly know on the average four more letters of the alphabet than those who do not watch the program, is that an educationally significant gain or not?

Second, given the emphasis on research design and statistical techniques, there is a tendency to fit the study to the technique rather than vice versa. Application of an appropriate technique often appears to be of more importance than pursuing a question of significance that does not mesh with available techniques. Important data, particularly those relating to developing attitudes, changes in program, and so forth are sometimes ignored. For example, an evaluation of two different approaches to beginning reading, using control groups and standardized tests, showed no significant difference between the children's reading achievement. A footnote indicated that the evaluator had noticed "incidentally" that one group of children liked reading and seemed to be more comfortable at school than the other group, but that information was not part of the "study" since it was not one of the preordained variables. In another evaluation, teachers stopped using some of the new curriculum materials (the necessary art supplies were simply not available), but the evaluation proceeded as if use of the materials had continued throughout the year.

Third, the emphasis on carefully selected and controlled studies, well-defined treatments or interactions, and appropriate quantitative analyses sharply reduces the length of "treatment" examined and the attention paid to the context or environment in which the study occurred. Eisner reported that a survey of research articles in the *American Educational Research Journal* over two volumes indicated an average of about forty minutes for the treatment.[8]

Fourth, the need to select variables before a study commences means that variables emerging as significant in the *particular* location in which a study is being undertaken cannot strictly speaking be included, since these differences are strained out of the conclusions in the effort to catch the generalizable. An evaluator of an art program had been led to expect that the children in each of the schools were to be largely engaged in painting. She planned accordingly. Not far into the term one of the teachers switched to textiles. Not only was the evaluator left with a set of inappropriate information-gathering techniques but also with no provision for noting the change and exploring it. Yet the change at that one location could have had real educational significance. In many ways the effect of the methodology was to iron out or ignore differences that were of immediate significance for those participating, and potentially significant for others working in similar settings.

Fifth, such evaluations frequently produce information about matters that are not seen as of immediate concern to participants, to those sponsoring the study, and to other interested groups. What is there is solid, but often low on "relevance" and is frequently expressed in language with little meaning for those not familiar with the research tradition to which the evaluation belongs.

Sixth, as implied in several of the points above, such an approach to evaluation rests heavily on predetermination: the evaluator has to decide in advance on the significant variables, on ways of gathering information, on procedures for analysis, on sources of information, and even on the outcomes to be sought. Evaluators are sometimes given only a short time to do a study of an educational program that gives heavy emphasis to experiential learning and to involvement of students. Moreover, the program could change direction in keeping with student needs. If something of mutual interest emerges under these circumstances, it is largely a matter of good fortune. Evaluators often wonder why teachers and administrators do not use their reports; teachers, for their part, wonder why the evaluator paid attention to the peculiar things he or she selected.

Finally, the extent to which evaluation in educational settings can be "controlled," in the sense required by classic research design, is limited. Traditional administrative research, for example, requires significant variables to be identified, to be separated clearly and consistently from other aspects of the situation, and to remain constant throughout the period of study. Within traditional research (and thus evaluation) design, such variables must be controlled through randomization using very large samples. Such an approach is demanding in terms of time and resources. But a more fundamental issue is that such control, if achieved, would lead to a laboratory exercise with little relevance to those actually working in educational settings outside the "controlled" ones.

Some Recent Developments in the Dominant Paradigm

COST-BENEFIT ANALYSIS

With the increased demands for accountability on the one hand, and the tightening of resources available to education during the 1970s on the other hand, quantitative techniques of a different kind have evolved. Chief among these has been the development of cost-benefit analysis. Such an approach addresses the concept of worth or value of a program by attempting to focus upon social values as delineated in terms of costs and benefits and by exploring the interactive consequences of alternate ways of distributing resources. The methodology involved has been derived from the field of economics and attempts to provide a satisfactory way of converting social values to costs and benefits. The whole procedure is intended as a way of assigning a monetary value to alternative choices.

Any society has limited resources; hence any shift in how those resources are assigned has both a cost factor and a benefit. For example, when a new program is installed in a school or a district, costs include not only those directly associated with the program (personnel, physical plant, materials, disruptions to ongoing programs, administration, student time) but also other opportunities that are foregone. Who receives what benefits from a program, from whose perspective it is a benefit, and who bears the brunt of the cost are the fundamental social issues addressed in cost-benefit analysis. As such, the cost-benefit paradigm views truth as demonstrable; truth is whatever can be demonstrated to be logically consistent with the basic values, axioms, and definitions of the system, and the focus is to make judgments on the worth of possible alternatives.[9]

Evaluation of the worth of an educational program to society or to a local community puts a premium on agreed-upon educational goals. As suggested above, the gains of one group within the educational system (for example, slow learners) and the gains and the losses of another group (for example, the gifted) need to be taken into account. However, differential weighting of costs and benefits for different subgroups in society carries with it deep-seated philosophical implications about equality. In practice, cost-benefit analysis in educational evaluation draws attention to the problems involved in obtaining the consensus on and commitment to the goals of the program itself.[10]

In general, the case for carrying out a cost-effective analysis of alternative educational programs or goals is a strong one, yet the branch of inquiry is still relatively young and techniques are still being developed. The judgments of the evaluator in setting out rules and guidelines for estimating costs and effects represent a crucial variable in determining the outcomes of the evaluation. The omission of particular cost components or program outcomes, the selection of a discount rate, and the projections of costs or results all represent areas where different judgments may alter appreciably the cost-effective ratings of alternatives.

The implications of the foregoing are that the cost-effectiveness analyst, and the user of his or her results, should feel professionally obligated to approach the analysis cautiously and with an awareness of its limitations. The user should recognize the fact that the conclusions of such studies do not in themselves define a policy action. They serve as useful sources of information that must be combined with factors not taken into account in the study in order to make public choices that are reasonable, efficient, and equitable.[11]

In a recent survey of evaluation of programs, Talmage noted that the philosophical base of the cost-benefit analyzers, including Levin, was essentially logico-analytic, the discipline was basically economics and accounting, and the focus of the methodology was on judging the worth of a program in terms of costs and benefits, defined in financial terms.[12] At the same time, the cost-benefit analyzers retained many of the hallmarks of quantitative evaluation: control or comparison groups were included wherever possible; the participants had no role in carrying out the evaluation; the evaluator was essentially independent of whatever program was being examined; and the evaluator could, and most often did, ignore both internal and external political pressures.

Another extension of quantitative techniques has been an increasing concern about such standards of science as objectivity, experimentation, and generalization as they apply to evaluation. Glass and Ellett concluded that "a large part of scientific judgment is knowing which circumstances are important and which are not. Such forms of knowing are largely tacit and qualitative, based on experience and involving assumptions of regularity, order, and stasis that are never formally checked as a part of science itself."[13] Clearly, statements such as this reach out beyond experimental design.

THE ECLECTICS

In response to concerns such as the above, evaluators have emerged in the last decade who supplement essentially a quantitative and experimental position through careful attention to context. In her appraisal of evaluation of programs, Talmage termed these evaluators "the eclectics."[14] As such, they do not reject experimental design but regard process and context as critical components of an evaluation study. Overall, they seriously question the value of large-scale experimental studies for many of the reasons noted above and acknowledge that the client-evaluator relationship influences the program.[15] Further, there is a concern about the overemphasis on achievement as the single most important outcome. Achievement is criticized as too narrow an indication of program goals,[16] and achievement testing itself is criticized as being culturally biased.[17]

In general the eclectics use quasi-experimental designs. Descriptive data are viewed as necessary to augment and enhance the interpretability of the quantitative data base. Hence descriptions of the process by which a program is implemented, as well as the social and political context in which it takes place, are viewed as important areas for data collection. Variables are still predetermined, but design is flexible enough to take into account issues that emerge in the course of the evaluation itself. The evaluator assumes a nonthreatening stance and consults with and includes program staff and participants wherever possible. Fundamentally, as Cronbach noted, evaluators are considered as educators.[18] They interact with program participants. The process of evaluation becomes, in a sense, a subspecies of the process of teaching and learning.

Qualitative Evaluation: An Alternative Paradigm

In the late 1960s, John Mann drew attention to the significance of aesthetic criticism for evaluation, in particular for curriculum evaluation.[19] Mann proposed a type of criticism in which the function of the critic-evaluator is to disclose the meaning in a particular curriculum of the choices made by its creator. In developing a critique, the critic selects on the basis of his personal knowledge of ethical reality. Mann argued that such an approach, while it might lack the precision of empirical methodology, would present the possibility of continuous discovery of new meanings in educational situations, particularly when taking the form of conversations among interested persons. Although Mann drew on a form of literary criticism, he noted that other forms of criticism were possible. The application of the techniques of literary criticism to evaluation has been further extended by Willis and by Kelly.[20] Both made it clear that it was the role of the evaluator as critic not only to disclose the meaning of the situation but to judge.

Eisner's work draws on a different critical perspective, that of art.[21] In doing so, he has consistently argued that the set of methods and procedures he and his colleagues have developed is intended to complement, not replace, the experimental ones commonly used in evaluation and research. In brief, he uses the twin concepts of educational connoisseurship and educational criticism, both drawn from the domain of art criticism. As connoisseur, the evaluator must be able not only to observe the range of subtle qualities present in an educational situation but also to see their significance. Connoisseurship is "the art of perception that makes the appreciation of such complexity possible."[22] As critic, he or she must be able to recreate that situation so that it is accessible to others in its complexity and nuances of meaning. It is, so to speak, the finely developed educational eye and palate of the connoisseur that provide the content for the critic. Once having seen as connoisseur, the educational critic writes, videotapes, or films the educational situation:

> What the critic aims at is not only to discern the character and qualities constituting the object or event [but also to provide] a rendering in linguistic terms of what it is that he or she has encountered so that others not possessing his level of connoisseurship can also enter into the work. . . . The function of criticism is educational. Its aim is to lift the veils that keep the eyes from seeing by providing the bridge needed by others to experience the qualities and relationships within some area of activity. . . . The critic must talk or write about what he has encountered; he must . . . provide a rendering of the qualities that constitute that work, its significance, and the quality of his experience when he interacts with it.[23]

The critic's work has three aspects to it: description, interpretation, and appraisal, which in practice are often intertwined in a single entity. The description is designed to give the reader or listener a visual picture of the educational situation as the connoisseur perceived it. Hence the critic makes use of metaphor, narrative, and even poetic language to enable a reader to enter the connoisseur's experience of that particular educational setting. Interpretation takes two forms: intrinsic and extrinsic.[24] Intrinsic interpretation concentrates on interpreting the events and meanings of the patterns of behavior in terms of the setting itself. Extrinsic interpretation relates these patterns of events and behavior to theories drawn from, for example, the social sciences. Finally, the role of the critic includes that of making an appraisal of the worth of the activity: "Education is a normative enterprise; it seeks to realize certain virtues. The educational critic attempts to facilitate this process by appraising what has been described and interpreted."[25] The outcome of curriculum criticism should be an illumination of the assumptions, convictions, and beliefs which, though often implicit, have served to guide the observed patterns of action and interaction. Given that, there is also the opportunity for those engaged in the activities to experience them as the educational critic has, and the opportunity for them and other readers to think about those educational activities as the curriculum connoisseur has.

The significance of the work in developing a critical approach in educational evaluation and research lies not only in the resources and challenges it offers but also in the fact that the approach comes from a nonscientific base and as such demonstrates that the scientific base is not the only one from which powerful and useful approaches to evaluation and research may be evolved.

Closely related to criticism as an approach to evaluation and research is the line of work that has its roots in phenomenological inquiry. A key difference between the two relates to the extent that criticism views the educational situation through the eye of the critic as connoisseur. The phenomenologist aims to view the educational situation through the eyes of the actors (students, teachers, and those others whom the central participants see as significant). The approach rests on the initial identification of the key participants in an educational situation and proceeds by examining the consciousness that each actor has of whatever objects or processes enter his or her field of perception. It moves on to establish how meanings develop for each of the actors and what the experience means to them. In so doing, the inquiry attempts to discover which qualities in the educational experience are most pervasive or widely shared among the group and most meaningful to participants. Willis suggests that, whereas in scientific evaluation the evaluator runs alongside the train making notes of what he or she observes through the window, the phenomenological evaluation is like boarding the train to interact with passengers and engineer.[26]

As the approach has been developed by Pinar and Grumet,[27] it has focused on enabling the actors in a particular educational setting to reflect on the meaning of their educational experience and to develop heightened consciousness and understanding. Willis and Allen argued that it is also possible, as the actors' individual "stories" develop and as they reflect on their educational experience, for common patterns to appear and for the commonalities of experience to emerge.[28] Bussis, Chittenden, and Amarel have similarly used the commonalities of experience among the actors and recurrent themes to depict the "lived in" experience of a curriculum.[29]

Methods used in phenomenological inquiry include observation, open-ended and conversational interviews with participants, autobiographic techniques, guided self-reflection, and questionnaires. The outcome of the inquiry should be an account of the educational situation seen through the eyes of the actors as individuals and as a group, as well as an interpretation of the significance of that experience. Willis suggests that one way of providing an illuminating interpretation is to provide a comparison of the experience as the actors see it against a background of ideas that will help to depict the educational significance of the situation.[30]

The set of approaches to evaluation and research that may be broadly termed naturalistic also rests on a different view of knowledge. Hamilton has characterized this emerging group of approaches to evaluation as "pluralist" in that they attempt to take account of the value positions of multiple audiences:

> Compared with the classic models, they tend to be more extensive (not necessarily centered on numerical data), more naturalistic (based on program activity rather than program intent), and more adaptable (not constrained by experimental and preordinate designs). In turn, they are likely to be sensitive

> to the different values of program participants, to endorse empirical methods which incorporate ethnographic fieldwork, to develop feedback materials which are couched in the natural language of the recipients, and to shift the locale of formal judgment from the evaluator to the participants.[31]

Wolf and Tymitz stressed that "naturalistic inquiry attempts to present "slice-of-life" episodes documented through natural language and representing as closely as possible how people feel, what they know, and what their concerns, beliefs, perceptions, and understandings are.[32]

Taken together, the definitions suggest a focus on people as subjects and on interactions with people, mainly through interviewing, as the typical method of gathering data. The emphasis on "slice-of-life" vignettes also conveys something of the informality of approach that has characterized much of the action research carried out in schools, using what is loosely termed "case-study methods." Guba and Lincoln have recently identified naturalistic approaches as the ones, in their view, that are typically most appropriate for educational evaluation and research.[33] Certainly in the last ten or more years there has been a rapid growth in work using such approaches and a great deal of argument as to appropriate methods, central issues, ethical principles, and so on.

We give here extracts from the work of three individuals to illustrate the approach in general and to indicate the differences in practice within it. The three are Robert Stake's responsive evaluation, Louis Smith's ethnographic studies, and Barry MacDonald's democratic evaluation.

Although Smith's work was published earlier, it was Stake's brief monograph that heralded the changing methodologies.[34] In this publication, circulated in draft three to five years earlier, Stake argued as follows:

> An educational evaluation is *responsive evaluation* if it orients more directly to program activities than to program intents, [if it] responds to audience requirements for information, and if the different value perspectives present are referred to in reporting the success and failure of the program. (p. 14)

The orientation of the evaluation is largely informed, proceeding on the basis of a great deal of interaction between evaluation and project participants.

To do a responsive evaluation, the evaluator conceives of a plan of observation and negotiations. He arranges for various persons to observe the program, and with their help prepares brief narratives, portrayals, product displays, graphs, and so forth. He finds out what is of value to his audience and gathers expressions of worth from various individuals whose points of view differ. Of course, he checks the quality of his records: he gets program personnel to react to the accuracy of his portrayals, authority figures to react to the importance of various findings, and audience members to react to the relevance of his findings. He does much of this informally, iterating and keeping a record of action and reaction. He chooses media accessible to his audiences to increase the likelihood and fidelity of communication. He might prepare a final written report; he might not, depending on what he and his clients have agreed on. (p. 14)

Stake makes quite explicit his reasons for suggesting a move away from the "preordinate" approach:

One of the principal reasons for backing away from the preordinate approach to evaluation is to improve communication with audiences. . . . The responsive approach tries to respond to the natural ways in which people assimilate information and arrive at understanding. Direct personal experience is an efficient, comprehensive, and satisfying way of creating understanding, but is not usually available to our audiences. (pp. 22-23)

The responsive evaluation approach means that the evaluator must have a real capacity to listen and the necessary technical skills to capture accurately and fully the response of others, even in situations where his or her own response is itself strongly felt and conceptualized. It also means reporting or portrayal of multiple rather than single viewpoints.

The evaluator in a responsive evaluation must be able to respond to each of those involved in the project in such a way that the individual responses, while being brought into relation with each other, are nevertheless kept distinct and presented in their own right. The role of respondent, on the one hand, thrusts one into intimate contact with the project, and on the other hand, must be kept distinct from the roles of workshop leaders, project coordinators, and other participants.

The application of ethnographic techniques to the study of education, originally a separate line of work but one that now is frequently merged with responsive approaches, is seen in Smith and Geoffrey's

Complexities of an Urban Classroom.[35] The study is based on a term-long participant observation of a single classroom in a high school. The resulting work not only gives a full description of that setting, but lays a firm basis for grounded theory through its deliberate and constant placing of observations into a theoretical framework. Smith and Schumacher took a similar approach in the evaluation of the Aesthetic Education Program developed at CEMREL.[36] Smith has written extensively about this methodology.[37] The overall thrust of his work is through close observation of the project, entailing extensive direct contact with project members in whatever settings they are working over a considerable period of time. Relevant data include: form and content of verbal action between participants; form and content of verbal interaction with researchers; nonverbal behavior: patterns of action and nonaction; and traces, archival records, artifacts, documents.

Records are kept in the form of audio tapes and field notes developed by the evaluator as well as in the form of materials that are part of the project: reports, student papers, tests, and comments from teachers. (Smith and Schumacher noted that "as always in this type of inquiring, we feel inundated with 'the data'.") The records are constantly sorted and sifted as the effort is made to develop grounded theory:

> The development of grounded theory is not haphazard. The researcher constantly tests his emerging hypotheses against the reality he is observing daily. Unlike the usual prestructured research designs, participant observation includes a constant necessity for testing theory against real data. . . . Because of his awareness of the setting, the researcher knows what situations are likely to provide discordant information. He enters these situations to confront this possibly negative evidence, probes to find out why the theory cannot account for what is observed, and gradually develops his theory. It makes sense, then, to think of participant observation as a series of studies which follow each other daily and build on each other in a cybernetic fashion.[38]

In the role of "noninterfering observer" the participant observer-evaluator has plenty of opportunities for providing project participants with feedback. Smith and Schumacher note the use of memos on specific issues, vignettes describing particular observations, and intensive discussion with project staff. This approach has a strong drive toward interpreting observations by drawing on relevant theoretical insights and then transforming these insights by redeveloping them in terms of the data gathered in this new setting. Further, as a deliberate policy, each evaluation report has included a substantial methodological appendix. These materials trace Smith's own development, while offering to others in the field a formidable corpus of practical and theoretical insights.

Democratic evaluation, as its originator Barry MacDonald sees it, is an information service to the whole community.[39] Sponsorship of the evaluation is not seen as providing any special claims on the service, pluralism of values is acknowledged explicitly, and the evaluator has a real commitment to the notion of an "informed citizenry." The evaluator constantly acts as an "honest broker" between the various groups involved in the educational program and employs a language that is readily understood by all parties. The evaluator's role is mainly to gather definitions of the program, as well as reactions to it. In so doing, confidentiality is guaranteed to program participants and those with whom the evaluator interacts. Further, program participants control the use of the information that the evaluator has gathered. No recommendations are made by the evaluator. The study is considered successful when it serves a range of audiences. The key concepts of democratic evaluation are confidentiality, negotiation, and accessibility.

As with many other approaches to evaluation one purpose is to provide relevant data for those in a position to make decisions. The decision makers, however, are seen as complex groups likely to hold and act from different value positions. Nevertheless, there is still the confidence that the information generated during the study will contribute to better decision making in the light of the priorities, values, and circumstances of those making the decisions.

MacDonald sees the knowledge emanating from such studies as democratic in that studies are only undertaken when the necessary negotiations have been concluded with sponsors to ensure the evaluator's independence and the signing over of the evaluation data to those who are evaluated. His position is that in a pluralist society the evaluator has no right to use his position to promote his personal values, or to choose which particular educational ideologies he will regard as legitimate. In order to control possible bias, both accounts and boundaries are negotiated with project participants. The first procedure means that each participant is given the opportunity to check any evaluation accounts in terms of their fairness, accuracy, and the relevance of the evaluator's representation of the participant's views. The negotiation of boundaries refers to the way participants are given control over the release of the accounts developed during the evaluation.

The methods used in the study are similar to those described in Stake's responsive evaluation, with the aim being to develop one or more case studies in the course of the evaluation. It is not in the actual methods used for gathering information that MacDonald's approach is distinctive, but rather in the way it raises directly the question of power and politics in educational evaluation research. MacDonald attempts to equalize the power relationships among sponsor, evaluator, and program participants by the procedures devised for negotiating the evaluator's independence of sponsors, for gathering the information, and for handling possible release of the case study to a wider audience.

Summary and Implications

The single most important implication is quite simply that the training of educational evaluators and researchers must change. The premises that human understanding is fostered through a variety of forms and that knowledge is not defined by any simple set of criteria but is multiple in character, carry direct implications for the way courses in educational research and evaluation are structured.

First, most courses currently offering such training assume a single paradigm of knowledge. Most training takes place within this (scientific) paradigm. Classes on information-gathering techniques concentrate on the formal approach, structured prior to the researcher's contact with the educational setting. Techniques for analysis are almost exclusively quantitative. (It is significant that most graduate courses in education include work on research design and statistical methods; few include courses on negotiating skills, developing case studies, or writing accounts that illuminate.) Those responsible for such courses might well argue that there is already too much that must be covered and that additional material, while of value, just cannot be "fitted in." But the premise that human knowledge exists in different forms implies that any form of knowledge is nonexclusive and should be presented as such. It would be a radical shift in research and evaluation training if classes in design and quantitative analysis noted the epistemological bases of the approach being advocated and that other valid alternatives for the pursuit of knowledge are available.

Second, the very existence of such diverse ways of knowing implies that those engaged in training educational evaluators and researchers should confront their students with the basic assumptions as to "what it means to know" in the context of the material used in the course. Alternative forms of knowing and understanding imply that there is no one form of knowledge with an exclusive monopoly on human understanding. Most research and evaluation material assumes that it informs, but from what premises? And what are the alternative bases?

Third, each of the alternatives noted above (and indeed the experimental model itself when used as a guide to the evaluation of educational programs) relates to work undertaken in field settings. Research and evaluation in education are activities that nearly always occur in field settings. Further, they are activities that lie in the domain of the practical rather than the theoretic. Both of these premises suggest that those seeking to train evaluators and researchers would do well to include in the training significant opportunities to practice the methodologies in the "real world" of schools and other educational settings. This, in turn, suggests that such programs should establish close links with local school systems. Both MacDonald and Smith commented on the extent to which case study techniques are perhaps most effectively taught in an "apprenticeship." Certainly the realities of the politics of evaluation and research, as well as the skills of negotiation, confidentiality, and accessibility, are difficult to emulate through abstract discussion or simply reading. In each case the heart of the matter lies in skillful performance; such skills are rarely acquired without practice. It is perhaps only in education that we could assume that performance skills of this kind are best learned without actual practice in them. Dancers make no such mistake.

Fourth, there is clearly a need for a course in evaluation and research that addresses more than one way of knowing and deliberately seeks to enable students to understand, and equips them to work within different frameworks of knowledge. Such a challenge is an ambitious one. Nevertheless, such courses are particularly important if the claims made that some research and evaluation problems are better suited to one or another approach are to be validated, or if the difficulties in combining information and insights gained from different knowledge bases are to be solved, and if the process is to be made public.

Fifth, it must be recognized that to limit the forms of training in research and evaluation to a single construct of knowledge is to restrict knowledge itself to that form. Since evaluation and research are intended to inform and to increase understanding, such a restriction implies a commitment at variance with the activity itself.

Sixth, if such training were to be undertaken, many graduate schools of education would require a different faculty. At present such schools draw heavily on the disciplines of sociology, psychology, history, and statistics. The interdisciplinary nature of an education school would be challenged either to extend itself or to form close working relationships with those in a variety of fields of knowledge: anthropologists, artists, those engaged in literary criticism and aesthetics, and so forth.

Seventh, it is at the level of techniques for presenting information that the changes implied are most graphically illustrated. Eisner has drawn attention to the importance of training in writing—not scientific reports—but living portraits of the classroom and the role of film and video in such training. Film and video also have a role in presenting the information gathered in evaluation and research. Training in these techniques of presenting information is often not easily accessible to graduate students in Schools of Education.

Eighth, the press to develop the evaluator's familiarity with different media is matched by the press to diversify his or her skill in different techniques for information gathering. For example, the development of techniques drawn from accountancy and economics requires particular quantitative skills. In contrast the demands of modes of knowing reflecting the interpersonal, the critical, the ethnographic, the responsive, and the democratic necessitate skills in open-ended interviewing, particular observation, interpreting nonverbal cues, and using documents, records, and unobtrusive measures.

Ninth, there are the implications for increased knowledge and understanding of the process of evaluation and research. The sort of argument that MacDonald indicates is necessary to attempt to deal with evaluation in a politically democratic way (and much of the work in school-based action research falls within this mold) means that the participants in the project control the release of information. That is, the participants "own" the data. This view endangers the development of the understanding and necessary sharing of the process involved unless there is also negotiated the evaluator's right to be able to depict the process used in the study, while at the same time protecting the confidentiality of those who "own" the data.

The issue of sharing of the process involved in evaluation and research studies is of particular importance. For many years, Louis Smith included study notes on the methodology involved as part of the evaluation reports. Information such as this is essential if the emerging models for educational evaluation are to be firmly grounded in practice, and are to give a basis for the development of theory. Significantly, there is the need for collaboration of the portrayal made in each of the phenomenological, critical, and naturalistic modes noted above. In each case there are particular problems relating to the referential adequacy of the account developed during the evaluation or research. One step in establishing such adequacy would be to develop a data archives providing the original study material (and noting that it may be in form of videos, slides, photographs, as well as audio tapes and written documents) against which the final report could be set.

Finally, most of the forms of knowledge currently reported on at conferences and in journals rest on the written word—indeed, on words that are used in a particular way: that of propositional logic. It is well to recognize that it is a convenient form for the dissemination of knowledge and understanding: it will go through the mail reasonably cheaply, it is amenable to reproduction, and it is reasonably cheap either to produce or present. However, the challenge of the emerging forms of educational evaluation and research is for the editors of journals and those planning conferences to make active provision for information to be conveyed in a range of written and spoken language media, and a range of media including video, film, electronic mail, and artifacts.

Footnotes

1. Malcolm Parlett and David Hamilton, *Evaluation as Illumination: New Approaches to the Study of Innovating Programs,* Occasional Paper 9 (Edinburgh: Center for Research in Educational Sciences, University of Edinburgh, 1972). Also in David Hamilton et al., ed., *Beyond the Numbers Game* (London: Macmillan Education, 1977).

2. Robert E. Stake, "Responsive Evaluation," mimeographed, 5 December 1972. See also, Robert E. Stake, ed., *Evaluating the Arts in Education: A Responsive Approach* (Columbus, Ohio: Charles E. Merrill, 1975).

3. Lee S. Shulman, "Disciplines of Inquiry in Education: An Overview," *Educational Researcher* 10 (June/July 1981): 5-12, 23.

4. Ray C. Rist, "On the Relations among Education Research Paradigms: From Disdain to Detente," *Anthropology and Education Quarterly* 8 (May 1977): 42-49.

5. See, for example, Ralph W. Tyler, "Changing Concepts of Educational Evaluation," in *Perspectives of Curriculum Evaluation*, ed. Ralph W. Tyler, Robert M. Gagné, and Michael Scriven (Chicago: Rand McNally, 1967), pp. 13-18.

6. Decker F. Walker and Jon J. Schaffarzick, "Comparing Curricula," *Review of Educational Research* 44 (Winter 1974):83-111.

7. Gene V Glass, "Quasi-experimental Research Methods in Education: Time Series Experiments," in *Alternative Research Methodologies in Educational Research*, ed. Richard M. Jaeger (Washington, D.C.: American Educational Research Association, 1980).

8. Elliot Eisner, "Can Educational Research Inform Educational Practice?" *Phi Delta Kappan* 65 (March 1984): 447-52.

9. Egon G. Guba and Yvonne S. Lincoln, *Effective Evaluation* (San Francisco: Jossey-Bass, 1981), p. 53.

10. Henry M. Levin, "Cost-Effectiveness Analysis in Evaluation Research," in *Handbook of Evaluation Research*, vol. 2, ed. Marcia Guttentag and Elmer L. Streuning (Beverly Hills, Calif.: Sage Publications, 1975).

11. Ibid., pp. 89-122.

12. Harriet Talmage, "Evaluation of Programs," in *Encyclopedia of Educational Research*, 5th ed. (New York: Free Press, 1982), p. 601.

13. Gene V Glass and Frederick S. Ellett, Jr., "Evaluation Research," in *Annual Review of Psychology*, ed. Mark R. Rosenzweig and Lyman W. Porter (Palo Alto, Calif.: Annual Reviews, Inc., 1980), p. 224.

14. Talmage, "Evaluation of Programs."

15. Lee J. Cronbach, "Beyond the Two Disciplines of Scientific Psychology," *American Psychologist* 30 (February 1975): 116-27.

16. William W. Cooley and Paul R. Lohnes, *Evaluation Research in Education* (New York: Wiley, 1976).

17. Vito Perrone, *The Abuses of Standardized Testing* (Bloomington, Ind.: Phi Delta Kappa, 1977).

18. Lee J. Cronbach and Associates, *Toward Reform of Program Evaluation* (San Francisco: Jossey-Bass, 1980).

19. John S. Mann, "Curriculum Criticism," *Curriculum Theory Network* 2 (Winter 1968-69): 2-14. Also in *Teachers College Record* 71 (September 1969): 27-40.

20. George Willis, "Curriculum Criticism and Literary Criticism," *Journal of Curriculum Studies* 7 (May 1975): 4-17. Reprinted in *Qualitative Evaluation: Concepts and Cases in Curriculum Policy*, ed. George Willis (Berkeley, Calif.: McCutchan Publishing Corp., 1978), pp. 93-111; Edward F. Kelly, "Curriculum Criticism and Literary Criticism: Comments on the Analogy," *Curriculum Theory Network* 5 no. 2 (1975): 87-106.

21. Elliot W. Eisner, "The Perceptive Eye: Toward the Reformation of Educational Evaluation," mimeographed, Stanford Evaluation Consortium, December, 1975.

22. Ibid., p. 1.

23. Ibid.

24. Gail McCutcheon, "Educational Criticism: Methods and Applications," *Journal of Curriculum Theorizing* 1, no. 2 (1979): 5-25.

25. Elliot W. Eisner, *Educational Imagination* (New York: Macmillan, 1979).

26. George Willis, "A Reconceptualist Perspective on Curriculum Evaluation," *Journal of Curriculum Theorizing* 3, no. 1 (1981): 185-93.

27. William F. Pinar, "Search for a Method," in *Curriculum Theorizing: The Reconceptualists*, ed. William F. Pinar (Berkeley, Calif.: McCutchan Publishing Corp., 1975). See also, idem, "The Analysis of Educational Experience" and "Existential and Phenomenological Foundations of Currere," in *Toward a Poor Curriculum*, ed. William F. Pinar and Madeline R. Grumet (Dubuque, Iowa: Kendall Hunt, 1976).

28. George Willis and Anthony Allen, "Patterns of Phenomenological Response to Curricula: Implications," in *Qualitative Evaluation*, ed. Willis; George Willis, "Phenomenological Methodologies in Curriculum," *Journal of Curriculum Theorizing* 1, no. 1 (1979): 65-78.

29. Anne M. Bussis, Edward A. Chittenden, and Marianne Amarel, *Beyond the Surface Curriculum* (Boulder, Colo.: Westview Press, 1976).

30. Willis, "A Reconceptualist Perspective on Curriculum Evaluation."

31. David Hamilton, "Making Sense of Curriculum Evaluation: Continuities and Discontinuities in an Educational Idea," in *Review of Research in Education*, ed. Lee S. Shulman (Itasca, Ill.: Peacock Publishing Co., 1977), p. 339.

32. Robert L. Wolf and Barbara L. Tymitz, "Toward a More Natural Inquiry in Education," *CEDR Quarterly* 10 (1977): 7-9.

33. Guba and Lincoln, *Effective Evaluation.*

34. Stake, *Evaluating the Arts in Education*; idem, "Responsive Evaluation."

35. Louis M. Smith and William Geoffrey, *The Complexities of an Urban Classroom* (New York: Holt, Rinehart and Winston, 1968).

36. Louis M. Smith and Sally Schumacher, *Extended Pilot Trials of an Aesthetic Education Program: A Qualitative Description, and Evaluation* (St. Louis, Mo.: Cemrel Inc., 1972).

37. Louis M. Smith and P. C. Carpenter, "General Reinforcement Package Project: Qualitative Observation and Interpretation," mimeographed (St. Louis, Mo.: Cemrel Inc., 1972), pp. 1-3. See also, Louis M. Smith and Pat Keith, *Social Psychological Aspects of School Building Design*, Cooperative Research Report, no. 5-223 (Washington, D.C.: U.S. Office of Education, 1967); Louis M. Smith and Paul A. Pohland, "Education Technology in the Rural Highlands," in *AERA Evaluation Monograph Series*, no. 8, ed. Douglas Sjogren (Chicago: Rand McNally, 1972); Louis M. Smith and John A. M. Brock, *Go, Bug Go!: Methodological Issues in Classroom Observational Research*, Occasional Paper, Series no. 5 (St. Ann, Mo.: Cemrel Inc., 1970).

38. Louis M. Smith, "Center for New Schools: Ethnographic Techniques in Educational Research," in *Beyond the Numbers Game*, ed. Hamilton, p. 200.

39. Barry MacDonald, "Evaluation and the Control of Education," in *Curriculum Evaluation Today: Trends and Implications*, ed. David Tawney (Aylesbury, Buckinghamshire: MacMillan, 1976).

Name Index

Subject Index

INFORMATION ABOUT MEMBERSHIP IN THE SOCIETY

From its small beginnings in the early 1900s, the National Society for the Study of Education has grown to a major educational organization with more than 3,000 members in the United States, Canada, and overseas. Members include professors, researchers, graduate students, and administrators in colleges and universities; teachers, supervisors, curriculum specialists, and administrators in elementary and secondary schools; and a considerable number of persons who are not formally connected with an educational institution. Membership in the Society is open to all persons who desire to receive its publications.

Since its establishment the Society has sought to promote its central purpose—the stimulation of investigations and discussions of important educational issues—through regular publication of a two-volume yearbook that is sent to all members. Many of these volumes have been so well received throughout the profession that they have gone into several printings. A recently inaugurated series of substantial paperbacks on Contemporary Educational Issues supplements the series of yearbooks and allows for treatment of a wider range of educational topics than can be addressed each year through the yearbooks alone.

Through membership in the Society one can add regularly to one's professional library at a very reasonable cost. Members also help to sustain a publication program that is widely recognized for its unique contributions to the literature of education.

The categories of membership, and the current dues in each category, are as follows:

Regular. The member receives a clothbound copy of each part of the two-volume yearbook (approximately 300 pages per volume). Annual dues, $20.

Comprehensive. The member receives clothbound copies of the two-volume yearbook and the two volumes in the current paperback series. Annual dues, $35.

Retirees and Graduate Students. Reduced dues—Regular, $16; Comprehensive, $31.
The above reduced dues are available to (a) those who have retired or are over sixty-five years of age and who have been members of the Society for at least ten years, and (b) graduate students in their first year of membership.

Life Membership. Persons sixty years of age or over may hold a Regular Membership for life upon payment of a lump sum based upon the life expectancy for their age group. Consult the Secretary-Treasurer for further details.

New members are required to pay an entrance fee of $1, in addition to the dues, in their first year of membership.

Membership is for the calendar year and dues are payable on or before January 1. A reinstatement fee of $.50 must be added to dues payments made after January 1.

In addition to receiving the publications of the Society as described above, members participate in the nomination and election of the six-member Board of Directors, which is responsible for managing the business and affairs of the Society, including the authorization of volumes to appear in the yearbook series. Two members of the Board are elected each year for three-year terms. Members of the Society who have contributed to its publications and who indicate a willingness to serve are eligible for election to the Board.

Members are urged to attend the one or more meetings of the Society that are arranged each year in conjunction with the annual meetings of major educational organizations. The purpose of such meetings is to present, discuss, and critique volumes in the current yearbook series. Announcements of meetings for the ensuing year are sent to members in December.

Upon written request from a member, the Secretary-Treasurer will send the current directory of members, synopses of meetings of the Board of Directors, and the annual financial report.

Persons desiring further information about membership may write to

KENNETH J. REHAGE, Secretary-Treasurer
National Society for the Study of Education

5835 Kimbark Ave.
Chicago, Ill. 60637

PUBLICATIONS OF THE NATIONAL SOCIETY FOR THE STUDY OF EDUCATION

1. The Yearbooks

NOTICE: Many of the early yearbooks of this series are now out of print. In the following list, those titles to which an asterisk is prefixed are not available for purchase.

*First Yearbook, 1902, Part I—*Some Principles in the Teaching of History.* Lucy M. Salmon.

*First Yearbook, 1902, Part II—*The Progress of Geography in the Schools.* W. M. Davis and H. M. Wilson.

*Second Yearbook, 1903, Part I—*The Course of Study in History in the Common School.* Isabel Lawrence, C. A. McMurry, Frank McMurry, E. C. Page, and E. J. Rice.

*Second Yearbook, 1903, Part II—*The Relation of Theory to Practice in Education.* M. J. Holmes, J. A. Keith, and Levi Seeley.

*Third Yearbook, 1904, Part I—*The Relation of Theory to Practice in the Education of Teachers.* John Dewey, Sarah C. Brooks, F. M. McMurry, *et al.*

*Third Yearbook, 1904, Part II—*Nature Study.* W. S. Jackman.

*Fourth Yearbook, 1905, Part I—*The Education and Training of Secondary Teachers.* E. C. Elliott, E. G. Dexter, M. J. Holmes, *et al.*

*Fourth Yearbook, 1905, Part II—*The Place of Vocational Subjects in the High-School Curriculum.* J. S. Brown, G. B. Morrison, and Ellen Richards.

*Fifth Yearbook, 1906, Part I—*On the Teaching of English in Elementary and High Schools.* G. P. Brown and Emerson Davis.

*Fifth Yearbook, 1906, Part II—*The Certification of Teachers.* E. P. Cubberley.

*Sixth Yearbook, 1907, Part I—*Vocational Studies for College Entrance.* C. A. Herrick, H. W. Holmes, T. deLaguna, V. Prettyman, and W. J. S. Bryan.

*Sixth Yearbook, 1907, Part II—*The Kindergarten and Its Relation to Elementary Education.* Ada Van Stone Harris, E. A. Kirkpatrick, Marie Kraus-Boelté, Patty S. Hill, Harriette M. Mills, and Nina Vandewalker.

*Seventh Yearbook, 1908, Part I—*The Relation of Superintendents and Principals to the Training and Professional Improvement of Their Teachers.* Charles D. Lowry.

*Seventh Yearbook, 1908, Part II—*The Co-ordination of the Kindergarten and the Elementary School.* B. C. Gregory, Jennie B. Merrill, Bertha Payne, and Margaret Giddings.

*Eighth Yearbook, 1909, Part I—*Education with Reference to Sex: Pathological, Economic, and Social Aspects.* C. R. Henderson.

*Eighth Yearbook, 1909, Part II—*Education with Reference to Sex: Agencies and Methods.* C. R. Henderson and Helen C. Putnam.

*Ninth Yearbook, 1910, Part I—*Health and Education.* T. D. Wood.

*Ninth Yearbook, 1910, Part II—*The Nurses in Education.* T. D. Wood, *et al.*.

*Tenth Yearbook, 1911, Part I—*The City School as a Community Center.* H. C. Leipziger, Sarah E. Hyre, R. D. Warden, C. Ward Crampton, E. W. Stitt, E. J. Ward, Mrs. E. C. Grice, and C. A. Perry.

*Tenth Yearbook, 1911, Part II—*The Rural School as a Community Center.* B. H. Crocheron, Jessie Field, F. W. Howe, E. C. Bishop, A. B. Graham, O. J. Kern, M. T. Scudder, and B. M. Davis.

*Eleventh Yearbook, 1912, Part I—*Industrial Education: Typical Experiments Described and Interpreted.* J. F. Barker, M. Bloomfield, B. W. Johnson, P. Johnston, L. M. Leavitt, G. A. Mirick, M. W. Murray, C. F. Perry, A. L. Safford, and H. B. Wilson.

*Eleventh Yearbook, 1912, Part II—*Agricultural Education in Secondary Schools.* A. C. Monahan, R. W. Stimson, D. J. Crosby, W. H. French, H. F. Button, F. R. Crane, W. R. Hart, and G. F. Warren.

*Twelfth Yearbook, 1913, Part I—*The Supervision of City Schools,* Franklin Bobbitt, J. W. Hall, and J. D. Wolcott.

*Twelfth Yearbook, 1913, Part II—*The Supervision of Rural Schools.* A. C. Monahan, L. J. Hanifan, J. E. Warren, Wallace Lund, U. J. Hoffman, A. S. Cook, E. M. Rapp, Jackson Davis, J. D. Wolcott.

*Thirteenth Yearbook, 1914, Part I—*Some Aspects of High-School Instruction and Administration.* H. C. Morrison, E. R. Breslich, W. A. Jessup, and L. D. Coffman.

*Thirteenth Yearbook, 1914, Part II—*Plans for Organizing School Surveys, with a Summary of Typical School Surveys.* Charles H. Judd and Henry L. Smith.

*Fourteenth Yearbook, 1915, Part I—*Minimum Essentials in Elementary School Subjects—Standards and Current Practices.* H. B. Wilson, H. W. Holmes, F. E. Thompson, R. G. Jones, S. A. Courtis, W. S. Gray, F. N. Freeman, H. C. Pryor, J. F. Hosic, W. A. Jessup, and W. C. Bagley.

*Fourteenth Yearbook, 1915, Part II—*Methods for Measuring Teachers' Efficiency.* Arthur C. Boyce.

*Fifteenth Yearbook, 1916, Part I—*Standards and Tests for the Measurement of the Efficiency of Schools and School Systems.* G. D. Strayer, Bird T. Baldwin, B. R. Buckingham, F. W. Ballou, D. C. Bliss, H. G. Childs, S. A. Courtis, E. P. Cubberley, C. H. Judd, George Melcher, E. E. Oberholtzer, J. B. Sears, Daniel Starch, M. R. Trabue, and G. M. Whipple.

*Fifteenth Yearbook, 1916, Part II—*The Relationship between Persistence in School and Home Conditions.* Charles E. Holley.

*Fifteenth Yearbook, 1916, Part III—*The Junior High School.* Aubrey A. Douglass.

*Sixteenth Yearbook, 1917, Part I—*Second Report of the Committee on Minimum Essentials in Elementary-School Subjects.* W. C. Bagley, W. W. Charters, F. N. Freeman, W. S. Gray, Ernest Horn, J. H. Hoskinson, W. S. Monroe, C. F. Munson, H. C. Pryor, L. W. Rapeer, G. M. Wilson, and H. B. Wilson.

*Sixteenth Yearbook, 1917, Part II—*The Efficiency of College Students as Conditioned by Age at Entrance and Size of High School.* B. F. Pittenger.

*Seventeenth Yearbook, 1918, Part I—*Third Report of the Committee on Economy of Time in Education.* W. C. Bagley, B. B. Bassett, M. E. Branom, Alice Camerer, J. E. Dealey, C. A. Ellwood, E. B. Greene, A. B. Hart, J. F. Hosic, E. T. Housh, W. H. Mace, L. R. Marston, H. C. McKown, A. E. Mitchell, W. C. Reavis, D. Snedden, and H. B. Wilson.

*Seventeenth Yearbook, 1918, Part II—*The Measurement of Educational Products.* E. J. Ashbaugh, W. A. Averill, L. P. Ayers, F. W. Ballou, Edna Bryner, B. R. Buckingham, S. A. Courtis, M. E. Haggerty, C. H. Judd, George Melcher, W. S. Monroe, E. A. Nifenecker, and E. L. Thorndike.

*Eighteenth Yearbook, 1919, Part I—*The Professional Preparation of High-School Teachers.* G. N. Cade, S. S. Colvin, Charles Fordyce, H. H. Foster, T. S. Gosling, W. S. Gray, L. V. Koos, A. R. Mead, H. L. Miller, F. C. Whitcomb, and Clifford Woody.

*Eighteenth Yearbook, 1919, Part II—*Fourth Report of Committee on Economy of Time in Education.* F. C. Ayer, F. N. Freeman, W. S. Gray, Ernest Horn, W. S. Monroe, and C. E. Seashore.

*Nineteenth Yearbook, 1920, Part I—*New Materials of Instruction.* Prepared by the Society's Committee on Materials of Instruction.

*Nineteenth Yearbook, 1920, Part II—*Classroom Problems in the Education of Gifted Children.* T. S. Henry.

*Twentieth Yearbook, 1921, Part I—*New Materials of Instruction.* Second Report by Society's Committee.

*Twentieth Yearbook, 1921, Part II—*Report of the Society's Committee on Silent Reading.* M. A. Burgess, S. A. Courtis, C. E. Germane, W. S. Gray, H. A. Greene, Reginia R. Heller, J. H. Hoover, J. A. O'Brien, J. L. Packer, Daniel Starch, W. W. Theisen, G. A. Yoakum, and representatives of other school systems.

*Twenty-first Yearbook, 1922, Parts I and II—*Intelligence Tests and Their Use,* Part I—*The Nature, History, and General Principles of Intelligence Testing.* E. L. Thorndike, S. S. Colvin, Harold Rugg, G. M. Whipple, Part II—*The Administrative Use of Intelligence Tests.* H. W. Holmes, W. K. Layton, Helen Davis, Agnes L. Rogers, Rudolf Pintner, M. R. Trabue, W. S. Miller, Bessie L. Gambrill, and others. The two parts are bound together.

*Twenty-second Yearbook, 1923, Part I—*English Composition: Its Aims, Methods and Measurements.* Earl Hudelson.

*Twenty-second Yearbook, 1923, Part II—*The Social Studies in the Elementary and Secondary School.* A. S. Barr, J. J. Coss, Henry Harap, R. W. Hatch, H. C. Hill, Ernest Horn, C. H. Judd, L. C. Marshall, F. M. McMurry, Earle Rugg, H. O. Rugg, Emma Schweppe, Mabel Snedaker, and C. W. Washburne.

*Twenty-third Yearbook, 1924, Part I—*The Education of Gifted Children.* Report of the Society's Committee, Guy M. Whipple, Chairman.

*Twenty-third Yearbook, 1924, Part II—*Vocational Guidance and Vocational Education for Industries.* A. H. Edgerton and others.

*Twenty-fourth Yearbook, 1925, Part I—*Report of the National Committee on Reading.* W. S. Gray, Chairman, F. W. Ballou, Rose L. Hardy, Ernest Horn, Francis Jenkins, S. A. Leonard, Estaline Wilson, and Laura Zirbes.

*Twenty-fourth Yearbook, 1925, Part II—*Adapting the Schools to Individual Differences.* Report of the Society's Committee. Carleton W. Washburne, Chairman.

*Twenty-fifth Yearbook, 1926, Part I—*The Present Status of Safety Education.* Report of the Society's Committee. Guy M. Whipple, Chairman.

*Twenty-fifth Yearbook, 1926, Part II—*Extra-Curricular Activities.* Report of the Society's Committee. Leonard V. Koos, Chairman.

*Twenty-sixth Yearbook, 1927, Part I—*Curriculum-making: Past and Present.* Report of the Society's Committee. Harold O. Rugg, Chairman.

*Twenty-sixth Yearbook, 1927, Part II—*The Foundations of Curriculum-making.* Prepared by individual members of the Society's Committee. Harold O. Rugg, Chairman.

*Twenty-seventh Yearbook, 1928, Part I—*Nature and Nurture: Their Influence upon Intelligence.* Prepared by the Society's Committee. Lewis M. Terman, Chairman.

*Twenty-seventh Yearbook, 1928, Part II—*Nature and Nurture: Their Influence upon Achievement.* Prepared by the Society's Committee. Lewis M. Terman, Chairman.

*Twenty-eighth Yearbook, 1929, Parts I and II—*Preschool and Parental Education.* Part I—*Organization and Development.* Part II—*Research and Method.* Prepared by the Society's Committee. Lois H. Meek, Chairman. Bound in one volume. Cloth.

*Twenty-ninth Yearbook, 1930, Parts I and II—*Report of the Society's Committee on Arithmetic.* Part I—*Some Aspects of Modern Thought on Arithmetic.* Part II—*Research in Arithmetic.* Prepared by the Society's Committee. F. B. Knight, Chairman. Bound in one volume.

*Thirtieth Yearbook, 1931, Part I—*The Status of Rural Education.* First Report of the Society's Committee on Rural Education. Orville G. Brim, Chairman.

Thirtieth Yearbook, 1931, Part II—*The Textbook in American Education.* Report of the Society's Committee on the Textbook. J. B. Edmonson, Chairman. Cloth. Paper.

*Thirty-first Yearbook, 1932, Part I—*A Program for Teaching Science.* Prepared by the Society's Committee on the Teaching of Science. S. Ralph Powers, Chairman.

*Thirty-first Yearbook, 1932, Part II—*Changes and Experiments in Liberal-Arts Education.* Prepared by Kathryn McHale, with numerous collaborators.

*Thirty-second Yearbook, 1933—*The Teaching of Geography.* Prepared by the Society's Committee on the Teaching of Geography. A. E. Parkins, Chairman.

*Thirty-third Yearbook, 1934, Part I—*The Planning and Construction of School Buildings.* Prepared by the Society's Committee on School Buildings. N. L. Engelhardt, Chairman.

*Thirty-third Yearbook, 1934, Part II—*The Activity Movement.* Prepared by the Society's Committee on the Activity Movement, Lois Coffey Mossman, Chairman.

Thirty-fourth Yearbook, 1935—*Educational Diagnosis.* Prepared by the Society's Committee on Educational Diagnosis. L. J. Brueckner, Chairman. Paper.

*Thirty-fifth Yearbook, 1936, Part I—*The Grouping of Pupils.* Prepared by the Society's Committee. W. W. Coxe, Chairman.

*Thirty-fifth Yearbook, 1936, Part II—*Music Education.* Prepared by the Society's Committee. W. L. Uhl, Chairman.

*Thirty-sixth Yearbook, 1937, Part I—*The Teaching of Reading.* Prepared by the Society's Committee. W. S. Gray, Chairman.

*Thirty-sixth Yearbook, 1937, Part II—*International Understanding through the Public-School Curriculum.* Prepared by the Society's Committee. I. L. Kandel, Chairman.

*Thirty-seventh Yearbook, 1938, Part I—*Guidance in Educational Institutions.* Prepared by the Society's Committee. G. N. Kefauver, Chairman.

*Thirty-seventh Yearbook, 1938, Part II—*The Scientific Movement in Education.* Prepared by the Society's Committee. F. N. Freeman, Chairman.

*Thirty-eighth Yearbook, 1939, Part I—*Child Development and the Curriculum.* Prepared by the Society's Committee. Carleton Washburne, Chairman.

*Thirty-eighth Yearbook, 1939, Part II—*General Education in the American College.* Prepared by the Society's Committee. Alvin Eurich, Chairman. Cloth.

*Thirty-ninth Yearbook, 1940, Part I—*Intelligence: Its Nature and Nurture. Comparative and Critical Exposition.* Prepared by the Society's Committee. G. D. Stoddard, Chairman.

*Thirty-ninth Yearbook, 1940, Part II—*Intelligence: Its Nature and Nurture. Original Studies and Experiments.* Prepared by the Society's Committee. G. D. Stoddard, Chairman.

*Fortieth Yearbook, 1941—*Art in American Life and Education.* Prepared by the Society's Committee. Thomas Munro, Chairman.

Forty-first Yearbook, 1942, Part I—*Philosophies of Education.* Prepared by the Society's Committee. John S. Brubacher, Chairman. Paper.

Forty-first Yearbook, 1942, Part II—*The Psychology of Learning.* Prepared by the Society's Committee. T. R. McConnell, Chairman. Cloth.

*Forty-second Yearbook, 1943, Part I—*Vocational Education.* Prepared by the Society's Committee. F. J. Keller, Chairman.

*Forty-second Yearbook, 1943, Part II—*The Library in General Education.* Prepared by the Society's Committee. L. R. Wilson, Chairman.

Forty-third Yearbook, 1944, Part I—*Adolescence.* Prepared by the Society's Committee. Harold E. Jones, Chairman. Paper.

*Forty-third Yearbook, 1944, Part II—*Teaching Language in the Elementary School.* Prepared by the Society's Committee. M. R. Trabue, Chairman.

*Forty-fourth Yearbook, 1945, Part I—*American Education in the Postwar Period: Curriculum Reconstruction.* Prepared by the Society's Committee. Ralph W. Tyler, Chairman.

*Forty-fourth Yearbook, 1945, Part II—*American Education in the Postwar Period: Structural Reorganization.* Prepared by the Society's Committee. Bess Goodykoontz, Chairman. Paper.

*Forty-fifth Yearbook, 1946, Part I—*The Measurement of Understanding.* Prepared by the Society's Committee. William A. Brownell, Chairman.

*Forty-fifth Yearbook, 1946, Part II—*Changing Conceptions in Educational Administration.* Prepared by the Society's Committee. Alonzo G. Grace, Chairman.

*Forty-sixth Yearbook, 1947, Part I—*Science Education in American Schools.* Prepared by the Society's Committee. Victor H. Noll, Chairman.

*Forty-sixth Yearbook, 1947, Part II—*Early Childhood Education.* Prepared by the Society's Committee. N. Searle Light, Chairman. Paper.

Forty-seventh Yearbook, 1948, Part I—*Juvenile Delinquency and the Schools.* Prepared by the Society's Committee. Ruth Strang, Chairman. Cloth.

Forty-seventh Yearbook, 1948, Part II—*Reading in the High School and College.* Prepared by the Society's Committee. William S. Gray, Chairman. Cloth. Paper.

*Forty-eighth Yearbook, 1949, Part I—*Audio-visual Materials of Instruction.* Prepared by the Society's Committee. Stephen M. Corey, Chairman. Cloth.

*Forty-eighth Yearbook, 1949, Part II—*Reading in the Elementary School.* Prepared by the Society's Committee. Arthur I. Gates, Chairman.

*Forty-ninth Yearbook, 1950, Part I—*Learning and Instruction.* Prepared by the Society's Committee. G. Lester Anderson, Chairman.

*Forty-ninth Yearbook, 1950, Part II—*The Education of Exceptional Children.* Prepared by the Society's Committee. Samuel A. Kirk, Chairman.

Fiftieth Yearbook, 1951, Part I—*Graduate Study in Education.* Prepared by the Society's Board of Directors. Ralph W. Tyler, Chairman. Paper.

Fiftieth Yearbook, 1951, Part II—*The Teaching of Arithmetic.* Prepared by the Society's Committee. G. T. Buswell, Chairman. Cloth, Paper.

Fifty-first Yearbook, 1952, Part I—*General Education.* Prepared by the Society's Committee. T. R. McConnell, Chairman. Cloth, Paper.

Fifty-first Yearbook, 1952, Part II—*Education in Rural Communities.* Prepared by the Society's Committee. Ruth Strang, Chairman. Cloth, Paper.

*Fifty-second Yearbook, 1953, Part I—*Adapting the Secondary-School Program to the Needs of Youth.* Prepared by the Society's Committee: William G. Brink, Chairman.

Fifty-second Yearbook, 1953, Part II—*The Community School.* Prepared by the Society's Committee. Maurice F. Seay, Chairman. Cloth.

Fifty-third Yearbook, 1954, Part I—*Citizen Cooperation for Better Public Schools.* Prepared by the Society's Committee. Edgar L. Morphet, Chairman. Cloth, Paper.

*Fifty-third Yearbook, 1954, Part II—*Mass Media and Education.* Prepared by the Society's Committee. Edgar Dale, Chairman.

*Fifty-fourth Yearbook, 1955, Part I—*Modern Philosophies and Education.* Prepared by the Society's Committee. John S. Brubacher, Chairman.

Fifty-fourth Yearbook, 1955, Part II—*Mental Health in Modern Education.* Prepared by the Society's Committee. Paul A. Witty, Chairman. Paper.

*Fifty-fifth Yearbook, 1956, Part I—*The Public Junior College.* Prepared by the Society's Committee. B. Lamar Johnson, Chairman.

*Fifty-fifth Yearbook, 1956, Part II—*Adult Reading.* Prepared by the Society's Committee. David H. Clift, Chairman.

*Fifty-sixth Yearbook, 1957, Part I—*In-service Education of Teachers, Supervisors, and Administrators.* Prepared by the Society's Committee. Stephen M. Corey, Chairman. Cloth.

Fifty-sixth Yearbook, 1957, Part II—*Social Studies in the Elementary School.* Prepared by the Society's Committee. Ralph C. Preston, Chairman. Cloth, Paper.

*Fifty-seventh Yearbook, 1958, Part I—*Basic Concepts in Music Education.* Prepared by the Society's Committee. Thurber H. Madison, Chairman. Cloth.

*Fifty-seventh Yearbook, 1958, Part II—*Education for the Gifted.* Prepared by the Society's Committee. Robert J. Havighurst, Chairman.

*Fifty-seventh Yearbook, 1958, Part III—*The Integration of Educational Experiences.* Prepared by the Society's Committee. Paul L. Dressel, Chairman. Cloth.

Fifty-eighth Yearbook, 1959, Part I—*Community Education: Principles and Practices from World-wide Experience.* Prepared by the Society's Committee. C. O. Arndt, Chairman. Cloth, Paper.

Fifty-eighth Yearbook, 1959, Part II—*Personnel Services in Education.* Prepared by the Society's Committee. Melvene D. Hardee, Chairman. Paper.

*Fifty-ninth Yearbook, 1960, Part I—*Rethinking Science Education.* Prepared by the Society's Committee. J. Darrell Barnard, Chairman.

*Fifty-ninth Yearbook, 1960, Part II—*The Dynamics of Instructional Groups.* Prepared by the Society's Committee. Gale E. Jensen, Chairman.

Sixtieth Yearbook, 1961, Part I—*Development in and through Reading.* Prepared by the Society's Committee. Paul A. Witty, Chairman. Cloth.

Sixtieth Yearbook, 1961, Part II—*Social Forces Influencing American Education.* Prepared by the Society's Committee. Ralph W. Tyler, Chairman. Cloth, Paper.

Sixty-first Yearbook, 1962, Part I—*Individualizing Instruction.* Prepared by the Society's Committee. Fred T. Tyler, Chairman. Cloth.

Sixty-first Yearbook, 1962, Part II—*Education for the Professions.* Prepared by the Society's Committee. G. Lester Anderson, Chairman. Cloth.

Sixty-second Yearbook, 1963, Part I—*Child Psychology.* Prepared by the Society's Committee. Harold W. Stevenson, Editor. Cloth.

Sixty-second Yearbook, 1963, Part II—*The Impact and Improvement of School Testing Programs.* Prepared by the Society's Committee. Warren G. Findley, Editor. Cloth.

Sixty-third Yearbook, 1964, Part I—*Theories of Learning and Instruction*. Prepared by the Society's Committee. Ernest R. Hilgard, Editor. Paper, Cloth.

Sixty-third Yearbook, 1964, Part II—*Behavioral Science and Educational Administration*. Prepared by the Society's Committee. Daniel E. Griffiths, Editor. Paper.

Sixty-fourth Yearbook, 1965, Part I—*Vocational Education*. Prepared by the Society's Committee. Melvin L. Barlow, Editor. Cloth.

*Sixty-fourth Yearbook, 1965, Part II—*Art Education*. Prepared by the Society's Committee. W. Reid Hastie, Editor.

Sixty-fifth Yearbook, 1966, Part I—*Social Deviancy among Youth*. Prepared by the Society's Committee. William W. Wattenberg, Editor. Cloth.

Sixty-fifth Yearbook, 1966, Part II—*The Changing American School*. Prepared by the Society's Committee. John I. Goodlad, Editor. Cloth.

*Sixty-sixth Yearbook, 1967, Part I—*The Educationally Retarded and Disadvantaged*. Prepared by the Society's Committee. Paul A. Witty, Editor. Cloth.

*Sixty-sixth Yearbook, 1967, Part II—*Programed Instruction*. Prepared by the Society's Committee. Phil C. Lange, Editor. Cloth.

Sixty-seventh Yearbook, 1968, Part I—*Metropolitanism: Its Challenge to Education*. Prepared by the Society's Committee. Robert J. Havighurst, Editor. Cloth.

Sixty-seventh Yearbook, 1968, Part II—*Innovation and Change in Reading Instruction*. Prepared by the Society's Committee. Helen M. Robinson, Editor. Cloth.

Sixty-eighth Yearbook, 1969, Part I—*The United States and International Education*. Prepared by the Society's Committee. Harold G. Shane, Editor. Cloth.

Sixty-eighth Yearbook, 1969, Part II—*Educational Evaluation: New Roles, New Means*. Prepared by the Society's Committee. Ralph W. Tyler, Editor. Paper.

*Sixty-ninth Yearbook, 1970, Part I—*Mathematics Education*. Prepared by the Society's Committee. Edward G. Begle, Editor. Cloth.

Sixty-ninth Yearbook, 1970, Part II—*Linguistics in School Programs*. Prepared by the Society's Committee. Albert H. Marckwardt, Editor. Cloth.

*Seventieth Yearbook, 1971, Part I—*The Curriculum: Retrospect and Prospect*. Prepared by the Society's Committee. Robert M. McClure, Editor. Paper.

Seventieth Yearbook, 1971, Part II—*Leaders in American Education*. Prepared by the Society's Committee. Robert J. Havighurst, Editor. Cloth.

Seventy-first Yearbook, 1972, Part I—*Philosophical Redirection of Educational Research*. Prepared by the Society's Committee. Lawrence G. Thomas, Editor. Cloth.

Seventy-first Yearbook, 1972, Part II—*Early Childhood Education*. Prepared by the Society's Committee. Ira J. Gordon, Editor. Paper.

*Seventy-second Yearbook, 1973, Part I—*Behavior Modification in Education*. Prepared by the Society's Committee. Carl E. Thoresen, Editor. Cloth.

Seventy-second Yearbook, 1973, Part II—*The Elementary School in the United States*. Prepared by the Society's Committee. John I. Goodlad and Harold G. Shane, Editors. Cloth.

Seventy-third Yearbook, 1974, Part I—*Media and Symbols: The Forms of Expression, Communication and Education*. Prepared by the Society's Committee. David R. Olson, Editor. Cloth.

Seventy-third Yearbook, 1974, Part II—*Uses of the Sociology of Education*. Prepared by the Society's Committee. C. Wayne Gordon, Editor. Cloth.

Seventy-fourth Yearbook, 1975, Part I—*Youth*. Prepared by the Society's Committee. Robert J. Havighurst and Phillip H. Dreyer, Editors. Cloth.

Seventy-fourth Yearbook, 1975, Part II—*Teacher Education*. Prepared by the Society's Committee. Kevin Ryan, Editor. Cloth.

Seventy-fifth Yearbook, 1976, Part I—*Psychology of Teaching Methods*. Prepared by the Society's Committee. N. L. Gage, Editor. Paper.

*Seventy-fifth Yearbook, 1976, Part II—*Issues in Secondary Education*. Prepared by the Society's Committee. William Van Til, Editor. Cloth.

Seventy-sixth Yearbook, 1977, Part I—*The Teaching of English*. Prepared by the Society's Committee. James R. Squire, Editor. Cloth.

Seventy-sixth Yearbook, 1977, Part II—*The Politics of Education*. Prepared by the Society's Committee. Jay D. Scribner, Editor. Paper.

Seventy-seventh Yearbook, 1978, Part I—*The Courts and Education*, Clifford P. Hooker, Editor. Cloth.

*Seventy-seventh Yearbook, 1978, Part II—*Education and the Brain*, Jeanne Chall and Allan F. Mirsky, Editors. Paper.

Seventy-eighth Yearbook, 1979, Part I—*The Gifted and the Talented: Their Education and Development*, A. Harry Passow, Editor. Paper.

Seventy-eighth Yearbook, 1979, Part II—*Classroom Management*, Daniel L. Duke, Editor, Paper.

Seventy-ninth Yearbook, 1980, Part I—*Toward Adolescence: The Middle School Years*. Mauritz Johnson, Editor. Cloth.

Seventy-ninth Yearbook, 1980, Part II—*Learning a Second Language*, Frank M. Grittner, Editor. Cloth.

Eightieth Yearbook, 1981, Part I—*Philosophy and Education*, Jonas F. Soltis, Editor. Cloth.

Eightieth Yearbook, 1981, Part II—*The Social Studies*, Howard D. Mehlinger and O. L. Davis, Jr., Editors. Cloth.

Eighty-first Yearbook, 1982, Part I—*Policy Making in Education*, Ann Lieberman and Milbrey W. McLaughlin, Editors. Cloth.

Eighty-first Yearbook, 1982, Part II—*Education and Work*, Harry F. Silberman, Editor. Cloth.

Eighty-second Yearbook, 1983, Part I—*Individual Differences and the Common Curriculum*, Gary D Fenstermacher and John I. Goodlad, Editors. Cloth.

Eighty-second Yearbook, 1983, Part II—*Staff Development*, Gary Griffin, Editor. Cloth.

Eighty-third Yearbook, 1984, Part I—*Becoming Readers in a Complex Society*, Alan C. Purves and Olive S. Niles, Editors. Cloth.

Eighty-third Yearbook, 1984, Part II—*The Humanities in Precollegiate Education*, Benjamin Ladnér, Editor. Cloth.

Eighty-fourth Yearbook, 1985, Part I—*Education in School and Nonschool Settings*, Mario D. Fantini and Robert L. Sinclair, Editors. Cloth.

Eighty-fourth Yearbook, 1985, Part II—*Learning and Teaching the Ways of Knowing*, Elliot Eisner, Editor. Cloth.

Yearbooks of the National Society are distributed by

UNIVERSITY OF CHICAGO PRESS, 5801 ELLIS AVE.,
CHICAGO, ILLINOIS 60637

Please direct inquiries regarding prices of volumes still available to the University of Chicago Press. Orders for these volumes should be sent to the University of Chicago Press, not to the offices of the National Society.

2. The Series on Contemporary Educational Issues

In addition to its Yearbooks the Society now publishes volumes in a series on Contemporary Educational Issues. These volumes are prepared under the supervision of the Society's Commission on an Expanded Publication Program.

The 1985 Titles

Adapting Instruction to Student Differences (Margaret C. Wang and Herbert J. Walberg, eds.)

Colleges of Education: Perspectives on Their Future (Charles W. Case and William A. Matthes, eds.)

The 1984 Titles

Women and Education: Equity or Equality? (Elizabeth Fennema and M. Jane Ayer, eds.)

Curriculum Development: Problems, Processes, and Programs (Glenys G. Unruh and Adolph Unruh, eds.)

The 1983 Titles

The Hidden Curriculum and Moral Education (Henry A. Giroux and David Purpel, eds.)

The Dynamics of Organizational Change in Education (J. Victor Baldridge and Terrance Deal, eds.)

The 1982 Titles

Improving Educational Standards and Productivity: The Research Basis for Policy (Herbert J. Walberg, ed.)

Schools in Conflict: The Politics of Education (Frederick M. Wirt and Michael W. Kirst)

The 1981 Titles

Psychology and Education: The State of the Union (Frank H. Farley and Neal J. Gordon, eds.)

Selected Issues in Mathematics Education (Mary M. Lindquist, ed.)

The 1980 Titles

Minimum Competency Achievement Testing: Motives, Models, Measures, and Consequences (Richard M. Jaeger and Carol K. Tittle, eds.)

Collective Bargaining in Public Education (Anthony M. Cresswell, Michael J. Murphy, with Charles T. Kerchner)

The 1979 Titles

Educational Environments and Effects: Evaluation, Policy, and Productivity (Herbert J. Walberg, ed.)

Research on Teaching: Concepts, Findings, and Implications (Penelope L. Peterson and Herbert J. Walberg, eds.)

The Principal in Metropolitan Schools (Donald A. Erickson and Theodore L. Reller, eds.)

The 1978 Titles

Aspects of Reading Education (Susanna Pflaum-Connor, ed.)

History, Education, and Public Policy: Recovering the American Educational Past (Donald R. Warren, ed.)

From Youth to Constructive Adult Life: The Role of the Public School (Ralph W. Tyler, ed.)

The 1977 Titles

Early Childhood Education: Issues and Insights (Bernard Spodek and Herbert J. Walberg, eds.)

The Future of Big City Schools: Desegregation Policies and Magnet Alternatives (Daniel U. Levine and Robert J. Havighurst, eds.)

Educational Administration: The Developing Decades (Luvern L. Cunningham, Walter G. Hack, and Raphael O. Nystrand, eds.)

The 1976 Titles

Prospects for Research and Development in Education (Ralph W. Tyler, ed.)

Public Testimony on Public Schools (Commission on Educational Governance)

Counseling Children and Adolescents (William M. Walsh, ed.)

The 1975 Titles

Schooling and the Rights of Children (Vernon Haubrich and Michael Apple, eds.)

Systems of Individualized Education (Harriet Talmage, ed.)

Educational Policy and International Assessment: Implications of the IEA Assessment of Achievement (Alan Purves and Daniel U. Levine, eds.)

The 1974 Titles

Crucial Issues in Testing (Ralph W. Tyler and Richard M. Wolf, eds.)

Conflicting Conceptions of Curriculum (Elliot Eisner and Elizabeth Vallance, eds.)

Cultural Pluralism (Edgar G. Epps, ed.)

Rethinking Educational Equality (Andrew T. Kopan and Herbert J. Walberg, eds.)

All of the preceding volumes may be ordered from

McCutchan Publishing Corporation
P.O. Box 774
Berkeley, California 94701

The 1972 Titles

Black Students in White Schools (Edgar G. Epps, ed.)

Flexibility in School Programs (W. J. Congreve and G. L. Rinehart, eds.)

Performance Contracting—1969-1971 (J. A. Mecklenburger)

The Potential of Educational Futures (Michael Marien and W. L. Ziegler, eds.)

Sex Differences and Discrimination in Education (Scarvia Anderson, ed.)

The 1971 Titles

Accountability in Education (Leon M. Lessinger and Ralph W. Tyler, eds.)

Farewell to Schools??? (D. U. Levine and R. J. Havighurst, eds.)

Models for Integrated Education (D. U. Levine, ed.)

PYGMALION *Reconsidered* (J. D. Elashoff and R. E. Snow)

Reactions to Silberman's CRISIS IN THE CLASSROOM (A. Harry Passow, ed.)

The 1971 and 1972 titles in this series are now out of print.